TEACHING SOFTBALL

Steps to Success

Diane L. Potter, EdD
Gretchen A. Brockmeyer, EdD
Springfield College
Springfield, Massachusetts

ARNULFO L OLIVEIRA MEMORIAL LIBRARY
1825 MAY STREET
BROWNSVILLE, TEXAS 78520

Leisure Press
Champaign, Illinois

Library of Congress Cataloging-in-Publication Data

Potter, Diane L., 1935-
    Teaching softball : steps to success / Diane L. Potter, Gretchen
A. Brockmeyer.
      p. cm. -- (Steps to success activity series)
    Bibliography: p.
    ISBN 0-88011-359-6
    1. Softball--Study and teaching. I. Brockmeyer, Gretchen A.,
1943-   . II. Title. III. Series.
   GV881.P68 1989
796.357'8--dc19   88-36782
                                          CIP

ISBN: 0-88011-359-6

Developmental Editor: Judy Patterson Wright, PhD
Production Director: Ernie Noa
Copy Editor: Peter Nelson
Assistant Editor: Robert King
Proofreader: Wendy Nelson
Typesetters: Sandra Meier, Brad Colson, and Yvonne Winsor
Text Design: Keith Blomberg
Text Layout: Kimberlie Henris
Cover Design: Jack Davis
Cover Photo: Bill Morrow
Illustrations By: Tim Offenstein and Gretchen Walters
Printed By: United Graphics, Inc.

Instructional Designer for the Steps to Success Activity Series: Joan N. Vickers, EdD, University of Calgary, Calgary, Alberta, Canada

Printed in the United States of America

10 9 8 7 6 5 4 3 2

Leisure Press
A Division of Human Kinetics Publishers, Inc.
Box 5076, Champaign, IL 61825-5076
1-800-747-4457

UK Office:
Human Kinetics Publishers (UK) Ltd.
PO Box 18
Rawdon, Leeds LS19 6TG
England
(0532) 504211

Contents

Series Preface

The Steps to Success Activity Series is a breakthrough in skill instruction through the development of complete learning progressions—the *steps to success*. These *steps* help students quickly perform basic skills successfully and prepare them to acquire advanced skills readily. At each step, students are encouraged to learn at their own pace and to integrate their new skills into the total action of the activity, which motivates them to achieve.

The unique features of the Steps to Success Activity Series are the result of comprehensive development—through analyzing existing activity books, incorporating the latest research from the sport sciences, and consulting with students, instructors, teacher educators, and administrators. This groundwork pointed up the need for three different types of books—for participants, instructors, and teacher educators—which we have created and together comprise the Steps to Success Activity Series.

The *participant book* for each activity is a self-paced, step-by-step guide; learners can use it as a primary resource for a beginning activity class or as a self-instructional guide. The unique features of each *step* in the participant book include

- sequential illustrations that clearly show proper technique for all basic skills,
- helpful suggestions for detecting and correcting errors,
- excellent drill progressions with accompanying *Success Goals* for measuring performance, and
- a complete checklist for each basic skill for a trained observer to rate the learner's technique.

A comprehensive *instructor guide* accompanies the participant's book for each activity, emphasizing how to individualize instruction. Each *step* of the instructor's guide promotes successful teaching and learning with

- teaching cues (*Keys to Success*) that emphasize fluidity, rhythm, and wholeness,

- criterion-referenced rating charts for evaluating a participant's initial skill level,
- suggestions for observing and correcting typical errors,
- tips for group management and safety,
- ideas for adapting every drill to increase or decrease the difficulty level,
- quantitative evaluations for all drills (*Success Goals*), and
- a complete test bank of written questions.

The series textbook, *Instructional Design for Teaching Physical Activities*, explains the *steps to success* model, which is the basis for the Steps to Success Activity Series. Teacher educators can use this text in their professional preparation classes to help future teachers and coaches learn how to design effective physical activity programs in school, recreation, or community teaching and coaching settings.

After identifying the need for participant, instructor, and teacher educator texts, we refined the *steps to success* instructional design model and developed prototypes for the participant and the instructor books. Once these prototypes were fine-tuned, we carefully selected authors for the activities who were not only thoroughly familiar with their sports but had years of experience in teaching them. Each author had to be known as a gifted instructor who understands the teaching of sport so thoroughly that he or she could readily apply the *steps to success* model.

Next, all of the participant and instructor manuscripts were carefully developed to meet the guidelines of the *steps to success* model. Then our production team, along with outstanding artists, created a highly visual, user-friendly series of books.

The result: The Steps to Success Activity Series is the premier sports instructional series available today. The participant books are the best available for helping you to become a master player, the instructor guides will help you to become a master teacher, and the teacher educator's text prepares you to design your own programs.

This series would not have been possible without the contributions of the following:

- Dr. Joan Vickers, instructional design expert,
- Dr. Rainer Martens, Publisher,
- the staff of Human Kinetics Publishers, and
- the *many* students, teachers, coaches, consultants, teacher educators, specialists, and administrators who shared their ideas—and dreams.

Judy Patterson Wright
Series Editor

The prospect of writing this book was exciting for two reasons. First, as teachers and teacher educators, we recognize the value of a book on softball that focuses on connecting theory and strategy to real-world teaching or coaching settings. Second, knowing that most softball books have been directed toward competitive coaching and playing settings, rather than instructional and recreational play, made us happy to accept the challenge of producing a book dedicated to those who teach the sport to students of varying ages and experience levels.

The purpose of this book is to provide a resource of softball materials for teachers of softball classes, coaches of youth teams, and teachers of professional preparation courses in softball. This book, used in conjunction with *Softball: Steps to Success*, provides instructional materials that will enable you to conduct meaningful learning experiences for students and players who wish to gain some expertise in the sport of softball. This book's approach is practical. Class management tips (such as ways to group students according to level of experience), instructional cues, and skill-specific feedback ideas are suggested to supplement the technical skill and drill materials found in the participant's book. Instructional directions are listed in chronological order to help you explain the drills to your students. A variety of instructional cues are suggested to provide both information and analogies that may help your students improve as they practice.

The drills are designed to enable your students to progress in skill proficiency and in tactical application of softball skills. A unique contribution of this instructor's guide to softball literature is the large number of drills and the possible modifications that increase or decrease the level of difficulty the drills require of your students.

In order to help you understand the drill factor (variable) being modified (manipulated) to require increased or decreased complexity of skill or knowledge by your students, a system of numbers (for cross-reference) has been placed within brackets at the end of each drill's "To Decrease Difficulty" and "To Increase Difficulty" sections. These numbers represent the variables of manipulation as identified by Dr. J. Rink, in her book *Teaching Physical Education for Learning*, that are most applicable to softball. The numbers and the variables of manipulation are defined as follows:

1. *Focus of Intent*: The student changes the reason for the practice. (Student changes from practicing to refine hitting technique to practicing to hit the ball to an alley.)
2. *Modification of equipment*: The student uses equipment that makes practice easier (a larger ball to hit) or more difficult (a golf ball to be hit by a wand rather than a bat).
3. *Conditions of performance*: The practice situation is modified to produce increased or decreased task demands. (The ball is hit harder to the fielders; or is rolled rather than hit to those fielders who are afraid of being hit by the ball.)
4. *Spatial arrangements*: Distances and amount of space are increased or decreased so that the skill executed is extended or reduced in difficulty or complexity. (The target for the throw from center field is second base for students with weak throwing arms and home plate for those with stronger arms.)
5. *Practice of parts*: A part of the skill or tactic is practiced in isolation from the rest. (The crow-hop is practiced without the overarm throw so the steps can be learned).
6. *Number of people involved*: The more people involved in the practice drill, the more complicated the task and the more decision-making required. (A fly ball is hit to an outfielder when there is a runner on first base only. Then a runner is added at third base. Now the outfielder must field the ball and decide which base to throw to.)

7. *Number of skills or actions combined*: When more skills are used in sequence, the task becomes more complex. (Fielding a ground ball hit directly to the fielder is made more difficult when the ball is hit so that the fielder first has to move to field the ball and then make a throw to a base.)

8. *Expansion of different responses*: A task is made more or less complex by the number of actions a student can do in response to the situation. (On a deep hit to the outfield, a relay person and a cut-off person move into position to play the ball. The situation will determine whether the cutoff person will be told to cut off the relay person's throw. Then the cutoff person, when told to cut off the ball, can either hold it or throw it to base. The different responses will be called for by the catcher.)

Further, the great many practice drills and the progression they and the variables of manipulation represent will enable you to develop a variety of practice sessions either for a single course unit or for a number of units covering several years of a student's tenure in school.

The management and safety tips presented in this book will help you utilize both a command style and a station style of instruction. There are guides to incorporating different skills and strategies simultaneously in practice sessions, by utilizing commonly available field areas and equipment in nontraditional ways. Thus, this book is designed to give you ideas on ways you can maximize student participation while attending to the different skill experience levels found in most classes and youth or recreational team settings.

The opportunity to focus our beliefs about both softball and teaching in one book was a challenge and a pleasure. We are indebted to Dr. Judy Patterson Wright for her faith in our ability and for her continual encouragement and assistance. The unique approach to this series, which combines the theoretical work of Dr. Joan Vickers and a concern for practical application of that theory to the real world of teaching and coaching, has provided us with the opportunity to present a resource that we hope will help you develop in your students a love of the game that comes from their successes in practice and play.

Diane L. Potter

Gretchen A. Brockmeyer

Implementing the Steps to Success Staircase

This book is meant to be flexible not only for your students' needs but for your own needs as well. It is common to hear that students' perceptions of a task change as the task is learned. However, it is often forgotten that teachers' perceptions and actions also change (Goc-Karp & Zakrajsek, 1987; Housner & Griffey, 1985; Imwold & Hoffman, 1983).

More experienced or master teachers tend to approach the teaching of activities in a similar manner. They are highly organized (e.g., they do not waste time getting groups together or using long explanations); they integrate information (e.g., from biomechanics, kinesiology, exercise physiology, motor learning, sport psychology, cognitive psychology, instructional design); and they relate basic skills to the larger game or performance context. This includes succinctly explaining why the basic skills, concepts, or tactics are important within the game or performance setting. Then, usually within a few minutes, they place their students into a game-like practice situation that unfolds in steps that follow logical manipulations of factors such as

- the equipment,
- the distance, force, and speed of the ball,
- the amount of player movement,
- the direction that the ball is being received or sent,
- the level (high, medium, or low) of the ball,
- the path of the bat swing, and
- the number of players, skills, and rules used in combination.

This book shows you how the basic softball skills, the game concepts and strategies, and selected physiological, psychological, and other pertinent knowledge are interrelated (see Appendix A for an overview). You can use this information not only to gain insights into the various interrelationships but also to define the subject matter for your softball course. The following questions offer specific suggestions for implementing this knowledge base and help you evaluate and improve your teaching methods, which include class organization, drills, objectives, progressions, and evaluations.

1. Under what conditions do you teach?
   - How much space is available?
   - What type of equipment is available? It may be necessary to use some readily available stationary field equipment, such as fences and goalposts, in creative ways.
   - What is the average class size?
   - How much time is allotted per class session?
   - How many class sessions do you teach?
   - Do you have any assistants?

2. What are your students' initial skill experience levels?
   - Look for the rating charts near the beginning of most steps (chapters) to identify the checkpoints that discriminate between students who are less experienced and more experienced in softball skills and game concepts.

3. What is the best order to teach softball skills?
   - Follow the sequence of steps (chapters) in this book.
   - The sequence of steps in this book can be used to reflect skill circuit use or long-term progression through the school years (grades 4 through 12 and college).
   - See Appendix B.1 for suggestions on when to introduce, review, or continue practicing each step.
   - Based on your answers to the previous questions, use the form in Appendix B.2 to put into order the steps that you will be able to cover in the time available.

4. What objectives do you want your students to accomplish by the end of a lesson, a unit, or a course?

- For your technique or qualitative objectives, select from the Student Keys to Success (or the Keys to Success Checklists in *Softball: Steps to Success*) that are provided for all basic skills.
- For your performance or quantitative objectives, select from the Success Goals provided for each drill.
- For written questions on safety, rules, technique, game concepts, and strategies, select from the Test Bank.
- See the Sample Individual Program (Appendix C.1) for selected technique and performance objectives for a 16-week unit.
- For unit objectives, adjust your total number of selected objectives to fit your unit length (use the form in Appendix C.2).
- For organizing daily objectives, see the Sample Lesson Plan in Appendix D.1 and modify the basic lesson plan form in Appendix D.2 to best fit your needs.

5. How will you evaluate your students?

- Read the Evaluation Ideas. You may use the Offensive Player Scorecard and the Defensive Player Scorecard in Step 23 of the participant's book, *Softball: Steps to Success*.
- Decide on your type of grading system, for example, letter grades, pass-fail, total points, percentages, skill experience levels, and so forth.

6. Which activities should be selected to achieve student objectives?

- Follow the drills and exercises for each step because they are specifically designed for large groups of students and are presented in a planned, easy-to-difficult order. Avoid a random approach to selecting drills and exercises.
- Modify any drill as necessary to best fit your students' skill experience levels by following the suggestions for decreasing and increasing each drill's difficulty level. See the Preface for an explanation of the numbers in brackets following each suggestion for decreasing and increasing each drill's difficulty level.
- Ask your students to meet the Success Goal listed for each drill.
- Use the cross-reference to the corresponding step and drill in the participant's book, *Softball: Steps to Success*, for assignments or makeups. The bracketed notation [new drill] after a drill title indicates that the drill appears only in this instructor's guide and will be new to your students.

7. What rules and expectations do you have for your class?

- For general management and safety guidelines, read the section "Preparing Your Class for Success."
- For specific guidelines, read the Group Management and Safety Tips included with each drill.
- Let your students know what your rules are during your first class orientation and the first day of class. Then post the rules and repeat them often.

Teaching is a complex task, requiring you to make many decisions that will affect both you and your students (see Figure 1). Use this book to create an effective and successful learning experience for you and everyone you teach. And remember, have fun, too!

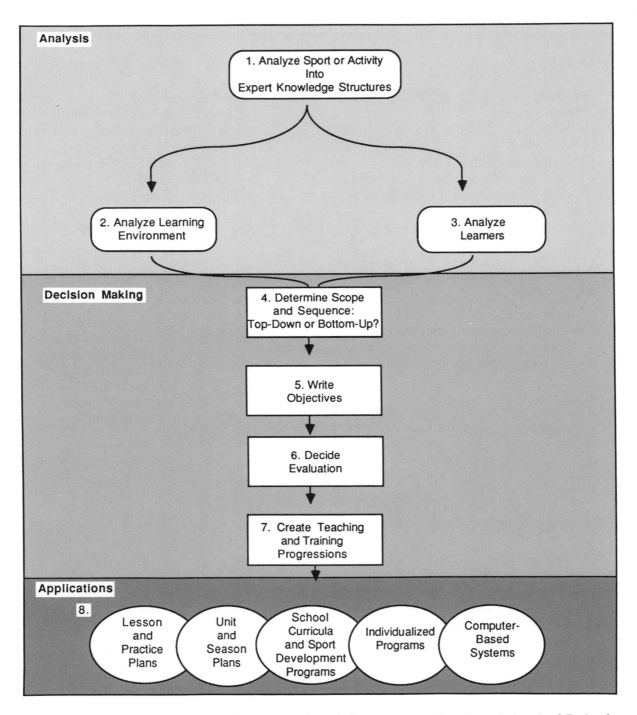

Figure 1 Instructional design model utilizing expert knowledge structures. *Note*. From *Instructional Design for Teaching Physical Activities* by J.N. Vickers, 1990, Champaign, IL: Human Kinetics. Copyright by Joan N. Vickers. Reprinted by permission. This instructional design model has appeared in earlier forms in *Badminton: A Structures of Knowledge Approach* (p. 1) by J.N. Vickers and D. Brecht, 1987, Calgary, AB: University Printing Services. Copyright 1987 by Joan N. Vickers; and in ''The Role of Expert Knowledge Structures in an Instructional Design Model for Physical Education'' by J.N. Vickers, 1983, *Journal of Teaching in Physical Education*, **2**(3), p. 20. Copyright 1983 by Joan N. Vickers.

Key

Position	Symbol	Pos. No.
Pitcher	P	1
Catcher	C	2
First Baseman	1b	3
Second Baseman	2b	4
Third Baseman	3b	5
Shortstop	SS	6
Left Fielder	LF	7
Center Fielder	CF	8
Right Fielder	RF	9
Short Fielder	SF	10
(slow pitch only)		

X	player
→	player movement
– – →	thrown ball
–·–·→	hit ball
～→	rolled ball
ᴑᴑᴑᴑ→	rebounding ball
H	hitter
F	fielder
BBR	batter-baserunner
B	baserunner
HP	home plate
DP	double play
OF	outfield
IF	infield
LE	less experienced
ME	more experienced
RH	right-handed player
LH	left-handed player
T	tosser or thrower
ST	sidearm thrower
R	relay person

Preparing Your Class
for Success

Teaching is an activity in which you make a series of decisions about procedures, organization, content, evaluation, equipment, and safety. Such decisions are often interrelated and interdependent; thus, your task of preparing and teaching a lesson is not a simple one. Teaching is a complex process when all the factors that contribute to decision making are considered.

One possible key to success in planning lessons that provide real opportunities for student learning is your establishment of the goal toward which each lesson is directed. In using this book as an aid to planning softball lessons for students of varying ages and skill experience levels, you will see that the format is designed to assist you in setting goals and developing learning tasks to support those goals. The "Student Keys to Success" and "Student Success Goals" sections provide qualitative and quantitative goals toward which the drills and game-like applications of each step (chapter) are directed.

A second key to success for planning skill lessons is the concept of maximum student participation. The "Group Management and Safety Tips" section of each step in this instructor's book contains many suggestions for maximizing student practice through facility utilization, drill organizational patterns, and adjustments for differences in student skill experience levels. The participant's book, *Softball*, and the instructor's book, *Teaching Softball*, are designed to be used together in your class planning. The materials contained in these books should provide you with class activities that can be effectively adjusted for classes of differing sizes and for special conditions in facilities, equipment, student skill levels, and student needs.

GENERAL CLASS ORGANIZATION AND MANAGEMENT

Softball is a sport that is made up of numerous skills that are nearly always used in combination with one another. The skills contained in the participant's book follow an order that is progressive in nature for one student to follow. However, there are times when it is impossible for all students in a class to be practicing the same skill drill simultaneously. Thus, it is not possible simply to move in serial order from one step to the next as you plan your softball unit.

Facility Utilization

Softball can be taught both indoors and outdoors. The indoor activities most often result from the necessity to do something with the class on rainy days. There are several skills that can be effectively practiced indoors with minimal loss of game-like realism. Thus, it is important to use time in a gymnasium for skill practice rather than the old standard whiffle-ball game.

Indoor softball practice is different from outdoor practice. However, it is possible to set up the gymnasium in ways that give significant practice time and still allow for safety and realism in the situation. Indoor practice is usually best used for individual skill work, the focus of which is refinement of skill technique. Individual skill practice is often repetitious, which is, of course, what advances skill development; however, repetition can also result in boredom. Thus, it is important for you to set up a variety of stations and activities to maintain student interest (see Diagram I.1). Practicing game concepts and game-like application of skills is not usually successful in the gymnasium. Too much room is required for game-like drills; the low number of students who can participate at one time creates problems.

Outdoor practice is certainly more realistic. Students can actually see their skill work applied in the drills and the games they play. They often focus inordinate attention on the outcome of their practice when they are practicing on a real softball diamond. Thus, even outdoors, many practice setups need to be divorced from the regulation field and the

LE stations

1. Fungo hitting ground balls

2. Fielding ground balls from throws and overhand throw

3. Hitting using the batting tee

4. Pitching using wall

ME stations

1. Fungo hitting and fielding ground balls

2. Soft toss hitting

3. Accuracy pitching using buckets and hoops

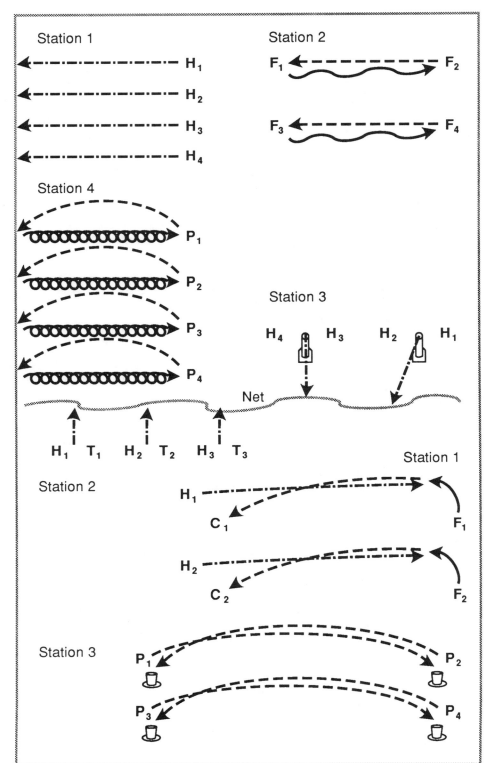

Diagram I.1 Gymnasium setup with experience-level stations.

rules of the game. When your students are ready to apply their skills to game-like situations, though, it is important to set up the facility to duplicate a regulation field. This is often not easily accomplished, because of the distances between bases, infield and outfield, and players. Many suggestions in the "Group Management and Safety Tips" sections of this instructor's book are directed toward adapting the facility to include several stations of game-like practice. If it is possible to utilize an area adjacent to the softball diamond for practice, you can effectively create more practice spaces for your class. Because softball does not make divots or holes in the grass, it is usually fine to set up practice areas on soccer fields, football fields, field hockey fields, and even baseball fields.

It is far better to have students practice skills on areas that are modified and oriented to the dimensions of a regulation softball diamond than to have them wait in long lines for their turns to try the skill on the real softball field. Of course, having the students spread out in different areas makes supervision more difficult. However, giving students the opportunity to practice repetitively should help avoid the discipline problems that occur when students are waiting for their turns to touch the equipment. The opportunity for sufficient practice trials should also help students experience success and develop increased levels of skill. A student who is purposefully practicing in realistic settings experiences success with goals because of the drill progression and will certainly be more motivated to stay on task and to continue participating. In this event, demands for supervision based upon prevention of and reaction to discipline problems may diminish.

Organizational Patterns

Suggestions are made in this instructor's book concerning ways to accommodate practice of different skills or practice of the same skill by students of differing skill levels. Two class organizational patterns that can be used for such practice are stations and skill circuits. For an example of the former, on a softball field set up for regulation play, there is limited space to practice fielding and throwing from shortstop to first base for a class of 30 or more students of differing skill levels. It is important to give the students practice in the real-distance throws, but this can be done as effectively in simulated settings as on the regulation field. You can design multiple drill stations, each with the shortstop-to-first base distance and a marker indicating the relative location of home plate. You can set up several of these stations at various locations on the regulation diamond and the adjacent practice areas. Specify directions according to skill level.

There are times when the skill being practiced requires so much room that it is impossible to safely set up a sufficient number of practice stations of the same skill. In this situation, a skill circuit might be best utilized for practice. A skill circuit is composed of stations at which different skills are practiced simultaneously (see Diagram I.2 for an example). One station could be a pitching practice drill. A second station could be the ball-toss hitting drill. A third station could be fungo hitting fly balls with outfielders catching the balls and making throws to a target. A fourth station could be mimetic practice of the footwork required for force plays at different bases. The students would spend a certain amount of time at each station, then rotate to a different one. Because the drills have different spatial requirements, they can be safely and effectively practiced simultaneously on the practice area available.

When you use skill circuit stations in organizing class practice, all the skills included in a given circuit should be at the same level of difficulty. This is important because the students rotate from one station in the circuit to another. Consequently, if you have students who are of different experience levels, you need either to develop two skill circuits located in different practice areas or to establish different success goals at each station in the circuit.

If each station in the circuit contains skill drills at a similar difficulty level, the order of the stations is unimportant. Students can practice successfully at any of the stations in

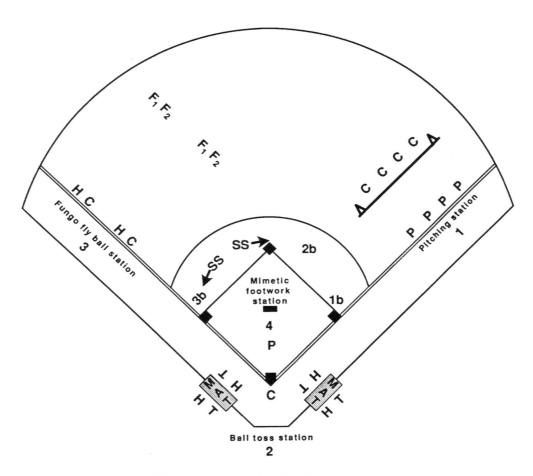

Diagram I.2 Sample skill circuit stations.

the circuit rather than having to progress from one station to the next in order of difficulty. Therefore, students can rotate through all the stations in one class period, or more than one class period can be used for completion of the skill circuit.

As you plan and carry out your softball unit, you will undoubtedly be able to combine skills and drills in stations or skill circuits that allow your students to most effectively practice the particular skills you are covering. Your individual teaching facility and the amount of equipment you have available will affect the format you will use for achieving maximum participation and learning. It is most likely that you will use a combination of organizational formats as you move through the unit. Suggestions in this instructor's book are made with the idea of helping you achieve maximum student participation.

Grouping by Experience Level

You are seldom so fortunate as to have an entire class of students with the same amount of experience in the activity you are teaching. It is difficult to motivate and foster skill improvement in more advanced students through the same instructions and drills used for the entire class. Furthermore, the differences in skill level between students in a class can produce legal liability concerns for you. Use ability grouping to place students with a similar skill level together. The rating charts in this book have been designed to help you divide the students into ability groups.

You will notice immediately that the skill categories in this book are different from the usual "beginner, intermediate, and advanced." We believe that dividing a class into three ability groups is very difficult when the time allotted for classes and units is usually small. We have found that it is much quicker and easier to divide a class into groups of only two ability levels. Then, when you are working with an individual student, you can easily give feedback, challenges, or remediation suggestions to adjust the task goal to the student's particular skill level. Thus, two skill level groups are identified on all of the skill rating charts.

Students are very often sensitive to the ability levels into which they are placed. Students often ascribe value to the *beginner* or *advanced* label. In an attempt to reduce the value connotation of low-ability and high-ability labels, the authors of this text use the terminology *less experienced* and *more experienced* (terms initially proposed by Dr. Betty Mann of Springfield College) to describe the skill level of the students. The thought underlying this terminology maintains that students who have had less experience in the skills of an activity are not lesser in ability, but simply more limited in experience. Thus, practice will increase that experience level. All persons who have achieved a particular skill level have done so through a combination of natural ability and practice. Most persons who are less experienced in an activity have not had the opportunity to develop their skill to their natural ability. Thus, you can emphasize that students at a higher skill level are not necessarily "better" or more valued than others, but are persons who have had greater opportunity to practice the skills being taught. Similarly, a student who is more experienced in some skills may be less experienced in others. Therefore, you can minimize student anxiety about labels by using *less experienced* and *more experienced* as measures of a student's previous practice, not his or her actual ability.

CLASS MANAGEMENT AND SAFETY CONCEPTS

Safety is critical in softball because hitting and throwing are key features of the game. Consequently, the first rule for safety is that all students are responsible for the safety of classmates. This means that they must look at the area to which they are throwing or hitting to make certain no one will be in jeopardy if the ball they throw is not caught. Similarly, when a student is going to swing a bat, he or she must be aware of the space all around the body. Students must be taught to swing bats only in specifically designated practice areas and to look around them in all directions before swinging bats.

The playing field and gymnasium must be set up for practice in ways that accommodate the swinging bats, the moving players, and the hit and thrown balls. The following principles can help establish practice and game environments that are safe and in which high-quality practice can take place:

- You must establish a *stop* signal to which your students will immediately respond.
- When balls are being thrown or hit as a part of a drill, orient the practice stations so that all hits and throws are going in the same general direction. Space the stations far enough apart that errant hits or throws from one station do not endanger students at other practice stations.
- Students should be cautioned not to enter practice stations other than their own to make plays on balls.
- When practice involves retrieving balls at a fence or wall, allow students to retrieve only after your signal.
- Locate the practice stations so that all your students are within view at all times.
- Students should not be allowed to wear jewelry to class.
- Students who are injured should be required to have a medical release before participating.
- All students should wear sneakers.
- Batting helmets should always be available for hitters and baserunners.
- Masks should be used by catchers any time a batter is in hitting position with a bat.
- Eyeglasses should be firmly attached; safety glass is recommended.
- Mark as out of play any dangerous place on the field or within the practice area.

- The students should pick up any softballs, bats, and gloves that are not being used in a drill and place them out of the practice or play area. A bucket for such equipment at each practice station is advantageous.
- Use cones or other markers to designate practice areas and starting lines. In softball the foul lines from home plate to the outfield fence serve as excellent markers for starting positions.
- When having students practice game skills in application settings, always orient them as if they were on a regulation field. Even on a nonfield practice area, students can be oriented to practice as though they were on the field by a cone (or a similar marker) placed in the ''home plate'' spot.
- Bats should never be used as golf clubs. They should not be used to hit rocks or any other nonregulation balls. It is okay to use the bats as ''air guitars,'' however.
- Empty containers such as buckets, plastic milk crates, and plastic bleach bottles can be used to retrieve balls and transfer them from one location to another. Balls sent to a target area can be caught or otherwise collected by a retriever and put into the container when no throw is called for by the drill. The retriever then simply brings the container to the performance site when it is his or her turn to practice the drill.
- Plan enough drill stations that only the lowest number of students called for by the drill structure are involved at one station.
- Set up your stations or skill circuit prior to the start of class.
- Have students help you break down your stations at the end of the class or the end of the day, whichever is called for.
- It is useful to have some type of warm-up review or practice posted at the practice facility so that students who come to class earlier than others can immediately become active. Often this warm-up will involve general stetching (to loosen up the arms, shoulders, and legs) and playing catch.
- Whenever possible, make targets visually appealing and vary their shapes. Nothing is more boring than using the same target day after day. If the target can make a sound when the ball hits it, it is usually more motivating to the student.
- Some targets that can be used in softball include
  - toss-backs, rebound nets;
  - hoops on the ground or attached to fences;
  - football goal posts;
  - lacrosse, soccer, field hockey goals;
  - cones to outline areas;
  - softball gloves;
  - loose bases or home plates;
  - buckets, boxes, barrels;
  - fences;
  - walls;
  - areas outlined with tape (use floor tape on floors and walls rather than masking tape, which is harder to remove), rope, string, ribbon, crepe paper; and
  - towels
- Many drills require the students to rotate between roles or stations. It is at times easy for the students to ''cheat'' themselves by not practicing when it is their turn. Thus, you may need to check occasionally to see that students are on task. This is particularly true when students are in stations separated by considerable distances. Hold students accountable for task practice.
- Do not waste time during class figuring out how to group your students for practice. Plan the management of practice groups prior to the start of class.
- Put all left-handed throwers or hitters at the same end of the practice line.

CLASS INSTRUCTIONAL CONCEPTS

Student practice is crucial to skill development. Skill development is crucial to successful game participation. Practicing skills in strategic, game-like situations is crucial to the development of a knowledgeable and skillful softball player. The class itself is a time for you to motivate, encourage, give feedback, and provide the support your students need to become active learners.

Here are some instructional ideas that facilitate the development of a positive class environment, including techniques for instruction, student self-management, and feedback.

Instructional Techniques:

- Make your skill explanations brief and concise. Use no more than four key points to describe the skill. Technical information is better given later, when you are working with individual students. You then know their readiness levels and can be as specific and technical as that readiness level warrants.
- Learn and use your students' names at all times.
- Use instructional aids whenever possible to clarify or enhance the skill being practiced. Targets are excellent when accuracy is the intended outcome of the drill. Charts that highlight skill technique facilitate analysis by partners or other peers. Modified equipment can make the skill easier (or less fear evoking).
- Involve the students in applying their skills to game-like situations as soon as possible. Students do not need to be perfect performers of skills before they can use them in controlled game conditions.
- Modify the game rules in any way that produces more practice and, hence, increased learning. The rules of the game are not sacred in a physical education class. Use rule modifications to allow students to practice in ways that reinforce concepts or refine skill techniques.
- If possible, end the class with some sort of culminating activity that combines all the skills practiced during the class period.

Student Self-Management Techniques:

- Allow the students to take some responsibility in the practice settings. If you have set them up in groups at different stations, there is no way you can monitor absolutely everything that happens.
- Encourage your students to use their practice time effectively. They will improve fast if they practice what they are sup-

posed to and in the ways that have been designed for maximum learning.
- From time to time, check the students' recording of their success scores in their participant's books. Also have them demonstrate for you the skills they have performed to achieve those scores. This will assist you in monitoring their accountability as they practice on their own.

Feedback Techniques:

- Try to get to every student to give help. Feedback on techniques is crucial if a student is going to proceed in skill development.
- Be certain that you watch a student long enough to see a consistent problem. Too often, only one practice trial is used to provide the basis for feedback and correction cues.
- Try to make your feedback as skill-specific as possible. Tell the students what they are doing that is correct. When they are making technical or strategic errors, try to tell them how to do the skills or strategies correctly. Try not to focus on what they have done incorrectly, unless they are highly skilled.
- Encourage your students to help one another in practice. The more experienced students can certainly help the less experienced students with skill practice. By filling in the skill checklists found in the participant's book, your less experienced students can help the more experienced students refine their skill techniques.
- Keep the students involved cognitively in the skill and game practice. Ask questions that cause the students to make decisions about correct procedures or techniques and about the application of concepts to game-like situations.
- If many students in the class are having the same problem, stop the class and give group feedback and cues about ways to perform the skill or strategy correctly.

CLASS WARM-UPS

Students often come into class thinking that they can simply begin practicing or playing without warming up. Failure to warm up, however, is one of the leading causes of injuries and muscle soreness. Many students will be less motivated if they come out of softball class sore. Students need to learn that gradually warming up and stretching the throwing arm is the best way to avoid the muscle soreness that comes from irregular play.

As the teacher, you should establish a class routine with warming up as the first activity of the class period. Because nearly every softball skill and game play concept involves movement requiring several muscle groups, the warm-up should involve the total body. First, to increase the heart rate, have students slowly jog either to the playing area or around the perimeter of the field. After heart rates are increased, the next order of the day should be stretching the neck, arms, back, legs, trunk, ankles, and, particularly, the shoulders. The warm-up exercises found in *Softball* in the section entitled "Preparing Your Body for Success" can be used at the beginning of class.

There are different ways to conduct stretching. You should teach your students the correct way to stretch. Be sure to emphasize that they should do static, not ballistic (bouncing), stretching. Have them slowly stretch until they notice tension, and hold that stretch for a count of 8 to 10. As the muscles accommodate, slightly increase the tension, and hold for 8 to 10 more counts. Repeat 3 times. When you are sure that your students know the stretches, then you can have students lead the preclass stretching. You can even ask them whether they know other stretches that work on the same muscles as the preclass stretches. Ask them to show you the stretches; when you have okayed these different stretches, have the students teach them to the class.

There are times when you will want to have the entire class stretch as a unit. This is probably the case at the beginning of your softball course. As the course progresses, however, you might make stretching out an individual responsibility.

Once the students have stretched out, they can execute the overhand throw in pairs. They should begin about 30 feet apart and gradually move farther apart as their arms begin to feel loose. Don't let them go too far apart, because they can hurt their arms by trying to throw the ball too great a distance; furthermore, they are usually not as accurate with long throws as with shorter throws.

Encourage your students to go through the full range of the throwing motion with their arms. In addition, the students should use the full body motion, including the turn and step in the direction of the throw. Many students stand in a stationary position and, with the arm only, use snap throws to toss the balls to their partner. This snapping action of a "cold" arm and shoulder can cause serious injury.

EQUIPMENT

Effective skill practice for students is largely dependent upon the availability of equipment. Throughout this book, the "Equipment" sections of the drills will direct you to set up practice stations with buckets of balls; bats of varying weights, lengths, and grip sizes; and gloves for every student. In addition, nonsoftball items are often called for, such as cones, hoops, wands, whiffle golf balls, tennis balls, and so forth. Skill proficiency is developed by hundreds of repetitions of motor acts with increasingly correct performances. In class situations the opportunity for 30 to 40 students to execute these repetitions can be provided only by having adequate equipment available.

Equipment Selection

If you are unfamiliar with softball equipment, go to your local sporting goods store and ask to see their selection of bats, balls, gloves, catcher's masks, bases, and home plates. Ask to see different grades (at proportionate costs) of the same type of item. In general, medium-grade items are the best for school use. The cheapest will not last, and the best are designed for the professional athlete.

The following section points out things for you to look for when selecting softball equipment. Your school system undoubtedly has specific purchasing regulations that you must follow. However, as the teacher in charge of an instructional area, you must have input into the decision-making process involved in buying equipment. Take a couple of knowledgeable students along, especially to help with bat selection. When making recommendations for the purchase of equipment for younger and smaller students, remember that the bat or the glove that feels good for you might be too heavy or too big for those students. The final general point on equipment selection is that you must keep up with new equipment trends. The IncrediBall® mentioned in this book is a relatively new product that has important implications not only for indoor practice but for playing situations where safety is a concern. The IncrediBall® is a cloth-covered, restricted flight ball that reacts in all other ways much like a regulation ball. An added advantage is that it can be thrown into the washer and dryer.

Softballs

Regulation softballs are available in three circumference sizes that are appropriate for class use: 12-inch (the most commonly used), 11-inch, and 16-inch balls. The 11-inch and 16-inch balls are designed for specific games. However, you can use these alternate-size balls to provide a smaller or a larger ball to either increase or decrease the difficulty of a practice task.

The composition, of both the inner material and the outside covering, is another factor to be considered when selecting softballs. The ''hard'' softball has a core that is designed to give the ball considerable flight. A ball made with a softer core is commonly called a ''restricted flight'' ball. As the name implies, the restricted flight ball does not travel as far when hit as a regular hard-core ball. Thus, the restricted flight ball has many advantages in a limited practice space.

The composition of the ball's outside covering is a major consideration when wet grass is a practice factor. Leather-covered balls become saturated with water quickly and become heavy, dirty, and slippery all at the same time. Both hard-core and restricted flight balls are available with a rubber (or similar) cover

that can be used in wet weather to prolong the life of the softballs.

Softball Bats

In general, the softball bat recommended for class use is the aluminum bat. Although wooden bats (if you can even find them) are cheaper, they do not last, and their replacement costs over a period of time would exceed the initial outlay for durable aluminum bats.

Softball bats vary in length, weight, barrel design, and grip composition and size. In general, shorter bats are also lighter in weight, but weights vary between bats of the same length. It is extremely important for you to provide bats with which your students can swing into and through the contact zone with minimal effort. Your smallest students will need bats from 28 to 31 inches in length (usually available in 1-inch increments). Your adult-size students should have 32-inch, 33-inch, and 34-inch bats to select from.

If possible, select bats within these length ranges that have differing weights (light to medium; in the low 20s, if measured in ounces; or low swing weights, if weight is given that way). Very heavy bats (30 or more ounces) are of little use in the class situation. Be wary of ordering bats from pictures in catalogues. A pastel color might be appealing, but unless the color is coding for weight and length (which some companies use), don't buy bats by color!

Barrel (the part of the bat that contacts the ball) design is usually a matter of preference for skilled hitters. Some prefer a large barrel, which provides more surface area for contact; others prefer a thin barrel, which is easier to whip through the contact zone. Some prefer a ''bottle bat'' style, in which the barrel stays the same diameter from the barrel end to within a few inches of the grip. Large-barrel bats, especially bottle bats, tend to be heavier than tapered bats. Select a variety of styles, concentrating more on the evenly tapered, lighter models.

Grip size and composition is the final bat factor to be considered. The size is, again, largely a matter of individual preference. Some people like a thin grip, others a thick grip. For your smallest students, be sure the grip is such that their fingers can surround the bat. In a technical sense, the thicker grip tends to slow down a swing. For most of your students, a slow swing is caused by too heavy a bat or too late a start; this is not a swing that anyone tries to develop. Again, select a variety of grip sizes so that the likes and dislikes of all students can be accommodated. Regarding the composition of the grip, choose one that offers a secure hand-hold for the batter and that will last. Aluminum bats usually have replaceable rubber tubing grips. You may not have many alternatives when it comes to grip composition. However, if the bats you order do have tubing grips, be sure to also order replacement tubes *and* the applicator for putting them on.

Fielder's Gloves

If you buy locally, check your sports store for closeouts on *baseball* gloves. The glove labeled a "softball glove" in most catalogues is small. Although perhaps appropriate in size for use in elementary schools, it is too small for middle school and high school use. Gloves have different webbing styles, finger lengths, and even number of fingers. None of these factors is critical to your selection of gloves for class use. Although bats and balls do not come in right- and left-handed versions, gloves do. Be sure to purchase an adequate number of left-handed gloves for your classes. Catcher's mitts and first baseman's mitts are not recommended for class use; regular fielder's gloves are perfectly adequate in a class situation for use by all players.

Catcher's Mask

Even though many adult slow pitch softball leagues do not require the catcher to wear a mask behind the plate, we recommend that for safety you require the use of the mask. A lightweight, wire softball mask is appropriate for class use.

Softball Bases and Home Plate

Your regular softball field, if used by a competitive team, may have bases and a home plate that are fixed in the ground. In addition to such permanent bases, you will need loose bases and home plates in order to set up stations in other field areas. Indoor rubber bases are useful, as are the thick bases typically anchored for game play by one or two straps and metal spikes driven into the ground. These bases, used without the spikes, can be effective for setting up diamonds on general field space. The Sav-a-Leg® home plate (with beveled edges) comes in both permanent and portable varieties; it is recommended for the class setting.

Batting Helmets

As with the catcher's mask, batting helmets are not usually worn by players in slow pitch games. However, there are times when they will create a safer practice situation. Helmets should meet the approved code for use in softball or baseball (stamped on the helmet). They are usually sized small, medium, large, and extra large or extra small. The adult sizes will not be appropriate for students with smaller heads; youth league sizes will be necessary to accommodate such persons.

Miscellaneous Softball Equipment

- Bat bags
- Ball bags
- Net bags (for gloves, balls, catcher's masks, etc.)
- Foul line marker (cord or twine to go from home plate to outfield) and machine for application
- Equipment transporter (grocery-style cart with larger wheels)

PRECLASS CHECKLIST

The success of any class is probably more dependent upon the preparation that goes into it than upon the actual teaching that occurs in the class setting itself. In order to ensure that your planning is not sabotaged by forgetfulness, the following checklist can be used as you plan each lesson and reviewed just before you go to class.

1. Check the equipment to make sure that you have what is required by your drills and that you have enough for everyone to be as active as possible.

2. Have extra balls in case some are lost.
3. Have extra cones or markers in case you need to adjust the drills in any way for groups or individual students.
4. Make sure that all your equipment is in good repair.
5. Count the equipment and mark the equipment carrier with the number of items made available to the class. This will facilitate your having the same amount of equipment at the end of class as at the beginning of class.
6. Check the practice areas to make sure there are no dangerous holes in the field (e.g., gopher holes, mole outcroppings).
7. Make sure that you have the station and target markers ready, either set up on the practice area or at the area ready to be set up so that students can help.
8. Be prepared with extra drill options for students in case they become bored or frustrated with the drills being done.
9. Have a rainy day plan ready.
10. Be positive and committed to student learning.

NINE LEGAL DUTIES

There are nine legal duties owed by an instructor to the students of a course to fulfill the obligation of liability. We list them here as they apply to a softball course.

1. Adequate Supervision

As an instructor, you must provide adequate supervision to protect students from inherent or extraneous hazards of the situation.

2. Sound Planning

You must also provide good, sound planning for the activities being conducted. Sound teaching progressions must be coupled with safe practice environments.

3. Inherent Risks

We have already mentioned the inherent risks involved in softball. You have a duty to the students to warn them adequately of such risks and to be sure they understand the risks.

4. Safe Environment

You must provide a practice area that is free of hidden or unmarked hazards. A safe environment also includes the surrounding area and the equipment available. You are expected to inspect the facility and equipment regularly and thoroughly and to pick up all balls and equipment daily.

5. Evaluating Students' Fitness for the Activity

You must evaluate your students' injuries or handicaps and determine to what extent such disabilities may limit their safe participation. You must also attempt to ascertain the mental attitudes of students where such attitudes may become a hazard to their safety.

6. Matching or Equating Students

When students are paired for active participation in a drill, you must be sure that each member of the pair can perform all of the skills you require of them both. A less experienced player should not be expected to keep up with a more experienced player assigned as a partner. However, at times more experienced players can serve as teaching partners, providing practice opportunities for less experienced players.

7. Emergency First Aid Procedures

In the event of an accident, you must be prepared to provide adequate medical assistance. It is your duty to your students to have planned and posted medical procedures that can be put immediately into action. Failure to provide this protection can result in court findings of negligence.

8. Other Legal Concerns

You cannot restrict your classes or your students in such a way as to violate their civil rights. Your legal duty is to provide for the legal rights and concerns of your students, staff, and any spectators allowed during the program.

9. General Legal Concerns

In today's lawsuit-happy environment, you must be aware of all the possibilities for liability and must take adequate measures to protect yourself. Always keep accurate records of your activities, especially in the event of an accident involving an injury. Keep such records for a minimum of 5 years. It is a wise practice for all instructors to carry adequate personal liability insurance. Rates for such insurance have risen dramatically in recent years, but you should consider very seriously the consequences of being uninsured.

Step 1   Catching

Catching the ball as it approaches is the fundamental defensive skill in softball. All defensive plays originate with some type of catch, so it is crucial that your students develop the correct catching patterns.

Catching the ball with two hands is a focal point that you, the instructor, can key in on. Two-handed catches secure the ball and make possible the smooth transition to the throw that nearly always follows a catch.

It is very important that the player catching the ball be directly in the line of the oncoming ball. This helps him or her see the ball clearly and get into the correct position to make the catch.

Less experienced players tend to move away from the ball as they catch it. They usually move to the side in order to avoid being hit if they should miss the ball. You can use a softer ball or a softer toss in order to help them overcome their fear.

STUDENT KEYS TO SUCCESS

- Get in line with oncoming ball
- Give with ball when it goes into glove
- Continuous motion from catch into throwing position

Catching Rating

CHECKPOINT	LESS EXPERIENCED	MORE EXPERIENCED
Preparation Stance	• Square foot and body position	• Feet in forward stride position, glove-side foot ahead
Tracking	• Begins late	• Begins when ball is tossed
Body Position	• Moves away from line of ball	• Stays in line with ball
Execution Number Hands Used Arm Action	• One-handed • Stiff at catch	• Two-handed • Gives with ball
Follow-Through Body Action Transition	• Faces forward • Two motions: catch, then turn to throw	• Turns to throw • Continuous motion: catch to preparation for throw

Error Detection and Correction for Catching

Errors in catching often occur for the less experienced players (LE) because of fear of the ball. You can help your students overcome this fear by helping them use correct catching techniques so they can become confident about their abilities. For the more experienced students (ME), the catching errors are usually those associated with the continuous motion from the catch to the throwing position.

The common catching errors following and in the participant's book should be the focal point of your observations of your students' practice. Be sure to focus on only one error at a time to correct, because your students should work on only one thing at a time.

ERROR

CORRECTION

1. The ball does not go into the glove (LE).

1. Have the student watch the ball from the toss all the way into the glove.

ERROR

CORRECTION

2. The ball is caught with the glove away from the body to the glove side (LE).

2. Have the student put his or her body in line with the oncoming ball. Have the student reach forward for the ball. Use a softer ball such as rubber ball or Rag Ball® or IncrediBall®.

3. The ball drops out of the glove (LE).

3. Tell the student that when feeling the ball hit the glove, he or she should close the glove hand and cover the ball with the throwing hand.

ERROR

CORRECTION

4. The student tries a one-handed catch (LE, ME).

4. Tell the student to cover the ball with the throwing hand.

5. The student has stiff arms at the catch.

5. Here are some cues for the student: "Give with the ball. Draw the ball in by bending the elbows. Cushion the ball like it's dropping into a blanket."

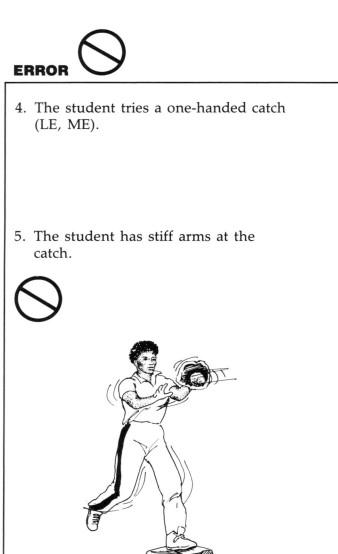

ERROR	CORRECTION
6. The catch is separate from the preparation for throwing (a discontinuous two-step motion).	6. The student needs to draw the ball into the throwing shoulder with both hands. The catch and the turn of the upper body should be one smooth movement.
7. There is no pivot on the follow-through.	7. The student needs to turn the glove side of the upper body toward the target while drawing the ball to the throwing shoulder.

Catching Drills

Note. For an explanation of the bracketed numbers after entries in the "To Decrease Difficulty" and "To Increase Difficulty" sections, see the Preface.

1. Mimetic Drill
[Corresponds to *Softball*, Step 1, Drill 1]

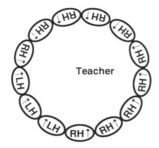

Group Management and Safety Tips

- All students can practice simultaneously. Have only your less experienced students do this drill. Start your more experienced students on Drill 3.
- Use lines or circles so you can see everyone. Put left-handed players together as a group. Place them so their throwing-hand side is beside the right-handers.
- Students could also pair up to watch one another. Be sure to focus observers' attention on the Student Keys to Success.

Equipment

- Gloves, 1 per student
- Mirrors, if available, when indoors

Instructions and Cues to Class

- "Start with your feet in the forward stride position, your glove-side foot forward."
- "Feel your body weight shift forward to make the catch."
- "As you catch the ball, feel your weight shift back and turn the glove-side of your body to the target."
- "In one continuous motion, reach for the ball, catch it, and draw it to your throwing shoulder."
- "Move slowly for the first 5 repetitions. Exaggerate the motions."

Student Options

- "After 10 repetitions, close your eyes and imagine you are catching a ball coming toward you. Make the catch and the movement to the throwing position one continuous, fluid motion. Say to yourself, 'Watch the ball, catch, and turn.' The turn consists of your moving continuously from the catch to the throwing position with a body pivot."
- "Have a partner watch you and tell you whether your motion is smooth and whether your body turns to the throwing position."
- "At home, practice the catching motion in front of a mirror. Check your technique according to the Keys to Success in your textbook."

Student Success Goals

- 10 repetitions with correct form: reach, give with ball, pivot glove-side of body toward target
- 10 repetitions with eyes closed, continuous motion from catch to throwing position
- 10 repetitions in front of a mirror

To Decrease Difficulty

- Not applicable

To Increase Difficulty

- Increase the speed of the action. [1]

2. Self-Toss Drill
[Corresponds to *Softball*, Step 1, Drill 2]

Group Management and Safety Tips

- Only less experienced students should do this drill.
- Have your students get into two lines facing one another, with about 15 feet between the lines.
- Space the students in line so that errant tosses will not hit others.

Equipment

- Softballs, 1 per student
- Nerf softballs, whiffle softballs, or Rag Balls®, 1 per 3 students (for students afraid of real softballs)

Instructions and Cues to Class

- "Toss the ball softly just higher than your head. Reach up with both hands to catch the ball."
- "Catch the ball and draw it to your throwing shoulder."
- "Remember to cushion the ball when you catch it."
- "Make the catch and the move to the throwing position a continuous motion."
- "Stop between repetitions. Toss, catch, move to the throwing position, and stop. Then repeat your toss."

Student Options

- "Have a partner watch your form to see whether you watch the ball go into your glove and whether you give with the catch."
- "Vary the height of your tosses."

Student Success Goal

- 20 tosses and catches without dropping the ball

To Decrease Difficulty

- Let your student use a softer or larger ball. [2]
- Have your student use a lower toss. [3]

To Increase Difficulty

- Make the student increase the height of the tosses. [3]
- Have your student catch the ball above head height. [1]
- Have the student use a smaller ball, such as a tennis ball or a baseball. [2]

3. *Move Into Position Drill*
[Corresponds to *Softball*, Step 1, Drill 3]

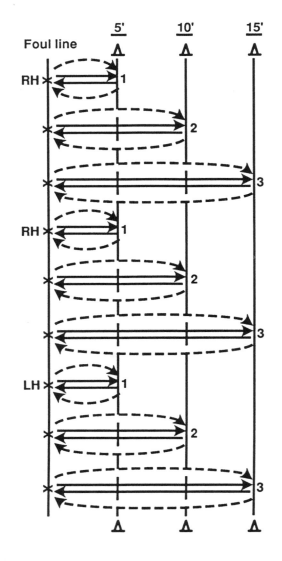

Group Management and Safety Tips

- This is the only drill in this step that more experienced players should do. They can practice this drill while the less experienced students do Drills 1 and 2.
- The setup for this drill is the same for both the less and the more experienced students.
- Mark lines 5 feet, 10 feet, and 15 feet from an outfield foul line or a line on a soccer or football field. You can use cones as markers for the three lines; put the cones at the two outer edges of the practice area

so that students do not trip over them.
- The students should start 5 to 7 feet apart on the foul line.
- Left-handed students should be grouped together at one end of the line.
- The students first face the three lines and do the drill.
- The students then turn and face in the direction of their throwing-arm sides (doing a 90-degree turn so their glove-side shoulders are at the foul line) and do the drill.
- Lastly, the students turn and face in the direction of their glove sides (doing a 180-degree turn so their throwing-side shoulders are at the foul line) and do the drill.

Equipment

- Gloves, 1 per student
- Softballs, 1 per student
- Cones, 6, or other line markers

Instructions and Cues to Class

- ''Toss the ball underhand up and forward so that it would come down on the first line, the 5-foot line. Move forward and catch it. Now turn toward your starting line and do the same thing. Repeat until you have made 4 tosses of 5 feet. Then repeat the drill with 10-foot and 15-foot tosses.''
- ''Move under the ball and catch it using correct form.''
- ''Watch the ball all the way into your glove.''
- ''Toss the ball high enough so that you have time to move under it and catch it above your head.''
- ''In one motion, move the ball from the catch to the throwing position.''
- ''Toss the ball sideways, then be sure to turn and run under it when making catches on tosses to your glove and throwing-hand sides.''

Student Option

- "The more experienced among you may toss the ball overhand, higher, or farther."

Student Success Goal

- 36 catches without dropping the ball

Forward direction	Glove-side toss	Throwing-side toss
4 at 5 feet	4 at 5 feet	4 at 5 feet
4 at 10 feet	4 at 10 feet	4 at 10 feet
4 at 15 feet	4 at 15 feet	4 at 15 feet

To Decrease Difficulty

- Use shorter distances. [4]
- Have a partner stand at the lines and toss the ball straight up into air for the other student to run under and catch. [4, 5]

To Increase Difficulty

- Have the student increase the distance of the toss and catch. [4]
- Have the student increase the height of the toss. [3]
- Make the student vary the height of the toss randomly. [1]
- Have your student vary the distance of the toss randomly. [1]

4. *Partner Toss Drill*
[Corresponds to *Softball*, Step 1, Drill 4]

Group Management and Safety Tips

- Only the less experienced students need to do this drill.
- Form students into two lines 10 feet apart, facing one another.
- People in a line should be 5 feet apart.
- The students should use soft, underhand tosses.

Equipment

- Gloves, 1 per student
- Balls, 1 per student pair
- Cones or other markers to mark lines
- Softer balls

Instructions and Cues to Class

- "Toss the ball underhand so your partner can catch it."
- "Make the toss catchable."
- "When catching, wait for the ball with your glove-side foot forward and your chest and head facing the tosser. Then you will be in position to throw as soon as you catch."
- "Watch the ball from the tosser's hand all the way into your glove. This is called *tracking* the ball and will help you catch it."
- "Catch the ball, pivot (turn your glove side to the tosser), and bring the ball to the throwing position. Now, hold that position so that the tosser can check to see whether your weight is back and your throwing arm is at your shoulder."
- "Remember, if the ball is above your waist, your fingers must point up; if the ball is below your waist, your fingers must point down. This way, the fingers provide a 'backstop' surface for the ball, and the pocket of the glove is open to the ball."
- "On a ball above your waist, if your fingers point down or toward the tosser, the ball will tend to bounce off the heel of your glove and into your body."
- "A ball to your waist is the hardest to catch. Point the glove fingers to the throwing side (with the thumb pointing down to the ground) and put your throwing hand under the glove. Then the pocket is open to the ball, and your throwing hand is ready to help with the catch."

Student Options

- "You may vary the height of the tosses: high, waist-level, or low."
- "You may vary the force of the tosses."
- "You may toss to random heights."

Student Success Goal

- 30 total catches at varying heights without dropping the ball

  10 of 10 above the waist

  10 of 10 below the waist

  10 of 10 at the waist

To Decrease Difficulty

- Have the tosser increase the distance of the toss, allowing longer tracking time by the catcher. [4]
- Have the tosser use a softer toss. [3]
- Let the students use a larger ball. [2]
- Let the pair use a softer ball. [2]

To Increase Difficulty

- Have the tosser use a more forceful toss. [3]
- Make the pair use a smaller ball, such as a tennis ball or a baseball. [2]
- Have the tosser vary the height of the toss. [4]
- Have the tosser vary the direction of the toss to the sides. [4]

Step 2 Throwing Overhand

The overhand throw is the strongest, most accurate, and most often used of the three basic throwing patterns. It is a fundamental skill used by all defensive players. It is the second part of the frequently used catch-and-throw combination. As with catching, the throwing skill has been isolated for practice in order that your students may focus primary attention on the throwing techniques before putting the catch and throw together.

You, the instructor, must make judgments regarding the amount of practice your students need on these two isolated skills before progressing to Step 3, "Combining Two Basics," which applies the two skills in practical, game-like practice drills. Typically, your less experienced students can benefit more from the isolated practices of Steps 1 and 2. Nevertheless, your more experienced students can use the isolated skill practice to quickly review correct technique and further refine their movements. They can then proceed to the combination drills in Step 3.

STUDENT KEYS TO SUCCESS

- Turn, step, throw
- Move your body in direction of throw
- Elbow up, leading
- Hand and ball high past head

Throwing Overhand Rating

CHECKPOINT	LESS EXPERIENCED	MORE EXPERIENCED
Preparation **Grip** **Body Position**	• Three or four fingers • Square to target	• Two fingers • Glove side toward target
Execution **Step** **Arm Action** **Center of Gravity (Weight Transfer)** **Wrist Action**	• With throwing-side foot • Hand leads • Elbow low, hand at shoulder height • Remains within stance • Remains extended throughout throw	• With glove-side foot • Elbow leads • Elbow high, hand above head height • Moves from back to front and outside stance, beyond front foot • Moves from flexed to extended position
Follow-Through **Body Position** **Throwing Hand** **Feet**	• Erect and in balance • Shoulder height • Forward stride with glove-side foot to the rear	• Knees bent, throwing-side shoulder forward • Low by glove-side knee • Throwing-side foot comes forward to balanced stance

Error Detection and Correction for Overhand Throwing

Less experienced students tend to make errors in the gross movements of the overhand throw. Stepping with the wrong foot, "pushing" the ball instead of throwing it, and using a sidearm rather than overhand movement pattern are typical beginner mistakes. As the instructor, you need to correct these major errors before dealing with the finer points of trajectory, accuracy, and force of the throw.

Errors committed by the more experienced students usually are associated with the finer motor control aspects and with the timing of the release.

Your knowledge of correct throwing technique, your ability to analyze movement, and your observation skills are all critical to your success in error detection and correction for your students.

ERROR 🚫

CORRECTION

1. The thrower steps with the wrong foot (LE).

2. The student "pushes" rather than throws the ball (LE).

3. The student throws sidearm rather than overhand.

1. Tell the thrower to step in the direction of the throw with the glove-side foot.

2. The student should lead the throw with the elbow, not the hand.

3. Have the student keep the elbow up and make sure the forearm passes through the vertical, with the hand passing above head height.

ERROR ⊘

CORRECTION

4. The ball's trajectory is too high.

4. The thrower should snap his or her wrist when releasing the ball, thrust the throwing-side shoulder forward when releasing the ball, or hold onto the ball a little longer.

5. The ball goes to the right or the left of the target.

5. Tell the thrower to be sure to use an overhand delivery, not a sidearm one, to step toward the target while throwing, and to "throw" the hand toward the target when releasing the ball.

Overhand Throwing Drills

1. Fence Drill

[Corresponds to *Softball*, Step 2, Drill 1]

Group Management and Safety Tips

- All students may practice at one time. However, have only the less experienced students do this drill; start the more experienced students on Drill 2.
- If using a wall for this drill, use cloth-covered balls such as a Rag Ball® or an IncrediBall®.
- If using a fence or a net, provide your students with several balls each because the balls will not rebound. Otherwise, have the students work in pairs in a peer (reciprocal) teaching setting. The partner at the fence observes the thrower's performance and suggests corrections based on the Keys to Success. This observer also returns the ball to the thrower.
- If there are enough softballs, give each pair of partners 5 balls. The thrower delivers 5 consecutive balls, and the observer looks for consistent performance errors.

Equipment

- Softballs, at least 1 per student (more will facilitate drill)
- Gloves, 1 per student

Instructions and Cues to Class

- "Stand 20 feet from the fence [net, wall]."
- "Repeat the phrase 'Turn, step, and throw' to yourself as you throw the ball against the fence [net, wall]."
- "Concentrate on your form."
- "Be sure to extend your arm all the way back before starting your throw. You want to use the full range of motion for your throw."
- "Make the entire throwing act one smooth, continuous motion."

Student Options

- "Work with a partner who observes your performance in a peer teaching setting. After 5 repetitions, your partner makes suggestions, based on the Keys to Success Checklist, on how you might improve your technique. Change roles after you have made a total of 10 throws."
- "At home, practice your throwing technique against the front steps, the side of the garage, a large flat rock in a stone wall, or any other relatively flat surface that you won't get yelled at for using. Use a tennis ball or any other kind of ball that will not harm the surface you are throwing against."

Student Success Goal

- 10 throws executed with correct form

To Decrease Difficulty

- Not applicable

To Increase Difficulty

- Increase the distance of the throw. [4]
- Have the student throw the ball both high and low against the fence (without throwing the ball over the fence). [3]

2. *Target Accuracy Drill*
[Corresponds to *Softball*, Step 2, Drill 2]

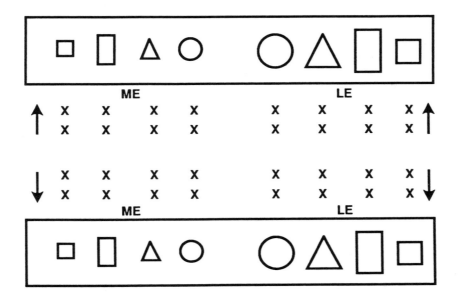

Group Management and Safety Tips

- More experienced students should start with this drill.
- Use large targets for the less experienced students and narrow targets for the more experienced.
- For interest, vary the shape of the targets, such as squares, rectangles, and triangles.
- For the more experienced player, place the targets chest high and knee high, simulating the targets for a force play and a tag play.
- If using walls as target backstops, arrange the targets so that rebounding balls do not cross paths. When using this drill in a gymnasium, line up your students in two lines, back to back and 10 feet apart, down the center of the gym. Place the less experienced students at the same end of both lines so they are back to back with one another.

- If outdoors, place the targets for the less experienced students on the outfield fence and those for the more experienced players on the side fences. The outfield fence is usually 6 to 8 feet high; this would provide a larger backstop than the typical side fence (4 to 5 feet high) for the off-target throws of the less experienced players.
- If your targets are limited in number, have more than one student throw at the same target.
- This drill can be set up with others in this step in a skills practice circuit.

Equipment

- Gloves, 1 per student
- Softballs, at least 1 per student, more if using a nonrebounding target backstop
- Targets, 1 per student, in varying sizes and shapes

Instructions and Cues to Class

- "Using the overhand throwing motion, throw the ball at the target."
- "During your first few throws, repeat to yourself the phrase 'Turn, step, and throw.' Primarily focus on going through the full range of your throwing motion with correct technique."
- "When you feel comfortable with your throwing motion and it feels smooth rather than jerky, throw 10 balls at the target, concentrating on the target throughout the action."

Student Options

- "Continue to focus on the throwing motion rather than on hitting the target if you are still having difficulty with the technique." (LE)

- "Challenge yourself by scoring a throw as on-target only if the ball hits entirely inside the target."
- "Change the height levels or size of the target."

Student Success Goal

- 20 total throws

    5 of 10 throws hit target (throwing action focus)

    8 of 10 throws hit target (target focus)

To Decrease Difficulty

- Increase the size of the target. [2]
- Shorten the distance of the throw. [4]

To Increase Difficulty

- Decrease the size of the target. [2]
- Lengthen the throwing distance. [4]

3. *Increase the Distance Drill*
[Corresponds to *Softball*, Step 2, Drill 3]

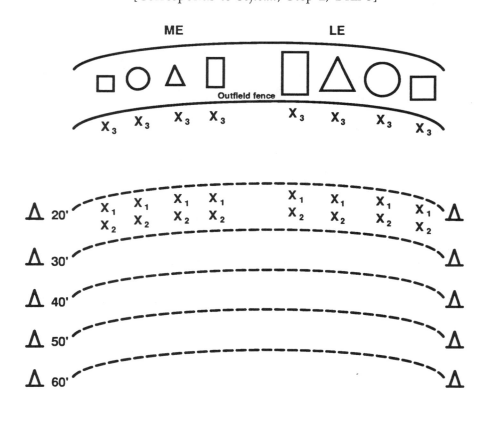

Group Management and Safety Tips

- Place targets 20 feet apart on one wall if in a gymnasium or on the outfield fence if on a field.
- Using larger targets for your less experienced students and smaller (narrower) targets for the more experienced, order targets by size so that the targets for the less experienced and those for more experienced are at opposite ends.
- Use cones, tape, or a line marker to mark off distances of 20, 30, 40, 50, and 60 feet from the targets.
- Group students by ability and by the number of available targets.
- Assign your groups to positions on the 20-foot line and opposite the appropriate target.
- The last person in the group to throw starts as ball retriever. Upon completion of the assigned number of throws, the thrower replaces the retriever.

Equipment

- Softballs, 1 per student (indoor ball for the gymnasium)
- Gloves, 1 per student
- Cones (10), tape, or line marker to mark off 5 lines
- Targets, one per group, in varying shapes and sizes

Instructions and Cues to Class

- "Using the overhand throw, each student in the group delivers 5 throws to the target."
- "The group moves back to the next mark when every group member hits the target at least once."
- "If the group fails to meet the criterion at a certain distance, the entire group repeats the throws for that distance until the criterion is met."
- "Although this is an accuracy drill, remember to concentrate on using correct throwing technique. Your accuracy in hitting the target is enhanced by the use of correct technique, especially as the distance increases."

Student Option

- Not appropriate

Group Success Goal

- Group moves back to 60 feet without having to repeat any throws

To Decrease Difficulty

- Reduce the number of people in the group who must have one throw hit the target in order to advance to the next mark. [6]

To Increase Difficulty

- Increase the number of on-target throws needed by each person in order for the group to advance to the next mark. [3]
- Reduce the size of the target by making it narrower. [2]
- Upon failure of the group to meet the criterion (at least one on-target throw by every member of the group), the group must return to the 20-foot mark and begin the drill again (see *Softball*, Step 2, Drill 4, H-O-R-S-E Drill). [3]

4. Vary the Direction Drill
[Corresponds to *Softball*, Step 2, Drill 5]

Group Management and Safety Tips

- Use the targets from Drill 2, Target Accuracy Drill.
- Divide the class into groups of three and place each group at a target.

Equipment

- Softballs, 5 per group of three
- Gloves, 1 per student
- Targets, 1 per group of three (target size does not matter)

Instructions and Cues to Class

- ''The thrower stands 30 feet from the target and delivers 10 balls into the area just outside and to the glove side of the target.''
- ''Each person in the group throws 10 balls to the glove side of the target; then each person throws 10 to the throwing side.''
- ''One of the other group members retrieves the balls for the thrower while the third gives feedback to the thrower.''
- ''Rotate roles within the group so that each person assumes each role.''
- ''Remember to step in the direction of your throw.''
- ''When you throw to the throwing-arm side of the target, you need to pivot to get your glove side pointed in the direction of the throw before taking your step and delivering the ball.''

Student Option

- Not appropriate

Student Success Goals

- 8 out of 10 throws hitting outside and to the glove side of the target
- 8 out of 10 throws hitting outside and to the throwing side of the target

To Decrease Difficulty

- Reduce the distance of the throw. [4]
- Reduce the number of required accurate throws. [3]

To Increase Difficulty

- Increase the distance of the throw. [4]
- Have the student alternate throwing to the glove and throwing sides in sets of 10. [1]

Step 3 Combining Two Basics

Catching and throwing almost never occur as isolated skills in a real softball game. It is very important for your students to develop skill in combining the actions of the catch and the throw into one sequential, fluid movement. The transition between the catching and throwing motions must be smooth and continuous. This enables the player to make plays on baserunners with greater dispatch than is possible if the catch and the throw are two distinct moves.

Less experienced players tend to catch the ball, have a short break in the action, then throw. The player with more experience is smoother in the transition between the two actions. Initially, the practice of the players should be focused upon moving from the catch directly into the throw. Look for the follow-through of the catch to be the starting position of the throw. Word cues that help the students "feel" and "see" the smooth, continuous transition between the two moves will facilitate their learning. The pattern is developed through practice, but it is mandatory that the practice be focused on the fluid transition. However, if there are problems with techniques particular to the isolated skills, have the students practice the skills in isolation to remedy the problems.

Another factor added to the combination of catching and throwing is the player's movement to the ball in order to make the initial catch. Here, the emphasis is really just a variation of the theme. The player must move quickly into position to make the catch and throw. As you observe the students practicing, make certain that they move into catching positions that enable them to catch and throw in one motion. The initial setup prior to fielding is a key to moving into a smooth, continuous transition between catching and throwing.

STUDENT KEYS TO SUCCESS

- Read path of ball
- Move quickly into path of ball
- Forward stride preparatory stance for catch and throw
- Catch, turn, step, throw in one continuous motion
- Step in direction of throw

Catching and Throwing Combination Rating

CHECKPOINT	LESS EXPERIENCED	MORE EXPERIENCED
Preparation **Body Location** **Body Position**	• Not in path of ball • Square to, or to side of, ball	• In line with oncoming ball • Forward stride, only shoulders square
Execution **Transition** **Throwing Step**	• Catch and throw two distinct actions • Jerky • Steps in direction moved to catch ball	• Catch and throw one continuous move • Smooth and fluid • Steps toward intended target

Error Detection and Correction for Catching and Throwing Combination

Beginning students tend to rush into the throw without making sure of the catch. They focus on the throw and neither quickly move into the path of the oncoming ball nor track the ball into the glove. These errors tend to make the catches erratic and the throws errant. They also cause the transition between the catch and throw to be jerky because the players are thinking about the two moves separately. As you observe and cue the students, remind them that catching and throwing are one move that begins when they are in proper catching position.

ERROR 🚫

CORRECTION

	ERROR		CORRECTION
1.	The student does not move directly into the path of the oncoming ball, probably because of slowly determining its direction (LE).	1.	Have the student practice watching the ball come out of a partner's throwing hand and moving into its path.
2.	The student does not assume the forward stride position to catch the ball because of being late getting to the spot where he or she must catch the ball (LE).	2.	Set two cones on the ground 5 feet apart. Have the student shuffle between the cones and assume the forward stride foot position at each cone. Gradually increase the distance between the cones and have the student turn and run to get to the cones.
3.	When the student catches the ball and throws it, the transition is jerky (ME) or nonexistent (LE).	3.	Have the student silently say, "Catch, turn, step, and throw" while miming the action. Then have him or her say the same thing while actually catching and throwing the ball. Doing this sets a rhythmic pattern.
4.	On the throw, the student steps in the direction moved to reach the ball rather than in the direction of the target.	4.	Have the student point the toe of the glove-side foot in the direction of the throwing target. Then have him or her "throw" the throwing shoulder at the target.

Catching and Throwing Combination Drills

1. Catch and Throw Drill
[Corresponds to *Softball*, Step 3, Drills 1, 2, 3, 4]

Group Management and Safety Tips

- This drill is for the less experienced players only. The more experienced players should begin with the next drill.
- The students should be at a wall that is taller than they are by about 6 feet. A backstop or a high fence could also be used. These drills could also be practiced indoors in a gymnasium, where the students need to use a rubber ball or an IncrediBall® (even a tennis ball that is a little "dead" could be used).
- The students need to be 10 to 15 feet from the wall.
- The students need to be about 10 feet apart so that they do not run into one another and so that errant balls do not interfere with other students.
- If indoors, caution the students not to throw the balls at or near windows or lights.
- If possible, put left-handed students into one group and have them do the drills at a different wall. If that is not possible, put all of the left-handed students at the left end of the line.

Equipment

- Gloves, 1 per student
- Balls, 1 per student
- Extra balls, in case some get thrown over the fence or lost in bleachers

Instructions and Cues to Class

- "Throw the ball high enough and hard enough so that it will bounce back to you and is easily catchable. Gradually make the catch harder."
- "Say to yourself, 'Catch, turn, step, and throw,' as you catch the ball coming off the wall."
- "The rhythm will help you develop a smooth transition from catching to throwing."
- "See the ball as it hits the wall and move fast enough to where you will catch it that you are waiting for it when it arrives."
- "Get in front of the ball and wait for it in forward stride position. Then your head is in position for you to watch the ball straight into your glove, and your body is ready to turn, step, and throw to the target."
- "Get a jump on the ball when it is going to your throwing-hand side, because you have to move farther to get into position to catch and throw."
- "The rhythm is 'move,' then 'catch, turn, step, throw.' Try to feel that rhythm as you are doing the drill."
- "Be sure that you turn after each catch and set up for the next throw to the wall. Periodically, between throwing sequences, put the ball at your feet and close your eyes and mimic two catch-turn-step-throw patterns, focusing on the rhythm."

Student Options

- ''Practice with a partner, who says, 'Catch, turn, step, throw' as you make the catch.''
- ''Have a partner watch you and help you make your transition from the catch to the throw smoother.''
- ''Have a partner watch you to see whether you always are in the forward stride position before you catch the ball. Tell him or her whether you think you were in the forward stride position. Your partner will then tell you whether you were correct.''

Student Success Goal

- 37 out of 40 total catches and throws off self-throws to wall

    15 catches and throws off rebound directly to chest

    8 of 10 catches and throws off rebound to glove side

7 of 10 catches and throws off rebound to throwing side

7 of 10 catches and throws off soft throw rebounding short

To Decrease Difficulty

- Have the student throw the ball higher on the wall so there is more time to track and get under it. [3]
- Have a partner toss softly to the catcher, who catches, turns, steps, and throws to the wall. [3]
- Use a softer or more ''dead'' ball. [2]

To Increase Difficulty

- Use a ''livelier'' ball. [2]
- Make the student throw the ball farther to the sides to force faster movement. [4]
- Have the student alternate throws to the glove side and the throwing side to increase the reaction speed. [1]

2. Throw, Move to Catch, Throw to Target Drill

[Corresponds to *Softball*, Step 3, Drill 5]

Group Management and Safety Tips

- This drill is for less experienced students, although the more experienced could also do it. The more experienced should throw the ball harder at the target so that they have to move into position faster.
- Targets need to be put about 12 feet apart on the walls, chest high, and 10 to 15 feet from catcher.
- Targets should be a diamond shape, 4 feet square.
- Students will be moving from side to side as they do the drill, so it would probably be best to pair them up. One partner can retrieve errant throws and give feedback to the thrower on the form and technique used. This observing partner should stand behind the thrower.

- Be sure the students have enough room to move without getting into one another's way.

Equipment

- Gloves, 1 per student
- Balls, 1 per student or per student pair
- Extra balls to replace any lost in the drill
- Tape for targets (or cardboard cutout targets that can be leaned against the wall)
- Toss-back or rebound net for students who are more skilled

Instructions and Cues to Class

- ''Use the full overhand motion in your throw to the target.''
- ''Reach for the target as you release the ball.''

- "Step right toward the target as you throw the ball. This way, your motion is moving in the direction you want the ball to go."
- "Move in front of the ball before it gets to you. Now, in one motion, catch and throw the ball to the target."
- "Don't throw too hard; otherwise, the ball will rebound too fast for you to make the catch. Make the rebound catchable."
- "Rhythm: Get into position, then catch, turn, step, throw."
- "Look for the target as you draw the ball to your shoulder and turn your glove side toward the target. You want to see the target before you release the ball. Your sight helps guide your throw to the target."
- "Bring that throwing arm right into throwing position as a part of the catch."

Student Option

- "Have a partner check your technique in the catch and throw motion. Have the partner help you make the catch and throw one smooth motion."

Student Success Goal

- Consecutive catches and on-target throws of balls that make the student move

    5 consecutive catches and throws of balls coming to the left

    5 consecutive catches and throws of balls coming to the right

    7 consecutive catches and throws of balls coming short or long

To Decrease Difficulty

- Make the target narrower and taller so the ball does not rebound so far to either side. [2]
- Move the catcher-thrower farther away from the target. [4]
- Make the target a square so there is more target to hit on the throw. [2]

To Increase Difficulty

- Make the target wider and shorter so hitting the corners takes a longer throw and so the ball rebounds farther away. [2]
- Move the catcher-thrower closer to the target. [4]
- Make the target smaller so there is less target to hit on the throw. [2]

3. *Throw and Catch and Quick Release Drill*
[Corresponds to *Softball*, Step 3, Drills 6, 7]

Group Management and Safety Tips

- Partners need to be paired so that less experienced players are with other less experienced ones, and more experienced ones are together.
- Put the less experienced pairs at one end of the lines and the more experienced pairs at the other end.
- One partner is on a foul line, and the other partner is facing him or her from 20 feet away.
- Position the lines so that the players do not have to look into the sun.
- There should be at least 6 feet between students on a line.

Equipment

- Gloves, 1 per student
- Balls, 1 per student
- Cones or other objects to mark lines

Instructions and Cues to Class

- "Make your throws catchable. You are responsible for the practice of your partner. If you make your partner better, you are also making yourself a better player."
- "Playing catch, get a rhythm going between the two of you. Catch, turn, step, and throw. Call out the rhythm for your partner as he or she catches your throw and throws it back."

- "When your rhythm goes out of whack, watch your partner to see whether he or she is in a forward stride position to catch the ball. If not, he or she cannot turn, step, and throw, and the rhythm is lost."
- "On the catch, imagine the force of the ball in your glove moves your throwing hand back to your shoulder and your weight onto your back foot. Without stopping the action, turn your body's glove side toward your partner, then step and throw toward your partner."
- "It's like Newton's law of action-reaction. The ball comes into your glove, which moves back to coil like a spring, then unwinds and reverses direction with the throw. It's all one move."
- "When both you and your partner are throwing simultaneously, one of you should throw slightly above the waist and the other slightly below. Partway through, switch."
- "Get a quick-release rhythm going when you are both throwing at the same time. Throw with the same force and timing as your partner."

Student Options

- "With your partner, set a pattern of high, medium, and low throws."
- "Change partners within your experience level and try to get a rhythm going between yourself and your new partner."

Student Success Goals

- 40 completed catches and throws by the partners
- 20 catches and throws in which both partners are completely successful

To Decrease Difficulty

- Move the partners closer together. [4]
- Let the partners slow down the rhythm of their catch-and-throw pattern. [3]
- Use softer balls. [2]
- Have the partners throw the ball with less force. [3]

To Increase Difficulty

- Move the partners farther apart. [4]
- Make the partners speed up the rhythm of their catch-and-throw pattern. [3]
- Have the partners throw the ball with more force. [3]
- Declare the partner's glove the target to hit on the throw. [2]

4. Accuracy Drills

[Corresponds to *Softball*, Step 3, Drill 8]

Group Management and Safety Tips

- Pair off the students according to experience level.
- One partner is on a foul line, and the other one is facing the first from 20 feet away (LE). More experienced partners can be 40 to 50 feet away from one another.
- Put the less experienced pairs toward one end of the lines.
- No one should be looking into the sun.

Equipment

- Gloves, 1 per student
- Balls, 1 per pair

Instructions and Cues to Class

- "Look at the target (partner's glove) as you throw and try to throw your throwing hand toward the target."
- "Step toward the target with your glove-side foot."
- "Catch the ball and smoothly move into position to throw."
- "Watch the ball into the glove and immediately look at the target."
- "Think about the target as you throw."
- "Feel the target pulling your throwing hand, arm, and shoulder to it."

- "Visualize the runner going into the tag play. Put the throw right where the fielder needs it." (ME)
- "If you are more experienced, challenge your partner's catching with a throw that makes him or her stretch."
- "If you stretch to get the ball, see how fast you can come to the throwing position. Try to make it a continuous, flowing move."

Student Options

- "Have your partner move the target slightly on every throw you make."
- "Catch the ball, then mimic a throw back to your partner. Think about where you are throwing the ball. Have your partner tell you where your imaginary throw seemed to be aimed. Were your body and arm going where you thought they were?"

Student Success Goals

- 31 of 40 total on-target throws and 31 of 40 total catches (LE and ME)

Less Experienced	More Experienced
9 of 10 direct throws	9 of 10 throws just below knees
8 of 10 glove-side throws	8 of 10 throws high and out front
7 of 10 throwing-side throws	7 of 10 head-high, glove-side throws
7 of 10 short throws	7 of 10 knee-high, throwing-side throws

- 28 of 40 total on-target throws (LE); or 36 of 40 on-target throws (ME)

Less Experienced	More Experienced
7 of 10 throws to throwing-side shoulder	9 of 10 throws below knees
7 of 10 waist-level throws	9 of 10 throws waist high
7 of 10 throws to glove-side hip	9 of 10 throws head-high to glove side
7 of 10 throws to throwing-side hip	9 of 10 throws knee-high to throwing side

To Decrease Difficulty

- Have the student move closer to the partner. [4]

To Increase Difficulty

- Have the pair move farther apart. [4]
- Have the pair continuously catch and throw the ball to the target areas rather than stopping after catching and preparing to throw. [1]
- Have the catcher vary the target setup (see *Softball*, Step 3, Drill 8). [1]

5. Line Drive, Leaping Line Drive, Continuous Line Drive Drills

[Corresponds to *Softball*, Step 3, Drills 9, 10, 11]

Group Management and Safety Tips

- Group the students according to experience level.
- Partners line up 60 feet away from one another. One partner is on a foul line, and the other is facing the first.
- Put the less experienced pairs toward one end of the lines.
- No student should be facing into the sun.
- Students on a line should be at least 15 feet apart.
- Emphasize that the students must throw the ball with control.
- After catching the ball, the students should come to the throwing position but should not throw the ball immediately.

Equipment

- Gloves, 1 per student
- Balls, 1 per pair

Instructions and Cues to Class

- ''Use the full overhand motion to throw a line drive.''
- ''Really snap your wrist on the release to add force to the throw.''
- ''Look at the target all the way through your throw.''
- ''Throw a catchable line drive. Do not overpower your throw; it would go off course.''
- ''Use your body weight shift and your step toward the target to increase your force.''

- ''Give with the ball as it comes in. Meet it in front of your body so that you can draw it in through a longer distance. This helps to absorb the force of stronger throws.''
- ''Use your body to absorb the force of the ball. Move backward onto your throwing-side foot as you draw the ball to your throwing shoulder. Now you're ready to 'fire' the ball on your throw.''
- ''Control your body and your throw. If your throws are not on target, reduce the force you are using. Find the right mix of force and accuracy.''
- ''Gradually increase the force of your throw. If you lose accuracy, cut back on the force.''

Student Options

- ''Try to hit the glove exactly where it is held by your partner.''
- ''Try to throw to exactly the same spot twice in a row.''
- ''Vary the force of the throw from hard to a little softer; check whether you are more accurate with one force level than another.''
- ''Analyze whether your line-drive throws are more accurate above the waist, below the waist, to the right, or to the left of the catcher. Set a goal for yourself to improve your weakest throw.''

Student Success Goals

- 36 of 48 total on-target line-drive throws and 24 of 30 total catches of line drives

  a. 6 of 8 throws above the waist

    in front of body

    to glove side of body

    to throwing side of body

  b. 6 of 8 throws below the waist

    in front of body

    to glove side of body

    to throwing side of body

  c. 4 of 6 catches above the waist

    in front of body

    to glove side of body

    backhand to throwing side of body

  d. 4 of 6 catches below the waist

    in front of body

    to glove side of body

    backhand to throwing side of body

To Decrease Difficulty

- Have the thrower use less force. [3]
- Use a target on the fence that is larger than glove. [2]
- Move the partners closer together to reduce the distance of the throws. [4]

To Increase Difficulty

- Have the pair shorten the time between throws. [3]
- Have the catcher move the target before each throw. [3]
- Have the thrower send line drives above the head of the catcher so the catcher will have to leap to make catches (see *Softball*, Step 3, Drill 10). [3]
- Make the pair throw continuous line drives. They must make the catches and return with line drives immediately, and in one motion (see *Softball*, Step 3, Drill 11). [3]
- Have the pair throw continuous line drives, the catcher changing the target for each throw. [1]

Step 4 Fielding a Ground Ball

Fielding ground balls should be introduced to your students as an extension of the catching and throwing that they have previously done. The principles of fielding ground balls and throwing are the same as those of catching and throwing, with the exception that the ball comes to the student on the ground. Consequently, you, as the teacher, can use the same cues and keys to success that you used before when working with your students on some parts of their fielding. Such similar keys include getting in the line of the oncoming ball; watching the ball into the glove; making the transition from catching to throwing a single, smooth motion; and following through in the direction of the throw.

In fielding ground balls, however, there are two additional movements for you to observe. The student must get into a low position (with the glove nearly on the ground) in front of the ball. The second difference is that, in the transition from fielding to throwing, the fielder comes to an erect throwing position while executing the turn and drawing the ball to the throwing shoulder. The less experienced player will have a tendency to stand too erect while attempting to field the grounder and to field the ball too close to the feet. The more experienced player will probably stay low and field the ball out in front of the feet, but even so will likely make the mistake of bringing the ball in to the stomach area rather than directly to the throwing position. Fielding is a most critical softball skill; your constant focus on solid, technical execution by your students will serve them well as they progress in this unit.

STUDENT KEYS TO SUCCESS

- Move quickly into position to field ball
- Body and glove low to ground as ball approaches
- Field ball ahead of feet
- Turn glove side to target and come to erect throwing position simultaneously (weight on back foot)
- Bring ball directly to throwing position on fielding follow-through
- Step toward target and throw

Fielding a Ground Ball Rating

CHECKPOINT	LESS EXPERIENCED	MORE EXPERIENCED
Preparation Stance	• Knees stiff • Bent at waist • Square stance	• Knees bent • Body low • Stagger stride
Focus	• Diffused, not on ball	• On ball

CHECKPOINT	LESS EXPERIENCED	MORE EXPERIENCED
Execution **Hand Position**	• Glove pocket down • Glove fingers point at ball • One hand	• Pocket open to ball • Glove fingers point to ground • Two hands
Fielding Point	• Between feet	• Ahead of feet
Head Position	• Eyes averted • Head up	• Eyes on ball • Head down
Follow-Through **Transition**	• Stands up after fielding • Weight balanced • Three- or four-finger grip	• Brings ball directly to throwing position • Weight moves front to back • Two-finger grip
Throw	• Separate action from fielding	• Continuous action with fielding

Error Detection and Correction for Fielding a Ground Ball

Your observation of your students as they practice fielding ground balls should be directed toward their preparatory body positions and their hand movements. The less experienced players are likely to be afraid of the ball; they "pull up" as the ball comes to their gloves. Concentrate your correction cues on low body fielding position and the fielder's bringing the ball directly to the throwing position while turning and coming to the erect throwing stance.

ERROR ⊘

CORRECTION

⊘

1. The student fields the ball to the side of the body.

1. The student should start to move into position to field as soon as the ball is seen, looking for the ball out of the hand of the thrower or directly off the wall. Recommend the Wall Fielding Drill (Drill 1), and have the student throw the ball off center in both directions.

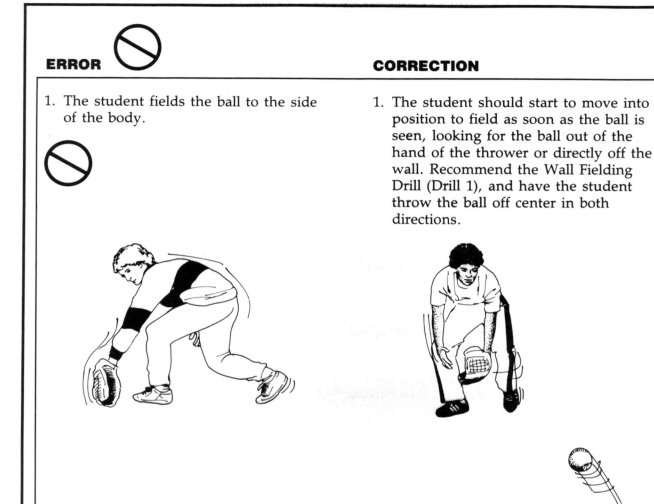

2. The fielder stays erect.

2. **Recommend the Footwork Drill (see *Softball*, Step 4, Drill 2) and the Two-Ball Drill (Drill 2). Have the student put the glove on the ground with the pocket facing up and toward the ball.**

ERROR   **CORRECTION**

3. The ball goes under the glove.

3. Have the student get into a low fielding position (knees bent, back parallel to ground) and hold it, then roll the ball to him or her. Tell the student to keep the head down and to field the ball directly under the eyes.

4. The ball bounces out of the glove.

4. Have the student be sure to cover the ball with the throwing hand as soon as the ball goes into the glove.

ERROR   **CORRECTION**

5. The fielder draws the ball in to the stomach.

5. Have the student repeatedly go from a fielding position to the throwing position with both hands. First have the student do the action mimetically. Then roll the ball slowly and have him or her focus on the flowing action of fielding and moving the hands immediately to the throwing shoulder.

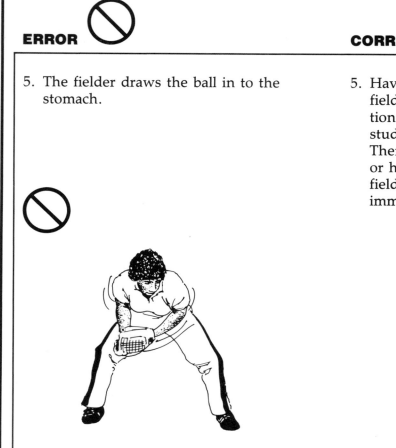

6. The transition to the throw is not smooth.

6. Have the student mime a smooth, slow-motion fielding-to-throwing action. Have him or her then field a slowly rolling ball and do a slow-motion transition. Have him or her gradually increase the speed of the transition action. Also, gradually increase the speed at which you roll the ball, so that the student can develop the proper pattern and rhythm.

Fielding Ground Ball Drills

1. Wall Fielding Drill
[Corresponds to *Softball*, Step 4, Drill 1]

Group Management and Safety Tips

- The students stand 15 feet away from a wall (or rebound net) from which the softball rebounds.
- If there is no wall available, a partner can roll the ball to the fielder.
- The students must be spaced so that they can move at least 10 feet in either direction to field the ball.
- The less experienced and more experienced groups should be at opposite ends of the line.

Equipment

- Gloves, 1 per student
- Balls, 1 per student (or per student pair)
- Cones or other line markers

Instructions and Cues to Class

- ''Throw at a wall 15 feet away so that the ball returns as a grounder.''
- ''Stay low on the ball so that it does not go under your glove.''
- ''Watch the ball all the way into the glove. Then you will not lift up your head and miss the grounder.''
- ''Once you see the ball in your glove, cover it with your throwing hand and look for your throwing target.''
- ''Field the ball ahead of your feet. This helps you see it, cuts down the distance it rolls, and makes it possible for you to come to the throwing position easier and faster.''
- ''Field the ball and bring it directly to your throwing shoulder. Don't bring the ball to your stomach, because that slows down the throwing action.''
- ''Think, 'Field, turn and come up, step toward target, and throw.' Get that rhythm pattern ingrained so that you have the same rhythm every time.''

Student Options

- ''Have a partner roll you the ball.''
- ''Have a partner stand behind you and hold a stick over your head so you can tell whether your head is staying down.''
- ''Have a partner analyze your form using the Fielding Ground Balls Checklist in the participant's book.''

Student Success Goal

- 10 consecutive good-form fielding plays of ground balls coming off the wall

To Decrease Difficulty

- Let the student use a softer ball. [2]
- Have the student stand farther away from the wall to increase the time to see and react to the ball. [4]
- Let your student use a softer throw to the wall. [3]
- Have a partner softly roll the ball to the fielder. [3]
- Let the student stop after fielding the ball rather than continue with another throw to the wall. [5]

To Increase Difficulty

- Move the student closer to the wall so the ball comes back faster and harder. [4]
- Have the student throw the ball to the wall with more force. [3]
- Make your student use a ball with more rebound (e.g., tennis ball). [3]
- Have your student increase the speed of fielding and throwing to the wall. [3]
- Have the student throw the ball off center so that he or she has to move to get into position to field the ball (see *Softball*, Step 4, Drill 2). [4]

2. Two-Ball Drill
[New Drill]

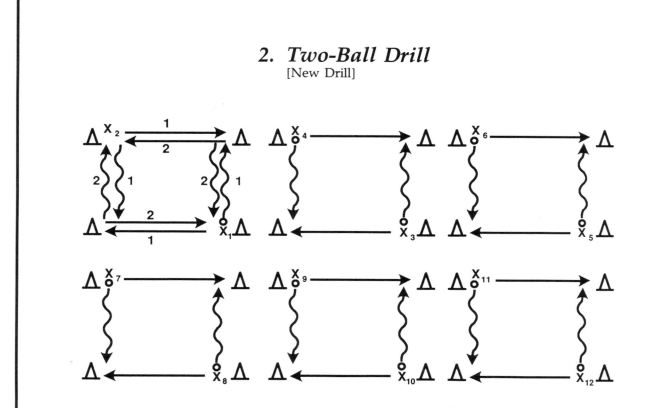

Group Management and Safety Tips

- Divide the students into less experienced and more experienced groups.
- Have the students pair up with others in their group.
- Each pair of students needs an area about 15 feet wide by 10 feet deep.
- Mark the corners of the area with cones or some other field marker.
- This drill can also be done in the gymnasium; simply decrease the size of each practice area.
- Set up the students so they are facing one another on opposite long sides of the practice rectangle. Each student is at the cone to his or her right.
- Each student should have a ball.
- All rectangles must be oriented in the same direction so that all pairs of students are facing the same way.
- Caution your students not to trip over the cones as they do this drill.
- Encourage your students to execute the drill in such a manner that their partners are challenged to do their best.

Equipment

- Gloves, 1 per student
- Balls, 1 per student (real balls, rubber balls, IncrediBalls® can all be used)

Instructions to Class

- "In this drill you roll the ball 1 foot to the inside of the cone directly opposite you. Both of you roll your softballs toward the cones at the same time."
- "When you release your softball, slide-step sideways toward the open cone on your side of the rectangle."
- "Stay low in the fielding position while you move to the spot where you will field the ball."
- "Get to where the ball is going to cross the line before it gets to that line. Reach forward and field it before it crosses the line."
- "Take the ball in your throwing hand, look at your partner, and simultaneously roll the ball straight ahead to the cone that your partner has just left."

- "Repeat this action until you have each fielded 20 grounders; rest a bit, then repeat the drill."
- "As you and your partner become more proficient, increase the speed of the rolling ball so that you have to move faster to get into position to field it."

Cues to Class

- "More experienced players can use the crossover step to get to the ball when it is impossible to get into position using the slide step."
- "This drill is not only good for patterning your low body position but also for moving laterally and for conditioning."
- "Get to the location to field the ball and be sure that your feet are in the forward stride (staggered) position. This is so that when you come up to throw the ball in a real game situation, you will be in good position to make the turn, step, and throw."

Student Options

- "Figure out how you and your partner could go all the way around the rectangle using the ideas of this drill. First go clockwise, then go counterclockwise. Remember, you always roll the ball to an open cone."
- "Change partners."

Student Success Goal

- Fielding 18 of 20 grounders

To Decrease Difficulty

- Increase the depth of the rectangle. [4]
- Decrease the width of the rectangle. [4]
- Have the students roll the ball slower. [3]
- Have the students use no gloves and a larger ball. [2]
- Let your students use a softer ball. [2]

To Increase Difficulty

- Decrease the depth of the rectangle. [4]
- Increase the width of the rectangle. [4]
- Make the students roll the ball faster. [3]
- Have the students vary the speed of the rolling ball. [8]
- Have the students vary the distance from which they roll the ball to the cone. [8]
- Make your students decrease the time between fielding and rolling the ball. [3]
- Have your students put spin on the ball. [3]

3. *Play Ground Ball Catch*
[Corresponds to *Softball*, Step 4, Drill 3]

Group Management and Safety Tips

- Divide your students into less experienced and more experienced groups.
- Have the students pair up with others they do not usually work with.
- The less experienced and the more experienced students should be in separate areas or on opposite ends of a line.
- One partner of a pair lines up on a foul line, and the other partner faces the first from about 30 feet. Make sure that no one is looking into the sun.

- In this drill, when fielders move laterally to field, make certain that left-handed and right-handed students are aware that they will be moving toward each other and need to be careful not to collide.
- Less experienced students should begin the drill with slow-rolling balls. More experienced students can begin with the balls rolling harder and faster.
- Because there are return throws from the fielder to the partner throwing the ground balls, all student pairs should be oriented in the same direction on the field. Then all throws will be going in the same direction, and errant throws will be less likely to hit other students.

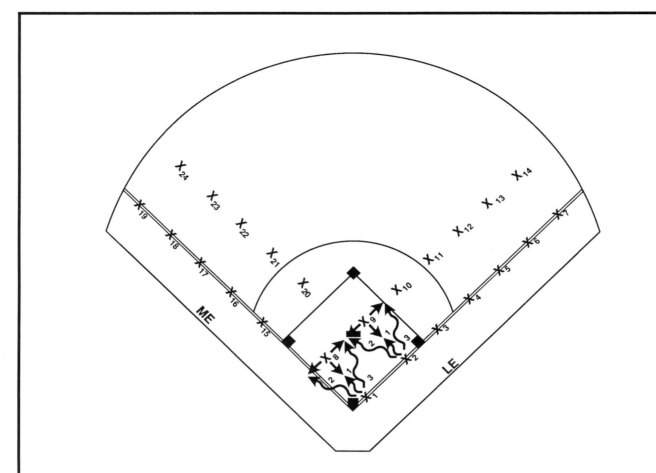

Equipment

- Gloves, 1 per student
- Balls, 1 per student pair
- Extra balls in case some are lost
- Softer balls for those still afraid of the ball

Instructions and Cues to Class

- "The partner on the foul line throws direct, short, glove side, and throwing side grounders to the fielder."
- "Work hard on moving quickly to the position where you will field the ball so that you are stationary and in the forward stride position awaiting the arrival of the ball."
- "Get low to field the ball. Stay down on the ball. Keep your head over your glove and watch the ball go into your glove."
- "Reach forward to field the ball ahead of your feet. Then you can see it better, and you get to it faster."
- "As soon as the ball is in your glove, move it to the throwing position and at the same time shift your body weight to your back foot, then turn to throw."
- "Make a smooth transition: Come up from fielding directly into the throwing position."
- "Look for your target immediately after you cover the ball in your glove with your throwing hand. Continue to look at the target as you move your body into throwing position. Step toward the target and throw."
- "Make sure your throw is a full overhand throw."

Student Options

- "When you consistently field the ball and throw to your partner, you and your partner can continuously field and throw to one another."
- "See how many grounders in a row you and your partner can field without an error."

- "Add a third partner and set up in a triangle. Throw grounders to one another first clockwise, then counterclockwise. Be sure to field the ball facing the partner who threw it, then turn toward the other partner to make your throw."

Student Success Goal

- 33 out of 40 total ground balls fielded and thrown

    9 of 10 ground balls directly at fielder

    9 of 10 short grounders

    8 of 10 glove-side grounders

    7 of 10 throwing-side grounders

To Decrease Difficulty

- Have the partner reduce the force of the grounder. [3]
- Let the student use a softer ball. [2]

- Increase the distance between partners. [4]
- Have the partner reduce the distance that lateral grounders go away from the fielder. [4]
- Have the partner roll the ball rather than throw the grounder. [3]

To Increase Difficulty

- Have the partner increase the force of the grounder. [3]
- Decrease the distance between partners. [4]
- Have the partner increase the distance that lateral grounders go away from the fielder. [4]
- Have the partner vary the speed or direction of the grounders, or both (see *Softball*, Step 4, Drill 4). [8]

4. React to the Bouncing Ground Ball Drill
[Corresponds to *Softball*, Step 4, Drill 5]

Group Management and Safety Tips

- See previous drill for management and safety tips.
- Have the student partners try to clear their fielding area of sticks or stones, which could make the bounce of the ball more erratic than desired and cause injury.

Equipment

- Gloves, 1 per student
- Balls, 1 per student pair

Instructions and Cues to Class

- "Move to the ball to field it; don't wait for it to come to you. You determine where you want to catch it. Then you will be planning your fielding position, and there will be less likelihood of the ball's bouncing away from your glove."
- "It is critical to stay down on the bouncing ball so that you know exactly where it is coming to you."

- "Do not take your eyes off the ball. Catch it ahead of your feet so that you can see where the bounce is going to take the ball."
- "Do not pull up your head. If you do, the ball will come up and hit you from either your glove or the ground."
- "Because there is more movement on this ball than on a rolling grounder, you need to watch the ball into the glove. Then immediately look up to the target and 'think your throw' to the target."
- "The bouncing ball will cause you to draw the ball in to your body more than a ball rolling on the ground. You need to concentrate to draw the ball in and up to the throwing position so that you can make the throw as soon as possible."

Student Options

- ''In a group of three, have one partner watch you field the bouncing balls and tell you whether you stayed down on the ball, fielded it ahead of your feet, and made the transition from fielding to throw a continuous motion. Also, have the partner watch to see where you draw the ball as you field it. It should go to the throwing shoulder.''
- ''Try to throw the ball to a position where the fielder can barely get to it by making a diving catch.'' (ME)

Student Success Goal

- 36 of 50 total bouncing grounders fielded and throws on target

   8 of 10 direct bouncing grounders

   8 of 10 right-side bouncing grounders

   8 of 10 left-side bouncing grounders

   12 of 20 random-direction bouncing grounders

To Decrease Difficulty

- Have the partner decrease the force of the grounder. [3]
- Have the partner decrease the number of bounces of the grounder. [3]
- Have the partner aim the first bounce a third of the way to the fielder. [4]
- Have the pair use a softer ball. [2]
- Have the partner decrease the lateral distance of the bouncing grounder. [4]
- Set an order to the varying directions of the grounder (e.g., forward, right, left, repeat). [3]

To Increase Difficulty

- Have the partner increase the force of the grounder. [3]
- Have the partner vary the distance of the first bounce from the fielder, beginning far away from the fielder and moving closer and closer. [4]
- Have the partner increase the lateral distance of the bouncing grounder. [4]
- Have the partner vary the lateral distance, the direction, or the force of the bouncing grounder. [8]
- Make the drill continuous. [3]
- Have the fielder turn the back to the thrower. When the thrower says ''turn'' (at the time of release of the ball), the fielder turns, locates the ball, reads its direction, moves into position, fields the ball, and throws it back using an overhand throw. [7]

5. Continuous Grounder Fielding Drill
[Corresponds to *Softball*, Step 4, Drill 6]

Group Management and Safety Tips

- See the tips in Drills 3 and 4.
- This drill is more appropriate for more experienced players than for less experienced ones.

Equipment

- Gloves, 1 per student
- Balls, 1 per student pair

Instructions and Cues to Class

- "Mix up your rolling and bouncing grounders. Vary the direction, speed, and distance you make your partner move to field the grounders."
- "Challenge your partner just the right amount. You want your partner to work hard and to be successful in fielding."
- "Practice your reactions in this drill. Read where the ball is going and how it is coming toward you: rolling or bouncing."
- "Pick up on the ball as it leaves your partner's hand, so that you have a jump on moving into position to field it."
- "Relax. Take a deep breath after fielding and throwing the ball for your partner to field."

Student Option

- "Make up a game where you field and throw ground balls. Score points for successes and take away points if you miss due to your own fault. Teach the game to another pair of students."

Student Success Goal

- 24 consecutive grounders fielded out of two sets of 30

To Decrease Difficulty

- Have the partner reduce the variety of throws. [3]
- Have the students set a pattern of throws, for example, 5 rolling throws alternating with 5 bouncing. [3]
- Increase the distance between the partners. [4]
- Have the partner decrease the force of the ball. [3]

To Increase Difficulty

- Decrease the distance between the partners. [4]
- Have the partner vary the force of the ball. [8]

Step 5 Hitting and Using the Batting Tee

Hitting is the most complex of all the skills in softball. It is very important for your students to have a *mental picture* of the full swing used to hit a pitched ball. However, the development of a full swing is facilitated by using some progressive steps that are designed to eliminate some of the complexities in the early stages.

It is important for you to explain the full swing and perhaps to have some of your more experienced students demonstrate hitting a pitched ball. Then use the batting tee drills to help your less experienced students begin to develop the swing and to give your more experienced students a review of the swing.

For less experienced students, stress the cues for initiating the swing, for the position of the body at the point of contact, and for completing the action (the follow-through). Less experienced students tend to swing with their arms only. Failing to take a good turn on the ball (swinging with arms only) eliminates the use of the large leg muscles, which add force to the swing. Novices also fail to swing through the ball, stopping the swing upon contact. The result is akin to stopping on first base instead of running over it. It makes the students slow down the swing before contact,

thus altering the level and reducing the force of the swing.

Your task with novices is to help them develop the pattern of the full hitting stroke, stressing correct technique in all three phases of this complex action. Eliminating the movement of the ball by using the batting tee makes it easier for early learners to pay attention to the body actions needed in the full swing.

Ironically, your task with more experienced learners may be more difficult, unless you were the instructor who taught them originally. You will probably need to break their old bad habits and establish correct new ones. This is often a more difficult task than working with someone who is strictly a beginner.

STUDENT KEYS TO SUCCESS

- Initiate swing with step and hip turn
- Take full turn on ball
- Contact ball off front foot with arms extended
- Hips square to target at contact
- Swing through ball
- Complete swing by wrapping bat around body

Hitting and Using the Batting Tee Rating

CHECKPOINT	LESS EXPERIENCED	MORE EXPERIENCED
Preparation **Grip** **Stance at Tee** **Body Position**	• Hammer grip • Hands separated • Midline of body opposite post of tee • Bat held in front of body • Body erect • Head unsteady • Focus diffused	• Middle knuckles aligned • Hands together • Front foot even with post • Bat back by rear shoulder • Knees bent, slight flex at waist • Head steady • Focus on ball
Execution **Initiation of Swing** **Contact Point**	• With hands and arms • Hips closed • Feet in square stance • Legs stiff • Arms flexed • Head flying • Shoulders and head pulled back • Weight on front foot	• With step and hips • Hips open, square to line of flight • Feet rotated on heel of front foot, ball of back foot • Front leg straight, back leg bent • Arms extended • Head down and still • Back shoulder at chin • Weight centered under back knee
Follow-Through **Bat Position** **Weight** **Head**	• Stops upon contact • On front foot • Up, flying	• Wraps around body • Under back knee • Down, steady

Error Detection and Correction for Hitting and Using the Batting Tee

Direct your observation first to your student's position at the tee, then to the swing. Improper stance at the tee makes a correct swing impossible. Remember, the contact point is the post of the tee (that's where the ball is). Less experienced students tend to stand directly opposite the post of the tee, especially if the post is mounted in the middle of home plate. Their contact point is then the midline of the body rather than ahead of the front foot. That is the main reason less experienced players bend their arms on contact with the ball on the tee. First, focus your cues on the initial position at the tee; then use cues that apply to initiating the swing, the contact point position, and swinging through the ball to complete the hitting action.

ERROR

CORRECTION

1. The hitter bends the arms at contact or contacts the ball on the handle of the bat.

1. Have your student move to stand with the front foot opposite the post of the tee.

ERROR

CORRECTION

2. The batter hits the ball off the end of the bat.

2. Have the student move closer to the tee, but in the position described in the previous correction.

3. The batter hits the tee under the ball.

3. The student should keep the back shoulder up and hit the middle of the ball.

4. The batter misses the ball entirely.

4. The student should keep the head down and steady, focusing on the ball.

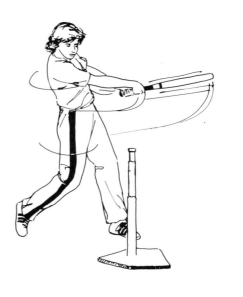

ERROR 🚫

CORRECTION

5. The batter steps and shifts weight onto the front foot.

🚫

5. Have the student step and open the hips, keeping the front leg straight and the back leg bent. The student should pivot on the heel of the front foot and the ball of the back foot, with weight under the back knee.

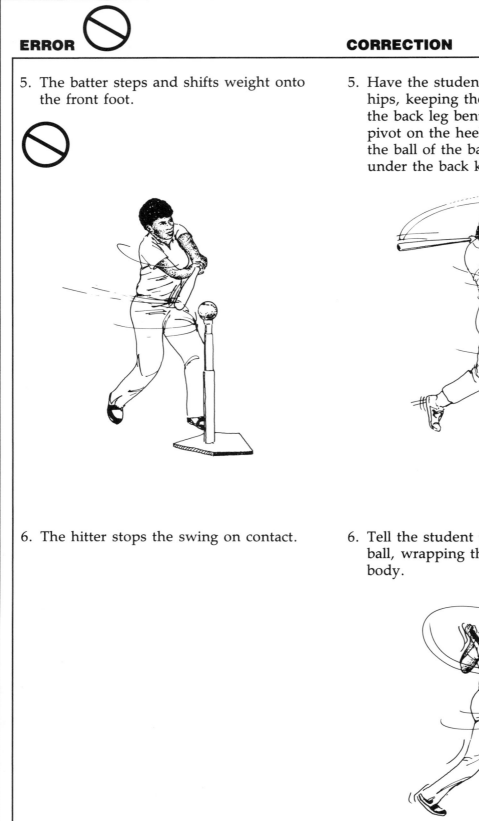

6. The hitter stops the swing on contact.

6. Tell the student to swing through the ball, wrapping the bat around the body.

Batting Tee Hitting Drills

Because it is most unlikely in a class situation that you would have a batting tee available for every student, the batting tee drills could probably be used as stations in a hitting or a multiple-skills circuit, or as individual work stations in a lesson in which students select an area of weakness to work on. Another way to use these drills is in combination with fielding and throwing practice.

The "Group Management" and "Equipment" sections are presented prior to the individual drills in this step because they are the same for all the drills.

Group Management and Safety Tips

- Hitting into a net or a blanket or using the tee with fielders is preferable to hitting into a fence such as the backstop at close range. For years batting tee and soft-toss (ball-toss) drills were done against the backstop or the outfield fence with regulation balls. The practice is not recommended now because of recent litigation brought for injury sustained because of the hitter's being hit by the rebounding ball (usually coming off the pipe framework). Two equipment modifications make the practice less hazardous: Tie a thick gymnastics mat to the fence and use a regulation softball, or a cloth-covered ball (IncrediBall®) against the bare wire fence.
- Use of a partner to set the ball on the tee facilitates the practice for the hitter.
- Caution the hitter to wait for the partner to clear the hitter's swinging range before swinging at the ball.
- Have the partner placing the ball on the tee observe the hitter's swing and give feedback on the performance.

Equipment

- Batting tees, 1 per student pair in a station setting, or 1 per station if combining hitting and fielding in a station
- Softballs, a bucket of 10 per tee
- Bats, a selection of lengths and weights for each tee

1. Net Drill
[Corresponds to *Softball*, Step 5, Drill 1]

Instructions and Cues to Class

- "Stand at the tee so that the ball on the tee is at the correct contact point, opposite your front foot."
- "Wait for your partner to place the ball on the tee and remove his or her hand and body from your swinging range before you begin your swing."
- "Start your hitting action with a slight step with your front foot, pointing the toes in the direction of the intended line of flight of the ball."
- "Start your hip turn before your arm swing."
- "Keep your head down and focus throughout your entire swing, first on the ball on the tee, then on the top of the tee's post where the ball was held."
- "Hit the middle of the ball; just make full contact."
- "Swing through the ball; do not stop your swing upon contact."
- "Have your hips square and your arms extended at the point of contact."

- ''The partner should watch the batter hit the ball. Using the points from the ''Keys to Success'' section, give feedback to the hitter about the technique used.''
- ''Switch roles after hitting the bucket of balls.''
- ''Repeat the drill so that each person hits the ball 20 times.''

Student Options

- ''Work alone, setting the ball on the tee yourself.''
- ''Close your eyes, visualize the ball on the tee, and hit the imaginary ball.''

Student Success Goal

- 16 of 20 hits with correct form and full contact

To Decrease Difficulty

- Have the student go through the full swing motion with no ball on the tee. [2]

To Increase Difficulty

- Have the student start with a two-handed grip on the bat but then use the bottom hand only to complete the swing (see *Softball*, Step 5, Drill 3). [5]

2. Net Target Drill
[Corresponds to *Softball*, Step 5, Drill 2]

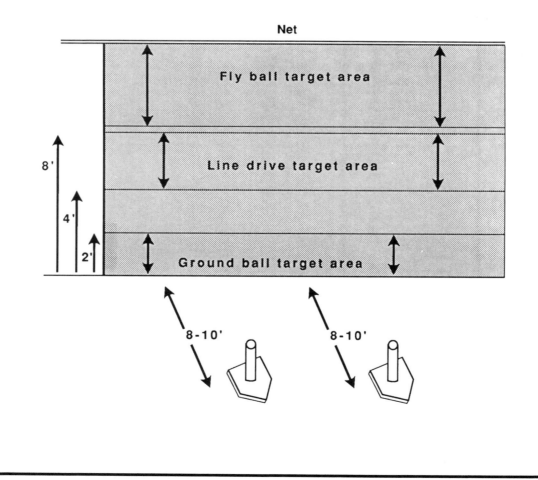

Equipment

- Tape for three lines on net, 2, 4, and 8 feet from the ground

Instructions and Cues to Class

- ''Use a high-to-low swing path to hit ground balls, aiming below the 2-foot line. Use a level swing to hit line drives, aiming between the 4-foot and 8-foot lines. Use a low-to-high swing path to hit fly balls, aiming above the 8-foot line.''
- ''When swinging high to low, start with the bat above the level of your rear shoulder. Make contact just above the middle of the ball. Swing forward, down, and through the ball.''
- ''When swinging low to high, start the bat back below the rear shoulder. Make contact just below the middle of the ball. Swing forward, up, and through the ball.''
- ''Hit 10 balls of each type.''

Student Options

- ''Work alone, setting the ball on the tee yourself.''
- ''Visualize the ball on the tee, close your eyes, and use the three swing paths to hit the imaginary ball.''

Student Success Goal

- 24 of 30 total on-target hits

    8 of 10 ground balls (low target)

    8 of 10 line drives (middle target)

    8 of 10 fly balls (high target)

To Decrease Difficulty

- Have the student close his or her eyes and practice the three swing paths. [1]

To Increase Difficulty

- Have the student vary the swing path on every hit. [8]
- Have a partner call for the type of hit to be made. [8]

3. Low-Ball/High-Ball Drill
[Corresponds to *Softball*, Step 5, Drill 4]

Instructions and Cues to Class

- ''Adjust the height of the tee so that the ball is low, below your waist.''
- ''Use the appropriate swing path to hit 20 ground balls at that setting.''
- ''Set the tee height so the ball is in the high part of your strike zone, above your waist.''
- ''Use the appropriate swing path to hit 10 line drives and 10 fly balls at that setting.''

Student Options

- ''Select a tee setting, either high or low, that is in your strength zone for hitting. Hit 20 balls using the appropriate swing path.''
- ''Select a height setting that is in a hitting weakness zone. Hit 20 balls.''

Student Success Goals

- 30 clean hits of 40 total swings, with no bat contact with the tee (fixed center-post tee)

  15 of 20 at the low setting

  15 of 20 at the high setting

- 60 clean hits of 80 total swings (adjustable center-post tee)

  15 of 20 at low inside setting

  15 of 20 at low outside setting

  15 of 20 at high inside setting

  15 of 20 at high outside setting

To Decrease Difficulty

- Have the student take a stance so that the ball is in the middle of the strike zone. [4]

To Increase Difficulty

- Have the student adjust the tee to place the ball on the corners of the plate: low outside, low inside, high outside, and high inside. [3]
- If using a tee with a fixed center post, have the student adjust his or her stance to place the ball in the relative inside and outside positions just described. [4]

Step 6 Fungo Hitting a Ground Ball

Fungo hitting serves two purposes for your students. It helps them develop bat control by requiring them to use hand-eye and bat-eye coordination. In addition, when your students are able to fungo hit ground balls, they can hit the ball to fielders. This facilitates practice of two skills simultaneously and also fosters game-like use of those skills. Consequently, you will want to teach your students to fungo hit in order to enable them to progress as softball players.

As you observe your students' practice, try to focus on those aspects of fungo hitting that strengthen the full-swing hitting pattern. You want to be sure that your students do not develop bad habits (improper hitting patterns) while fungo hitting. Bad habits are likely to develop because the batters will undoubtedly be thinking primarily about getting ground balls to the fielders. However, you should reinforce the idea that they will be able to get the ball to go where they want when they use proper technique.

The less experienced players will probably swing and miss the ball fairly often. In addition, they will tend to try to hit with their weight on their back foot. This will cause the ball to go up into the air rather than onto the ground. With these players, you should concentrate your feedback on eye-bat coordination. They must watch the ball and see it hit by the bat.

The more experienced players will probably be able to fungo hit the ball more consistently, but they have a tendency to use just their arms in the swing. Your explaining to them that they need to use this skill to increase their bat control and their swing pattern should reinforce their concentration on batting technique. As you observe the more experienced students, try to focus on the grip and the hip rotation into the swing.

Because fungo hitting is used to give fielders practice on fielding ground balls, the fungo hitters should always try to hit the ball just where the fielders need it. This means that the fungo hitters should practice placing ground balls to desired points. Encourage the fungo hitters to watch the fielders closely and try to place the grounder to points that will extend the skill of the fielder. The fungo hitters can help themselves develop bat control and at the same time assist their partners in improving their skills in fielding ground balls.

STUDENT KEYS TO SUCCESS

- Bat swing pattern high to low
- Ball toss falls in line with front foot
- Body weight pivots to front foot on swing
- Focus on ball throughout toss and hit
- Contact ball off front foot and slightly below waist level

Fungo Hitting a Ground Ball Rating

CHECKPOINT	LESS EXPERIENCED	MORE EXPERIENCED
Preparation Stance Focus Bat Position	• Open foot position • Looking at fielder • Bat laid back and parallel to ground	• Square foot position • Down, looking at ball • Bat held high
Execution Toss Swing Pattern Body Pivot Focus	• Out and away from body • Level, or low-to-high • Nonexistent • Where ball is to go	• Ahead of front foot • High-to-low • Hips turn toward intended hit • On ball and bat contact point
Follow-Through Body Position Bat Position	• Weight on back foot • At shoulder height	• Weight on front foot • Below shoulder

Error Detection and Correction for Fungo Hitting a Ground Ball

ERROR

CORRECTION

1. The ball is hit up into the air rather than onto the ground.

1. Have the student toss the ball lower, start the bat high above the back shoulder, and wait for the ball to drop below the waist.

ERROR  **CORRECTION**

2. The ball goes off target to the right or left.

2. Both feet should point in the direction of the target. The ball toss must be opposite where the front foot is after the step that begins the swing pattern. The batter must contact the ball directly in line with the front foot.

3. The ball is missed completely.

3. Have your student watch the ball all the time, not looking at the fielder while swinging but seeing the ball being hit by the bat.

Fungo Hitting Ground Ball Drills

1. *Fungo Hitting Ground Ball Wall Drill*

[Corresponds to *Softball*, Step 6, Drill 1]

Group Management and Safety Tips

- All students can do this drill: The less experienced players will need to practice longer; the more experienced players can use it for a quick review. You might be able to use this drill to determine ability groupings: Students who can hit the floor target consistently are more experienced.
- Because wall (fence) space is undoubtedly limited, it is unlikely that all students can do the drill simultaneously. If this is the case, have the students pair up. One student fungo hits, and the other serves as a peer teacher, giving feedback on the form of the fungo hitter.
- The hitters should be at least 15 feet from the wall. All hitters must be the same distance away from the wall. Mark a hitting line with cones or some other marker.
- The hitters should be at least 6 feet from one another on the hitting line. Have them check their swing pattern slowly to make sure that they are far enough away from—in front of and behind—the other hitters.
- The left-handed batters should be on one end of the line so that they are facing the right-handed batters.
- The partner who is observing the hitter should stand to the bat-hand side of the hitter, facing the wall.
- Mark a line about 5 feet in front of the wall, between the wall and the fungo hitter. This is the target for the ground ball.
- Watch the students to make sure that they do not "creep" toward the wall or toward other fungo hitters as they are doing the drill.
- If there are not enough bats for everyone to do the drill simultaneously, the more experienced students could set up a fungo hitting and fielding drill. Put together one fungo hitter, one catcher for the fungo hitter, and two fielders about 15 to 20 feet from the fungo hitter. The fungo hitter alternates hits to the fielders, who field the ball and throw it overhand to the catcher.

Equipment

- Bats, various weights and lengths (primarily shorter and lighter ones, which are easier to control), as many as are available
- Balls, 2 for each batter hitting to a wall, or 5 to 10 for each batter hitting to a fence
- Cones or other markers to mark the hitting line and the target line
- Buckets or containers for retrieving the balls (if hitting to a fence)

Instructions to Class

- "Hit the ball to the wall (fence), but aim for the target line 5 feet in front of the wall. This will help you hit the ball down."
- "Keep hitting until 5 balls in a row hit the ground before they hit the wall. Count how many tries it takes before you get 5 in a row."
- "If the ball rebounds off the wall after hitting the ground first, field it with your tossing hand. Hang on to the bat with your top hand."

- "If balls stay at the wall, do not go to retrieve them until you hear my cue. Others will be hitting, so we must not retrieve balls until everyone is ready to do so."
- "Work on the fungo hitting until you consistently feel and hear a good solid contact of the bat on the ball."

Cues to Class

- "Start the bat high behind your shoulder so that you can swing down on the ball. If you want the ball to go down to the ground, then you must have the bat contact the ball on the downswing."
- "Step toward the wall with your front foot. You need to step in the direction that you want the ball to go."
- "Be sure to pivot, just like at the tee. When you are swinging, your hips should be turning toward the target."
- "Remember, your hips cannot turn toward the target if your feet do not pivot so that your toes face the target."
- "Think about hitting technique as you fungo hit. Good technique will help you hit the ball consistently and where you want it to go."
- "Watch the ball all the time. You should see the bat hit the ball. Once you see the bat hit the ball, then you can look to see where it has gone. If you look too early, you will either miss the ball or it will not go where you intended it to go."

Student Options

- "Have your partner observe your fungo hitting. Ask him or her to watch your technique, particularly your swing path (high to low), your body and foot pivot, and your focus on the ball. Observer, you need to watch for one hitting aspect at a time. Then help your partner practice doing the skill correctly by working on the errors one at a time."
- "Between each fungo hit of a real ball, close your eyes and take three mimetic swings. Visualize the high-to-low swing pattern and the body and foot pivots."

Student Success Goal

- 5 consecutive fungo hits that hit the ground in front of the wall in less than 15 attempts

To Decrease Difficulty

- Let the student hit with a lighter and shorter bat. [2]
- Have the student "choke up" on the bat. [2]
- Have your student practice the toss alone (without swinging the bat) until it is consistent. [5]
- Have your student practice the fungo hit swing mimetically. [5]

To Increase Difficulty

- Have the student move closer to or farther from the wall while aiming for the same ground target (move this student to one end of the line). [4]

2. *Accuracy Drill*
[Corresponds to *Softball*, Step 6, Drill 2]

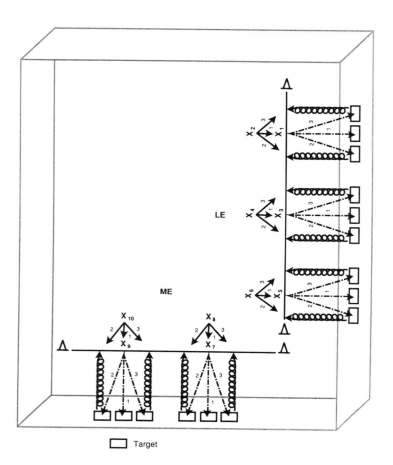

▭ Target

Group Management and Safety Tips

- Put targets on the ground along the base of a wall or a fence, 10 feet apart. If you can create targets 3 feet by 3 feet, do so. Otherwise, just place a cone or a disk every 10 feet along the wall.
- Students should be divided into less experienced and more experienced groups. They should pair up to work together.
- More experienced players should be toward one end of the hitting line.
- Each student pair consists of a hitter and a fielder.

- The hitters stand on a hitting line that is at least 20 feet from the wall. The left-handed hitters should all be at one end of the line, facing the right-handed hitters.
- Place the fungo hitters so that each is in the center of a 10-foot space (visualize the targets spaced every 10 feet extended as lines through the hitting line).
- The fielding partners stand behind the hitting line, facing the wall and the fungo hitter.
- The partner fielding the rebounding ball may not go in front of the hitting line.

- If the balls do not rebound but stay at the fence, all the students must go to collect the balls at the same time.
- If there is not enough equipment or space, have the more experienced players do this drill in the setup given in the previous drill.
- All fungo hitters should hit to the targets to the right and the targets to the left at the same time. Do not let them go right and left on their own.

Equipment

- Bats, light and short, as many as are available
- Balls, as many as are available: at least 5 per fungo hitter
- Buckets to retrieve balls, if they are not fielded
- Gloves, at least 1 per student pair
- Cones or other target markers (disks, gloves, flags, pinnies, scrimmage vests, rags)

Instructions to Class

- "Fungo hit grounders to the middle target area 5 feet from the wall. Try to have the ball hit the center of your target. The ball should hit the target on the ground before it hits the wall [fence]."
- "Fungo hit 10 balls to the center target, then switch roles with your partner. Count how many hit the target."
- "The fielding partner should field the ball as it rebounds off the wall and crosses the hitting line. Do not go in front of the hitting line to field the ball. Other hitters are fungo hitting, and an errant ball could hit you."
- "If the ball does not rebound off the wall or fence, do not go to retrieve it until I give the retrieval signal."
- "After hitting 10 balls to the center target area, hit 10 balls to the target area to your left. Remember to step with the front foot in the direction of the target."
- "After each of you has hit 10 balls to the left target area, hit 10 balls to the right target area. Be sure to step with the front foot toward the target."

Cues to Class

- "Be sure that you toss the ball so it would come down just opposite your front foot if you missed it. This will help you hit the ball in the direction you want it to go."
- "Wait for the ball to come down to waist level before you swing. Hit it when it is below your waist. This will help only if you start with the bat high above your shoulder."
- "At the end of each hit, check your feet. Are they pointing in the direction of the target?"

Student Options

- "Have your partner watch your swing. This time, he or she should focus on your step. Is it toward the target area? Do you pivot so that your feet point in the direction of the target?"
- "Alternate target areas: left, center, right."

Student Success Goal

- 24 of 30 fungo hits contacting the target areas before the wall

  8 of 10 on-target hits, center target

  8 of 10 on-target hits, left target

  8 of 10 on-target hits, right target

To Decrease Difficulty

- Let the student use a lighter or shorter bat. [2]
- Make the target areas bigger. [3]
- Move the targets closer together. [4]

To Increase Difficulty

- Make the targets smaller. [3]
- Move the targets farther apart. [4]
- Make the batter focus on hitting a particular area within the target. [1]
- Have the batter hit the targets alternately, then randomly, making things tougher for both the hitter and the fielder. [6, 8]
- Move the targets so that they are different distances apart (e.g., 10 feet and 8 feet). [4, 8]
- Have the batter move farther away from the targets, then closer to the targets. [4]

3. *Partner Call Target Drill*
[Corresponds to *Softball*, Step 6, Drill 3]

Group Management and Safety Tips

- The target setup is exactly the same as in the previous drill.
- In this drill, each student pair must have at least 30 feet of line space to work in.
- It would be possible to have only a portion of the class do this game, while the others work in an open area on the batting tee.
- Those at the batting tee should work on hitting to the right and the left, and there should be fielders who are fielding the balls hit off the tee.
- Students doing the Partner Call Target Game must have three target areas to do the drill: center, right, and left target areas.
- The fielding partner moves into position to field the ball after the fungo hitter has made contact with the ball.
- Watch carefully that the fungo hitter and partner do not ''creep'' from the center of their space on the hit to the target. They must both begin each hit in the center of their space.

Equipment

- Bats, as many as are available
- Balls, as many as are available—at least 3 per student pair if possible
- Gloves, 1 per student pair
- Batting tees, if there are batting tee stations

Instructions and Cues to Class

- ''The fungo hitter hits ground balls to the target area called for by the fielding partner.''
- ''The call of which target area to hit must come just prior to the toss by the fungo hitter.''
- ''Fielder, you are to cleanly field the ball before it stops rolling.''
- ''The hitter gets a point if the fungo hit goes to the correct target. The fielder gets a point if he or she fields the ball (without bobbling it) before it stops rolling. Keep track of your points because you will compare them at the end of the game to see who has more.''
- ''An 'inning' is equal to each of you fungo hitting 10 balls. See who gets more points in 3 innings and who wins more innings.''
- ''Fungo hitter, be sure to watch the ball and see the contact of the bat on the ball. You don't want to miss the ball.''
- ''Fungo hitter, try both to hit the target and to make your partner move a long distance to field the ball. Then it will be harder for him or her to score points.''
- ''Fielder, watch the ball go off of the bat so that you get a jump on where it is going.''
- ''Fielder, sometimes it helps if you look at the direction of the hitter's step with the front foot. Then you know what the direction of the hit will be.''

Student Options

- ''To work more on fielding, have the fungo hitter decide where to hit the ball. Then the fielder has to react to the hit and move into position to field the ground ball.''
- ''You can play this as a doubles game, with one pair of partners challenging another pair of partners. The fungo hitter and fielder are a team, and they score points in the same manner as in the other game. However, the *other* pair calls out the direction for the fungo hit. Each team gets 10 hits—5 by each partner. See which team scores more points and wins more innings.''
- ''You can make this a cutthroat game. You will need a group of three people. The fungo hitter hits ground balls to any of the targets. The two fielders attempt to field the ball before it stops rolling. Points are scored by the fungo hitter when the ball hits the target. The fielder scores when the ball is cleanly fielded before it stops rolling. Each inning is comprised of each person fungo hitting 10 balls. See who scores the most points in one inning.''

Student Success Goals

- Scoring more points overall
- Winning more innings

To Decrease Difficulty

- Have the fielder call the target early so that the fungo hitter has more time to set up for the hit. [3]
- Let the fungo hitter decide which target to hit the ball to. [3]

To Increase Difficulty

- Have the fielder call the target later so that the fungo hitter can step in the target direction only as the toss descends. [3]
- Move the targets farther apart. [4]
- Make the targets smaller. [2]
- Make the fielder stay stationary until the ball is actually hit. [3]

Step 7 Four-Skill Combination

Your students are now ready to apply the skills they have practiced thus far to more realistic, game-like drills. This application of the skills as they are combined in real game settings will enable your students to make the transition from practice to game play more easily. It is very difficult to practice the skills as isolated entities and then to be able to use them under the conditions that occur in game play. Consequently, the drills in this step are designed to give your students practice combining the skills of fielding ground balls that come off hits, throwing various distances to bases (as outfielders and infielders), and throwing in a variety of directions (as to different bases). These drills also enable your students to extend their ability to move to and field ground balls hit at a range of speeds.

As you observe your students and give them feedback on their skills, try to direct your cues and other information toward the skill combinations and the techniques needed to be successful in game play. If your students still need work on the isolated skills, have them go back to the earlier steps and try some of the options, variations, or difficulty adjustments identified there. The practice they are doing in this step is directed toward their application of skills in game-like settings; thus, you need to focus your attention on their use of the skill combinations.

Students, as they practice the drills in this step, will undoubtedly be very outcome oriented; they will be motivated to complete the play and get the ball to the proper player. You can help them also keep in mind the technical execution of the skills by reminding them that the technique used in one skill often affects the manner in which the other combined skills are executed. The less experienced students will be likely to try to rush the fielding skills and focus attention on the throw. Consequently, they will probably not keep their heads down as they field the ball, and they will have a tendency to muff the fielding play. Remind them that the throw is an extension of the follow-through of fielding and that they have to field the ball before they can throw it. Try to help them calm down as the ball comes to them. If they consistently have trouble fielding the ball, reduce the difficulty of the fielding action by having their partners deliver the ball with less force or hit the ball closer to them.

The more experienced players, on the other hand, will probably be quite proficient at these drills. Your feedback to them should be directed toward motivating them to try to refine their skills to rote, patterned execution. More experienced players should work on fielding the ball by charging it as it comes to them. They should try to make their throws go directly to the glove target given by the person catching their throws. Help them set goals for success in these drills that will enable them to perform the skill combination in game situations without having to think about it. You are trying to get the more experienced players to increase their ability to read where the ball is going and to react quickly so that they can simply use their established motor pattern to successfully execute the plays required.

STUDENT KEYS TO SUCCESS
- Watch ball
- Charge ball
- Focus on target
- Throw to glove of base player

Four-Skill Combination Drills

Some of the drills in this step are organized for practicing skill combinations as they are executed in games on the regulation field. However, it will be impossible to put all of your students on the regulation field and have them practice simultaneously. Consequently, reference is made in the drill setups to players being ''as at'' a particular position. This is done to describe the relative position of one person to another and the distances involved. These drills can be set up anywhere, and the distance can be adjusted to the ability level of the participants.

1. *Direct Grounders Drill*

[Corresponds to *Softball*, Step 7, Drill 1]

Group Management and Safety Tips

- Divide the students into less experienced and more experienced groups.
- Within each experience group, the students must be further divided into groups of three. One player starts the drill as the hitter, one as the catcher for the hitter, and the third as the fielder.
- The hitter and the catcher stand on a foul line, with the catcher 3 feet away from and facing the hitter.
- The hitter and the catcher must be at least 10 feet away from other hitters and catchers who are on the foul line.
- You can have pairs of students on both foul lines as long as any ball that got by the fielder would not endanger students fielding balls hit from the other line.
- The fielder stands 70 feet away from the hitter, facing the hitter and the catcher.
- If your class is large, you can divide the students into groups of four. The fourth person is a backup fielder. He or she stands 8 feet behind the other fielder and fields any balls that are not stopped by the other. If that backup fielder fields the ball, he or she should toss it to the other fielder, who makes the throw to the catcher. To rotate, simply have the hitter and catcher switch positions and the initial fielder and backup fielder switch. Repeat the drill.
- If you are unable to have all your students doing this drill simultaneously, some students could go on to Step 8, ''Pitching.'' After an appropriate amount of practice, the students would change practice stations with each other. Thus, you would have two skills being practiced at the same time. This way, your available space would be maximized.
- Be on the alert that as the fielders move about fielding the ground balls they do not wander into the space used by another group.

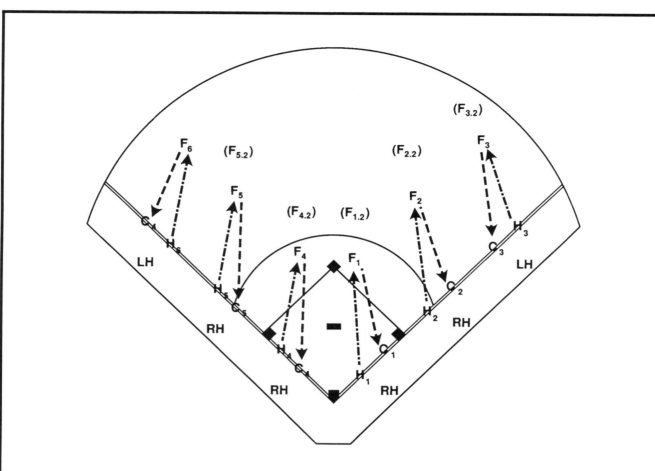

Equipment

- Balls, 1 per student
- Bats, 1 per group of three students (have a variety of weight and lengths so that students have a choice)
- Extra softballs

Instructions and Cues to Class

- "When you are the hitter, be sure that you hit the ground balls directly at the fielder so that he or she can concentrate on combining fielding and throwing into one motion."
- "As the fielder, start in the ready position (body low, feet in forward stride, eyes on hitter), watch the ball into the glove, and make the transition to the throw smooth and continuous."
- "Think about what you are going to do before the hitter hits the ball. Then just do what you thought about."
- "Don't get overanxious. Let the ball come to you. Field it and in one motion throw it to the catcher." (LE)

- "Look for the target as soon as you have the ball securely in your glove."
- "When you are the catcher, be sure that you give the fielder a big target so that he or she can easily pick it up visually and throw directly to it. When the ball comes in to you on the fly, be sure to move in front of it and give with the ball as it enters your glove. Then toss the ball to the hitter."

Student Options

- "Have the hitter watch your technique and give you feedback about your body position as you field the ball. Are you down low? Are your feet in forward stride position? Are you looking for the target at the correct time? Are you stepping in the direction of your throw?"
- "When you feel you are consistent on your fielding, have the catcher give you different targets for your throw."

Student Success Goals

- 8 of 10 fungo hit ground balls
- 8 of 10 successful fielding and throwing combinations
- 9 of 10 catches of the thrown ball

To Decrease Difficulty

- Have the batter hit the ball with less force. [3]
- Reduce the distance of the throw. [4]
- Use a softer ball, such as a Rag Ball® or an IncrediBall®. [2]

To Increase Difficulty

- Have the batter hit the ball with greater force. [3]

- Have the batter hit the ball so that fielder has to move to field it:
  Fielder moves to glove side,
  fielder moves to throwing side, or
  fielder moves to glove side and throwing side alternately [8]
- Have the batter hit the ball so that the fielder does not know the direction it will go or the speed at which it will come (see *Softball*, Step 7, Drill 2, Moving to the Ball Drill). [8]
- Make the fielder charge the ball as it is coming. [1]
- Have the catcher give different targets for the throw. [3]

2. *Triangle Drill*
[Corresponds to *Softball*, Step 7, Drill 4]

Group Management and Safety Tips

- Less experienced players and more experienced players should be in different groups.
- Groups of four are needed for the drill. One pair is a catcher and a hitter, positioned as in the previous drill. The other pair are fielders positioned as at first base and third base.
- This drill can be set up with four hitter-catcher pairs in four corners of a large square on a field. There must be enough room inside the square that the pairs of fielders are not in danger of being hit by overthrows and errant hits.
- If you have extra students, place two in outfield positions, one backing up the fielder at first base and one backing up at third. If the infielder should miss the ground ball, the outfielder will field the ball and throw it to the catcher.
- The students should switch roles within their pairs after 5 repetitions and repeat the drill. Then the home plate pair should switch roles with the fielding pair and repeat the drill.

- Watch that the students do not creep toward other groups, thus being endangered by possible overthrows.

Equipment

- Gloves, 1 per student
- Balls, 1 per student (all 4 or 6 balls are at home plate)
- Markers to designate zones for each drill station (if you need to do so)
- Bats, 2 or 3 of various lengths and weights at each hitting location

Instructions and Cues to Class

- ''Hitter, first hit ground balls to the fielder at the first base location. Then hit the next ball to the fielder in the third base location. Repeat 5 times so that each fielder gets 5 fielding tries.''
- ''Hitter, hit ground balls that the fielders can field. As the fielders become more consistent, vary the speed, the direction, and the range of the ground balls. Then you will be helping the fielders improve while practicing fielding balls the way they will come to them in a game.''

- "The fielder making the fielding play on the grounder should get in front of the ball, watch the ball into the glove, and in one motion turn the glove side to the other fielder, step toward the fielder, and throw the ball."
- "The fielder making the play on the grounder should field the ball first, then immediately look for the target while bringing the ball into the throwing position and shifting the weight back."
- "The fielder making the play on the grounder shouldn't rush the throw. Step and use the full overhand motion; then the throw will be strong and fast enough to get there on time."
- "The fielder catching the throw should make a big target with the glove for the ground ball fielder."

- "The fielder catching the throw should reach out in front to catch the ball. If the throw is off target, the fielder should move into the line of the throw to make the catch."
- "The fielder catching the throw should call out the number of his or her base (1 or 3) as the other fielder is playing the ground ball. This will help the player fielding the ground ball focus attention on the direction of the target."
- "Catcher at home plate, make sure that you get out ahead of the hitter to make the catch. You need to protect the hitter."
- "Catcher, reach out for the ball as it approaches you and give with the ball once it is in your glove."
- "Catcher, make sure that the hitter is looking when you toss the ball."
- "Think about what you are supposed to do in each role when you are in it. Then, when you are executing the skills required, it will be nearly automatic."

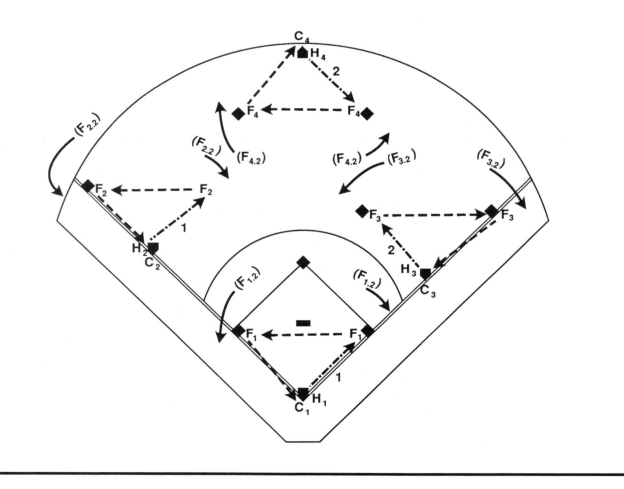

Student Options

- "When you are a fielder, have the hitter hit grounders to your glove side and to your throwing side so that you can practice moving both directions to the ball and then throwing to both first and third bases."
- "Have the other fielder change the place of the target he or she is making with the glove."
- "As you field and throw the ball, verbally repeat the rhythmic pattern from your earlier practice. 'Field, turn, step, and throw.' Try to become as smooth as you can in the fielding and throwing action."

Student Success Goals

- 8 of 10 fungo ground balls hit
- 9 of 10 catches at home position

Fielder at first base

- 4 of 5 fielding plays at first-base side
- 3 of 5 throws from first-base side

Fielder at third base

- 4 of 5 fielding plays at third-base side
- 4 of 5 throws from third-base side

To Decrease Difficulty

- Let the hitter use the batting tee. [5]
- Let the fielder play a rolled ball. [3]
- Use a softer ball. [2]
- Decrease the distance of the throw from the fielder to the base. [4]
- Lengthen the distance from the hitter to the fielder. [4]

To Increase Difficulty

- Have the hitter vary the force of the hit. [8]
- Have the hitter vary the direction of the ground ball:
  Glove side,
  throwing side,
  alternate sides, or
  random mixture of direct, glove-side, and throwing-side grounders [8]
- Have the hitter vary both the direction and the force of the hit. [8]
- Make the fielder charge the ball to field it earlier. [1]
- Have the catching fielder move the target from chest level to knee level. [3]
- Move one fielder from the third base position to the shortstop position and do the Get One Out Drill (see *Softball*, Step 7, Drill 5). [8]

3. *Outfielder Drill*
[Corresponds to *Softball*, Step 7, Drill 6]

Group Management and Safety Tips

- Use the same management for groups and roles within the group as in Drill 1, Direct Grounders Drill.
- The fielder is 100 feet from the hitter and catcher.
- The hitter fungo hits a ground ball to the fielder.
- The fielder fields the ball and throws the ball to the catcher, who is standing beside the hitter, facing the hitter.

- Make sure that there is sufficient room between the groups of three so that the fielder can move at least 15 feet in either direction.

Equipment

- Gloves, 1 per student
- Balls, 1 per student (all 3 balls per group at home plate)
- Bats, 2 or 3 of varying lengths and weights shared by two adjoining hitting stations

Instructions and Cues to Class

- "Hitter, hit grounders that are fieldable by the outfielder."
- "Fielder, move in line with the ball before it gets to you. Field the ball, and as you bring the ball to the throwing position, crow-hop and make the throw to the catcher."
- "The crow-hop is taking a step with the glove-side foot and hopping onto the throwing-side foot (step-hop-step) while bringing the ball to the throwing position. You do it to put some forward momentum into the throw."
- "Practice the crow-hop until it becomes automatic."
- "If you can't throw the ball in the air all the way to the catcher, make a one-bounce throw. Aim for a spot 10 to 15 feet in front of the catcher. Try to throw the ball to that spot on as straight a path as possible. The ball will rebound to the catcher. This will make the ball easier to catch, and it takes less time to get to the catcher than a high, looping throw."
- "Field and throw. Read the ball direction, move, field, and throw. React to the ball as it is hit. These cues should help you get the rhythm and the pattern you want to make automatic."
- "After 10 grounders, change roles."

Student Options

- "After 5 successfully fielded grounders, the hitter could hit the ball so the fielder has to move to field it."
- "If you have trouble reading where ground balls are going, stand behind another person who is fielding a ball. Watch for the ball to come off the bat. See the fielder move into the proper fielding position in the proper ball path."

- "If you find it easy to read the path of the ground ball, try to charge the ball to field it earlier. Remember, you get into the proper position first so that you can charge the ball by moving straight ahead."
- "Imagine that a runner is running to home and that your throw has to get to the catcher on the fly or on one bounce." (ME)

Student Success Goals

- 8 of 10 on-target hits
- 8 of 10 fielding attempts and on-target throws
- 8 of 10 catches at home position

To Decrease Difficulty

- Have the hitter decrease the force of the ground ball by rolling it or hitting it softly. [3]
- Use a softer ball. [2]
- Decrease the distance of the throw from the fielder to the catcher. [4]
- Let the hitter use a batting tee if fungo hitting is difficult. [5]
- Change the drill's focus from throwing to merely fielding the grounder. [1]

To Increase Difficulty

- Have the hitter increase the force of the ground ball. [3]
- Have the hitter vary the direction and speed of the ground ball. [8]
- Have the fielder charge the ball. [1]
- Have the catcher vary the height of the target from chest height to knee height. [3]

4. Rapid Fire Drill

[New Drill]

Group Management and Safety Tips

- This drill is for more experienced players only.
- This should be done on a regulation infield.
- Less experienced students can be practicing the earlier drills.
- No fielder is to charge the ball when fielding it.

Equipment

- Gloves, 1 per student
- Bases and home plates
- Bats, 3 or 4 per station of various lengths and weights (mostly light)
- Balls, 5 at each hitting station

Instructions to Class

- "Divide into groups of six. In each group of six, divide into two trios."
- "One trio consists of a hitter (H1) near third base, a third baseman (3b), and a fielder (F1) at second base. The other trio consists of a hitter (H2) near first base, a first baseman (1b), and a fielder (F2) at shortstop. The hitters stand in foul territory, 10 feet from the base (facing the baseman who is at the base)."
- "The hitter at third base (H1) hits ground balls to the person in the second-base fielding position (F1). The fielder makes overhand throws to the third baseman (3b)."
- "The hitter at first base (H2) hits ground balls to the person in the shortstop fielding position (F2). The fielder makes overhand throws to the first baseman (1b)."
- "The third and first basemen then toss the balls to the hitters."
- "You could get mixed up on this drill, so think first where your hits and throws are to go. Remember, the second baseman throws to third base, and the shortstop throws to first base."
- "The ground balls are hit simultaneously and, therefore, are crossing in the infield. You must hit the balls *directly* at the fielders. The fielders must stay *behind* the baseline to field the ball."
- "Fielders, do *not* charge a poorly hit ball."
- "Fielders, work on good fielding and quick releases on the throws."
- "After 10 repetitions, the players rotate within the group of three:
  H1 goes to 3b
  3b goes to F1
  F1 goes to H1
  F2 goes to 1b
  1b goes to H2
  H2 goes to F2
- Continue the counterclockwise rotation after each set of 10 repetitions until each player has played each position in his or her group. Then groups exchange positions and continue with rotation as before.

Student Option

- None

Student Success Goals

- 8 of 10 fungo hits directly to the fielder
- 8 of 10 combined fields and on-target throws at second base position
- 8 of 10 combined fields and on-target throws at shortstop position
- 8 of 10 catches at each base

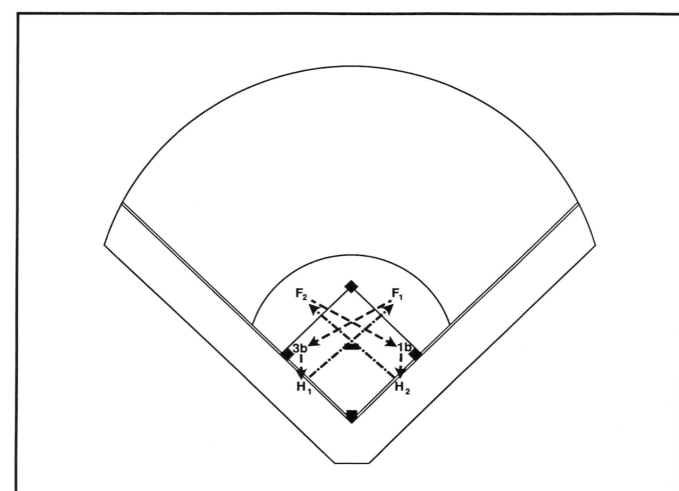

To Decrease Difficulty

- Have the hitters go in sequence—first, third baseline hitter, then first baseline hitter. [5]
- Have the hitter slow the series by pausing between hits to the fielder. [3]

To Increase Difficulty

- Have the hitter speed up the drill by barely waiting before hitting the next ground ball. [3]
- Have the hitter move the fielder to the right and left (no more than 4 feet) to field the ball. [4]

- Have the catcher make a target at chest height, then at knee height. [3]
- Use two balls so that as soon as the fielder has thrown the ball to the catcher, the hitter hits a second ball to the fielder. This makes a rapid-fire drill. If this is done, it may be helpful to have an additional catcher with the hitter so that he or she can toss the extra ball to the hitter, then receive the toss from the other catcher. [2, 8]

Step 8 Pitching

You could introduce pitching to your students at any time. Although in a game the pitch precedes the hitting act, they are completely isolated skills performed by two different people. Pitching is not a part of any combination skill, such as fielding and throwing; therefore, it is not linked in progression with any other skill.

Because of the complex nature of hitting and the opportunities to practice the skill without the pitch, hitting was presented prior to pitching in *Softball*. Your students need more time to develop their hitting technique than to develop their slow pitch pitching prowess. The mechanics of the slow pitch pitch are relatively simple, and most of your students should be able to master the skill in a very short time.

Because pitching is not a part of any particular progression, your students can practice it in conjunction with other skills. You can present different skills to halves of the class and rotate the groups either within the same class period or from day to day; this can help you maximize use of your facilities. Slow pitch pitching is a skill you can effectively pair up with any number of other skills or combinations. Using the outfield foul lines well beyond first and third base as the pitching rubbers or having your students pitch back and forth over the outfield fence allows you to free the infield area for other practice.

The underhand pendulum pitching movement, once patterned, results in a pitch that is on line with the target. The major problems encountered by all students learning to execute the slow pitch pitching action are distance and arc. These problems have to do with the amount of force needed to bring the ball to the plate and with the proper point of release to create the 6- to 12-foot arc required of a regulation slow pitch. Once your students have begun to pattern the pendulum movement, focus your cues on point of release and force production.

Fast-pitch windmill and slingshot deliveries are not presented in *Softball*, because the development and use of those techniques by every student is not realistic in a class situation. Eliminating the arc of the regulation slow pitch pitch and using the modified version (straight pendulum action with backswing restricted to shoulder height) would be a realistic alternative to the slow pitch pitch for class use.

Above all, teach your students to pitch, and use them as pitchers in game situations. Do not take yourself out of the teaching role by being the pitcher because you are the only one who can get the ball over the plate.

STUDENT KEYS TO SUCCESS
- Pivot foot on rubber
- Present ball with full stop
- Focus on target just to rear of back point of home plate
- Step with glove-side foot
- Smooth pendulum motion with throwing arm
- Underhand delivery with fingers under ball
- Step with pivot foot into good fielding position

Pitching Rating

CHECKPOINT	LESS EXPERIENCED	MORE EXPERIENCED
Preparation Grip Stance Focus	• Four fingers • Both feet square on rubber • Diffused	• Three fingers • Pivot foot on rubber, glove-side foot to rear • On back point of plate
Execution Weight Step Arm Swing Release Point Force Application Hand Position at Release	• Balanced on both feet • With throwing-side foot • Jerky, broken swing • Inconsistent • Inconsistent • Inconsistent	• Shifts from rear to pivot foot • With glove-side foot • Smooth backswing, forward swing • Less inconsistent • Less inconsistent • Behind and under ball
Follow-Through Step Throwing Arm Position Fielding Position	• Leaves pivot foot on rubber • Parallel with ground • Nonexistent	• Steps with pivot foot to balanced fielding position • Extended above head • Knees bent, stance square, hands ready, focus on ball

Error Detection and Correction for Pitching

Direct your observation of your students first to their stance on the pitching rubber. Check for the separation of the feet, with the pivot foot on the rubber and the stepping foot back. Liken the gross movement of the pitch to that of throwing: stepping with the opposite foot, following through in the direction of the throw (pitch), and shifting the weight from back to front. Concentrate your cues on those things that affect distance and arc, such as the amount (length) of the arm swing, a slow backswing with force applied to the forward swing, the point of release, and the hand and fingers under and behind the ball at release.

ERROR

CORRECTION

1. The arc is inconsistent, both too low and too high.

1. Recommend the Pitching Wall Drill (LE) and the Fence Drill (LE and ME) (see Drills 1 and 2). Cue a consistent point of release past the hip.

2. The distance is inconsistent, both too long and too short.

2. Have the students focus on the back point of the plate and attempt to drop the ball on it. Have the student visualize the high point in the arc as being two thirds of the distance to the plate and aim the ball to hit that point.

3. The student fails to assume the correct fielding position after releasing the ball.

3. Have the catcher roll the ball back to the pitcher, who must field it, then take the position to pitch again.

Pitching Drills

1. *Pitching Wall Drill*
[Corresponds to *Softball*, Step 8, Drill 1]

Group Management and Safety Tips

- This is a good rainy-day drill for the gymnasium.
- Have the students first practice independently against a wall for a short time. Thus, they all warm up and are better able to focus on the technique.
- Pair up a less experienced student with a more experienced student.
- Have the student pairs work as peer teachers, each partner using the Pitching Checklist for *Softball*, Step 8, for the observer to identify what to look for in each of the three phases of the skill. It would be helpful for you to go over the checklist with the students; possibly have a model student pitch while you identify the points to be observed.
- Have the pitcher identify points for the observer to watch and to give feedback upon. More experienced students should try to identify the points without looking at the checklist, whereas the less experienced may need to consult the list.

- If the more experienced student has good control of the pitching motion, have her or him purposely make errors for the less experienced student to pick out, focusing on one phase of the motion at a time.
- Use the same ball for all pitching drills that you intend to use in game situations. Especially in pitching, it is important for the students to get used to the feel and weight of the game ball.
- Be sure the groups are spaced around the walls of the gymnasium so that rebounding balls do not interfere with another group. Do not let groups overlap in the corners of the gymnasium.

Equipment

- Game-type softballs, 1 per student, and extras to replace those that get lost in the bleachers.
- Gloves, 1 per student
- Tape for wall markings
- Cones (or tape) for pitching rubber or pitching distance marks

Instructions to Class

- "Individually work on your pitching technique using the 6- and 12-foot marks on the wall to guide the height of the arc of your pitch."
- "Imagine a pitching rubber if you do not have an actual line. Be sure to stand with your pivot foot on the 'rubber' and your stepping foot to the rear."
- "Relax on the backswing and exert enough force on the forward swing to make the ball hit the base of the wall between the 1-foot line and the floor. This is just like dropping the ball on the back point of the plate. However, barely nicking the wall will cause the ball to rebound back to you so you won't have to chase it."
- "Aim the ball so that the high point of the arc is a spot about two thirds of the distance to home plate (the base of the wall). If the high point of the arc is close to the 12-foot mark, the two-thirds distance aiming point should bring the ball on target. If the high point of the arc is lower, closer

to the 6-foot mark, the aiming point will have to be closer to the target spot. Remember, the arc must be between 6 and 12 feet."
- "As you move your body into good fielding position, watch the ball come off the wall, field it, and bring it up to the throwing position as if you were making a play on the batter or another runner. Practice fielding and getting into position to throw to all the different bases."

Cues to Class

- "Use a smooth, straight, pendulum movement arm swing. This will cause the ball to go directly toward home plate."
- "Release the ball with your fingers under the ball so that you can lift the ball into the correct arc."
- "After you release the ball, be sure to step forward with your pivot foot into a good fielding position. In a regular game, you are closer to the hitter than any other player in fair territory. You need to learn to protect yourself and also to be in position to field the ball and make the out should the batter hit the ball back to you."

Student Option

- "Have a partner observe your pitching and, using the checklist, give you feedback on your performance."

Student Success Goal

- 7 of 10 on-target pitches

To Decrease Difficulty

- Shorten the distance of the pitch. [4]
- Have the student focus mainly on the execution phase by having a partner field the ball as it comes off the wall. [1]

To Increase Difficulty

- Mark the target area the width of the plate; have the pitcher aim the pitch for the inside corner and the outside corner. [4]
- Place a bucket at the base of the wall; have the pitcher try to get the pitch to hit the wall and go into the bucket. [2, 3, 4]

2. Fence Drill
[Corresponds to *Softball*, Step 8, Drill 2]

Group Management and Safety Tips

- Pair up your students so that a more experienced student and a less experienced student are together.
- The partners will pitch the ball back and forth over the outfield fence.
- Each student stands 23 feet from the fence (approximately 8 paces), making the 46-foot pitching distance between partners.
- If your class is large, use the other fences in addition to the outfield fence. Stretch a rope from the backstop to a broom or rake handle attached securely to the fence to create a higher obstacle to arc the pitches over (side fences are usually shorter than the outfield fence).

Equipment

- Balls, 1 per student pair
- Gloves, 1 per student
- Ropes and temporary posts attached to the fence to raise the height of the obstacle
- Cones to mark distance (optional)

Instructions and Cues to Class

- "The outfield fence is (#) feet high, and the sideline fences are (#) feet high to the rope. Remember, the slow-pitch arc must be between 6 and 12 feet. Using the fence as a guide, work on the correct arc for your pitch."
- "Pitch the ball back and forth over the fence so that your partner does not have to move to catch the ball. This would mean that the pitch would be very close to the strike zone for the batter."
- "Even though you do not have a line or a pitching rubber to work from, use the correct starting position, with your pivot foot ahead of your stepping foot. You do

not want to develop bad habits while doing this drill, so imagine you are stepping on a pitching rubber."
- "Use a relaxed backswing. Control the arc of the pitch with the force of your forward swing and your point of release."
- "Take your follow-through step with your pivot foot to move into the correct fielding position. You know the ball will not be hit back at you in this drill, but you want to work on all aspects of the pitching motion, including the follow-through."
- "Work on consistency. Try to pitch 10 consecutive balls that clear the fence and go to your partner."

Student Options

- "Work alone. Place a hoop on the ground on the far side of the fence into which you attempt to pitch the ball. Use a bucket of balls."
- "Start the drill with each partner 12 feet from the fence. Gradually increase the distance until each partner is 23 feet from the fence."

Student Success Goal

- 10 consecutive pitches clearing the fence and going to your partner

To Decrease Difficulty

- Shorten the distance of the pitch. [4]

To Increase the Difficulty

- Place ropes at 12 feet high and 10 feet high at the midpoint of the pitching distance. Have the student pitch the ball the 46-foot distance so that the ball goes between the two ropes. [3]
- Have the pitcher put spins on the ball. [1]

3. *Bucket Drill*
[Corresponds to *Softball*, Step 8, Drill 3]

Group Management and Safety Tips

- Allow each student to select a partner.
- Each person has a bucket, a milk crate, or a similar container.
- Position one of the partners on the foul line and the other 46 feet away.
- Allow 10-foot spacing between students on the lines.

Equipment

- Buckets, 1 per student (or per student pair, if equipment is limited)
- Balls, 1 per student pair (or more if using only 1 bucket)
- Cones to mark distance

Instructions and Cues to Class

- "Pitch the ball into the bucket, making it traverse the legal arc."
- "Use correct technique for all three phases of the pitch."
- "Score 2 points if the pitch goes into the bucket (even if it pops out) and 1 point if the ball hits the bucket on the fly."

Student Options

- "Work alone with a bucket and 10 balls."
- "Have your partner use the checklist to give you feedback on your form."

Student Success Goal

- 14 points on 10 pitches

To Decrease Difficulty

- Shorten the distance. [4]
- Let the student use a bigger bucket (or a big cardboard box, or a laundry basket). [2]

To Increase the Difficulty

- Have the student use two smaller buckets set a plate-width apart and try to pitch balls into them. [2, 3, 4]

4. Ball and Strike Drill

[Corresponds to *Softball*, Step 8, Drill 4]

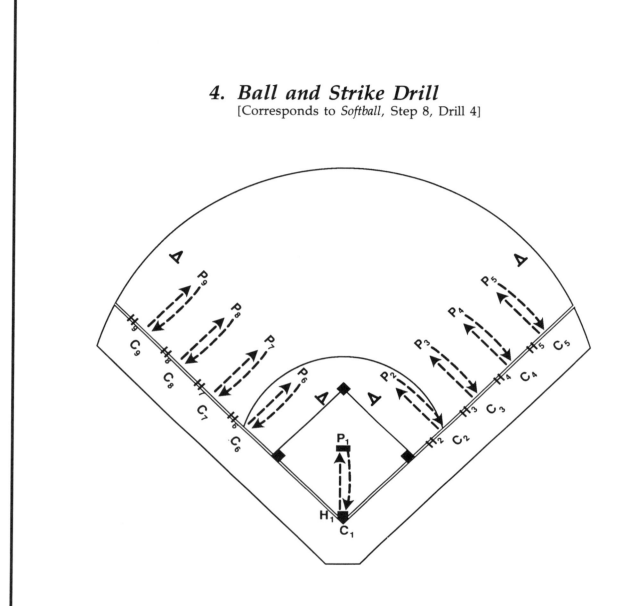

Group Management and Safety Tips

- Divide the class into groups of three: a pitcher, a catcher, and a hitter.
- Use the same setup on the foul lines as in the previous drill, but increase the spacing between students on the lines.
- If the batter is going to stand holding a bat, the catcher must wear a mask.
- The system for scoring points is outlined in the participant's book.

Equipment

- Balls, 1 per three-student group
- Gloves, 1 per student (the hitter's glove serves as home plate)
- Bats and catcher's masks, 1 each per three-student group (optional but together)
- Cones to mark distance

Instructions and Cues to the Class

- "The pitcher is practicing the pitching technique and is attempting to throw strikes without placing the ball in the middle of the plate. Try to hit the corners to make it more difficult for the batter to correctly call the pitch. Pitch high and low in the strike zone for the same reason."
- "The batter is practicing watching the pitched ball and making judgments about its position in the strike zone. Change your position at the plate: Crowd it; stand deep in the box; use closed, open, and square stances. All of these may affect the pitcher's concentration."
- "The batter needs to follow the ball all the way to the catcher's glove. See the ball cross the plate, and call it a 'strike' or a 'ball'."
- "The catcher is the facilitator for the drill. You must follow the ball and note its position as it crosses the plate in order to verify or dispute the call of the batter."

Student Option

- None

Student Success Goal

- Scoring 6 points before the opponent

To Decrease Difficulty

- Reduce the distance of the pitch and increase the size of the strike zone. [4]

To Increase Difficulty

- Count only pitches on the corners and reduce the size of the strike zone. [4]

Step 9   Baserunning

Baserunning is an offensive skill that you, as the teacher, can use both to give the students practice in technique and decision making and to condition them aerobically. Most students think that baserunning is a skill that needs no practice because, after all, ''everyone knows how to run.'' Your task is to convince them that there are proper techniques involved in baserunning that can help a slow runner overcome, to some extent, his or her lack of speed. Smart baserunning can make a fast runner even faster.

As you present the baserunning techniques, it is important to let your students know that the technical skills involved vary according to the offensive situation that the baserunner is involved in. Running from home to first base on a single is different from going from home to second base on a double. Additionally, beginning the baserunning from a base (rather than from home plate) involves different sets of techniques depending upon whether the hit ball goes to an infielder or an outfielder, whether the ball is a ground ball or a fly ball, and whether the play to be made on the baserunner is a force play or a tag play.

There are many options in baserunning where the baserunner must make decisions, and others where he or she must rely on the decision made by a base coach. For a less experienced player, the sheer variety of options can make baserunning confusing. Consequently, you might want to divide this step into a series of ministeps, each of which you can use as a station in conjunction with the skills of other steps that follow in this book. The more experienced players should be directed to refine their techniques, particularly in rounding bases and tagging up on fly balls. It would be helpful to have them practice their baserunning skill in game-like conditions so that their baserunning decision making would be sharpened. There are several drills in this step that focus on the decision-making opportunities available in softball game play.

STUDENT KEYS TO SUCCESS FOR OVERRUNNING FIRST BASE

- Run through (over) the base
- Run in foul territory
- Step out of batter's box with back foot
- After crossing base, turn to left (toward fair territory) to determine whether to stay on first or try to advance

Overrunning First Base Rating

CHECKPOINT	LESS EXPERIENCED	MORE EXPERIENCED
Preparation **Initial Move** **Direction**	• Steps with front foot • Runs in fair territory	• Steps with back foot • Starts in fair territory, moves into foul territory
Speed **Bat**	• Accelerates late • Throws bat or carries it to base	• Accelerates immediately • Drops bat just outside batter's box

CHECKPOINT	LESS EXPERIENCED	MORE EXPERIENCED
Execution **Direction** **Speed** **Contact With Base**	• Runs on baseline • Breaks speed to step on the base • Stops on base	• Runs in foul territory • Maintains speed through base • Overruns base
Follow-Through **Direction**	• Turns to right	• Turns to left and looks

Error Detection and Correction for Overrunning First Base

There are three basic errors made in running from home to first base. The less experienced player tends to make all three errors simply because the techniques involved are not ones that are a part of normal running or sandlot play. The more experienced player should be reminded about the need to run through the base, turn left, and look. After a quick review of the baserunning technique, the more experienced players should be directed to practice baserunning with the decision-making elements added. The less experienced players, on the other hand, need to focus on developing technical skill in baserunning so that they develop a consistent pattern. Then, when they run to first base, they will have developed a reaction that requires no thought, and they are more likely to be safe.

ERROR

CORRECTION

1. The runner starts out of the batter's box on the front foot.

1. Have the batter-baserunner swing and make sure that the weight is on the front foot at the follow-through. Recommend the Leave the Batter's Box Drill (see Drill 1).

2. The runner leaps for first base or breaks stride (intersperses short with long strides).

2. Have the runner focus on running through the base, contacting it on the front outside corner.

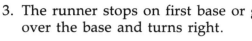

ERROR   **CORRECTION**

3. The runner stops on first base or goes over the base and turns right.

3. Have the runner think about running through to a line 3 feet beyond the base before slowing and turning to the left.

STUDENT KEYS TO SUCCESS FOR ROUNDING A BASE

- Run straight toward base
- At 15 feet from base, swing out in small arc to right
- Contact inside corner of base with left foot
- Look for ball or base coach to make decision whether to advance

Rounding a Base Rating

CHECKPOINT	LESS EXPERIENCED	MORE EXPERIENCED
Preparation **Approach to Base**	• Runs in big arc from one base to next	• Begins running in straight line toward base
Rounding Arc	• Begins early, big arc	• Begins about 15 feet from base, small arc
Body Position	• Upright	• Leans to left

Rounding a Base Rating

CHECKPOINT	LESS EXPERIENCED	MORE EXPERIENCED
Execution		
Contact of Base	• Top of base	• Edge of base facing next base
Contact Foot	• Inconsistent	• More consistent
Focus	• On base being rounded	• On play or base coach
Follow-Through		
Beginning Direction to Next Base	• Curved line	• Straight line
Advancing	• Reacceleration to base	• Continued acceleration
Not advancing	• Stops abruptly	• Stops and pivots to left on left foot

Error Detection and Correction for Rounding a Base

Correct execution of the skill of rounding a base can spell the difference between safely advancing a base when a play is going to be close or being put out because the ball arrives before the baserunner. As you observe your students and give them feedback, encourage them to develop proper technical skill in baserunning. A player can make up for lack of speed by properly rounding a base, thereby not wasting time by running too far.

The errors in rounding a base that you can expect to see are fairly easy to pick out. Additionally, both the less experienced players and the more experienced players are likely to commit the same errors. The differences between the two levels of students will tend to be related to the degree of error. For example, a less experienced player will tend to run a big arc from the initial base all the way to the base he or she is advancing toward. A more experienced player, however, will run in a straighter line to the base, but when swinging out to round the base may still make too big an arc. All students will have some difficulty hitting the inside corner of the base with the left foot while rounding the base. As you give cues, try to get your students to realize that they are trying to enable themselves to run as straight as possible toward the bases and turn in as small a space as possible. While they are running and rounding bases, they are attempting to keep up the fastest speed they can. After all, their goal is to safely advance as many bases as possible.

Look for the size of the arc (it should be small), when it begins (15 feet from the base), and where the base is contacted and with which foot (front inside corner with left foot). These three variables, adjusted proportionately, will help the person round the base efficiently and run the least distance possible while maintaining speed.

ERROR ⊘	CORRECTION
1. The baserunner ends up in the outfield when making the turn.	1. Your student should begin the turn earlier. Recommend the Swing-Out Drill (Drill 4).
2. The baserunner slows down to make a turn.	2. Have the student swing out about 15 feet from the base so he or she can continue close to full speed and on a straight path to the next base.
3. The runner doesn't know whether to advance.	3. The runner must listen for the base coach, or keep eyes up and watch the play if there is no base coach.

Baserunning Drills

1. Leave the Batter's Box Drill
[Corresponds to *Softball*, Step 9, Drill 1]

Group Management and Safety Tips

- The basic physical setup for all the drills in this section will be the same. Each group of students needs a base to serve as first base. There must also be some sort of base or marker to serve as home plate. If these can be put on some sort of line (foul line, baseline, yardage line on a playing field), it will help orient the baserunners to fair and foul territory.
- Students do not have to be divided into less experienced and more experienced groups for any of these drills.
- Because running is the basic movement in these drills, it is possible to have four players at a single home-to-first setup.
- This baserunning skill subsection can be used as one lesson or as a station with other skills in a lesson. Running from home to first is different from rounding the bases.

- When more than one person is running at a setup, be sure that they turn left after crossing the base, look, and then return to the starting position without getting in the way of subsequent runners. Often they can return to the end of the line by jogging on the infield side of the baseline.
- Be certain that the baserunners are crossing the base on the outside (toward the foul line), so that when the first baseman is added there will be no collisions at the base.

Equipment

- Bases (indoor, outdoor, carpet squares, tape on the floor of a gymnasium if indoors), 1 for every three to four students
- Bats, short and light, 1 per home-to-first setup

Instructions to Class

- ''Swing at an imaginary ball and run half-way down the baseline.''
- ''Concentrate on the follow-through of your swing so that your weight is on your front foot and you are leaning toward first base. Otherwise you will be slowed down taking off out of the box.''
- ''Swing, drive out of the batter's box, run six or eight strides, and drop the bat before your sixth stride.''
- ''Get into foul territory before your fourth stride. This protects you from being called out if you are hit by the thrown ball while in fair territory as you run to first base.''

Cues to Class

- ''Drive out of the batter's box. Feel like you are a track sprinter and you must get a quick and strong start to win the race.''
- ''Concentrate on taking your first step with your back foot and moving it toward foul territory.''
- ''Just as the throw flows continuously from the fielding action, the drive out of the box and the run toward first blend into a continuous action.''

Student Options

- ''Have a partner watch you as you swing and drive out of the box. Your partner should watch to see that you leave the box with your back foot, move to foul territory, and drop the bat.''
- ''Close your eyes, swing the bat, and run four strides toward first base. Open your eyes and check to see whether you are in foul territory.''
- ''Try the drill from both the right and the left batter's boxes. See whether it is easier from one box or the other.''

Student Success Goal

- 5 consecutive sequences using correct swing technique, leading out of the box with the back foot, and getting into foul territory within 10 feet of home plate

To Decrease Difficulty

- Have the student swing, drive out of the box, and take the first three steps all in slow motion. [3]

To Increase Difficulty

- Increase the distance of the run to first base. [4]
- Make the student practice from the opposite batter's box. [3]

2. *Over-the-Base Drill*
[Corresponds to *Softball*, Step 9, Drill 2]

Group Management and Safety Tips

- The tips here are the same as in the previous drill.

Equipment

- Use the same equipment as in the previous drill
- Batting tees, 1 per home-to-first setup
- Softballs, as many as possible and of all types
- Buckets or other containers

Instructions and Cues to Class

- ''By now you should be able to consistently swing and leave the batter's box using the correct techniques. Now swing at an imaginary pitch and actually run to first base.''
- ''As you run to first base, stay in foul territory.''
- ''Be sure you run over, or through, first base. Do not slow down before the base. You want to get there as fast as you can. If you try to stop on the base, you will slow down before you get there.''

- ''Think of running 3 feet beyond the base before slowing down.''
- ''Swing, get out of the box fast, run in foul territory, and keep your full speed all the way over the base.''
- ''Run over the outside of the base. The first baseman is going to be on the inside of the base, and you don't want to collide.''
- ''Run beyond the base, slow down, and turn left. Look to where you hit the ball. Go back to the base. Then come back to the end of the line by jogging on the infield side of the baseline.''
- ''Be sure you turn left and look after you cross the base. You are not out if you turn left. In a game, you will look and decide whether to go directly back to first base or whether you can continue running to second base. If you return directly to first base, you are not open to being put out. If you make a move toward second base after you turn to the left, you can be put out either at second base (if you are running to it) or at first (if you change your mind and come back to first base).''

Student Options

- ''You can start this drill from either the right or the left batter's box.''
- ''Have someone time you as you practice. Try to lower your time by focusing on driving out of the batter's box with your back leg five times. The next five times, focus your attention on running through first base and not slowing down until you have crossed the base.''

Student Success Goal

- 10 consecutive error-free sequences of running over first base

To Decrease Difficulty

- Use an indoor base so that the height of the ''bag'' does not make the runner fearful of tripping over the base. [2]
- Decrease the distance so that the runner can maintain full speed. [4]
- Have the runner go from home to first base without using a bat in the swing. [5]

To Increase Difficulty

- Have the runner, after crossing the base and turning to the left, make a move toward second base, hesitate, then continue 8 steps at full speed toward an imaginary second base. [7]
- Have the runner, after crossing the base and turning to the left, make a move toward second base, change his or her mind, run back to first base (the outfield baseline corner), and stop on the base. [7]
- Have the batter-baserunner use a batting tee and actually hit a ground ball and run to first base (see *Softball*, Step 9, Drill 3). This can be done alone or in a group. It can also be combined with fielding so that one person hits the ball and runs, one person fields the hit ball and puts it into a bucket, and a third person sets the ball on the tee for the next batter. [7, 8]

3. *Overrun Base With First Baseman Drill*
[Corresponds to *Softball*, Step 9, Drill 4]

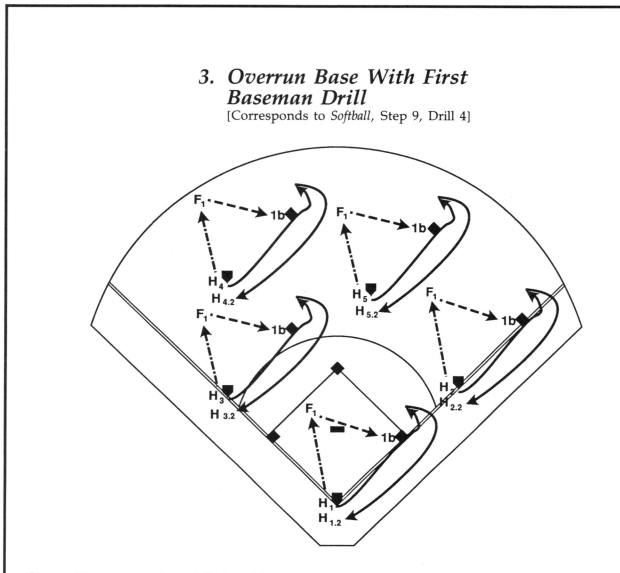

Group Management and Safety Tips

- Home-to-first-base setups are the same as in the previous drills except that there needs to be additional space between drill stations.
- In these drills there is a ball hit and a fielder who fields it. Thus, all stations must be oriented in the same direction so that all ground balls are hit in the same direction.
- It is crucial that the person playing first base stand on the side of first base toward second base and that the baserunner run over the outside (foul side) of first base. This prevents collisions.
- After running over first base, turning left, and stopping, the baserunner must return to the batting area without getting in the running path of the next batter or the path of the ground ball hit by him or her.
- This drill should be done with at least four players so that there are two batter-baserunners who take turns. The fielder and the first baseman should switch roles after half of the total number of practice trials of the two batter-baserunners have been completed.
- This drill should first be done with no throw to the first baseman. The fielder should field the ball and simply put it into a container.

Equipment

- The same equipment as in the previous drill
- Gloves, 2 per home-to-first setup

Instructions to Class

- ''In this drill there is a first baseman on first base as the batter-baserunner overruns it. This is the way it will be in games.''
- ''The first baseman plays on the inside of the base because he or she wants a free view of the ball. The runner crosses the base on the outside edge so as not to collide with the first baseman while running full speed.''
- ''The batter hits a grounder so the fielder can practice fielding the ball. The fielder fields the ball and simply drops it into a container or rolls it back to the hitting station out of the way of the batter.''
- ''First baseman, straddle the inside corners of the base with your feet. Just before the baserunner gets to the base, imagine that you are going to catch a throw from the infielder. Step toward the infielder with your glove-side foot and reach for the ball. As you step toward the throw, shift your throwing-side foot to touch the inside edge of the base with your toes.''

Cues to Class

- ''Baserunner, the first three times you hit the ball and run to first base, concentrate on running in foul territory. The next three times, concentrate on running full speed over the base. The last four times, imagine that the throw is coming and that, as you cross the base and turn left, you see that the imaginary throw was missed by the first baseman. Run six strides toward second base before returning to the batting site.''
- ''Challenge yourself, baserunner, to touch the front outside corner of first base with your foot.''
- ''You're not finished with your run to first base until you have turned to the left to see what has happened with the ball.''

Student Options

- ''Imagine situations where the thrown ball is either caught or missed by the first baseman, then either run toward second base or go directly back to first base. See whether you can think of times when you would advance to second base after having crossed first base.''
- ''Sometimes have your batting partner shout 'Bad throw, go!' after you have crossed first base. When you hear your partner shout as you turn left, run six steps toward second base. When you do not hear your partner yell, look and go back to first base.''

Student Success Goal

- 4 of 5 runs to first base in which your foot contacts the front outside corner of the base

To Decrease Difficulty

- Use an indoor base. [2]
- Decrease the distance to first base. [4]
- Let the student swing without the ball and batting tee. [1]

To Increase Difficulty

- Have the infielder throw the ball to the first baseman (see *Softball*, Step 9, Drill 4b). In this drill, if the throw is off target, the first baseman should just let it go; do not allow him or her to move toward it. Also, in this drill the batter-baserunner must wear a batting helmet. [1, 7]
- Have the batter-baserunner try to hit a ground ball that the infielder has to move two or three steps to the right or left to field. [3]
- Make a game of the drill variation in which the ball is thrown to the first baseman (see *Softball*, Step 9, Drill 4b). Play this game with the four players. Keep a team score. One team is composed of two batter-baserunners. The other team consists of the fielder and the first baseman. A point is scored for each run to first base in which the batter-baserunner is safe. Each baserunner team gets five times each at bat, then the two batter-baserunners rotate to the fielding and first base positions. Have the students keep track of the number of points they score as a team. [3, 6]

4. Swing-Out Drill

[Corresponds to *Softball*, Step 9, Drill 6]

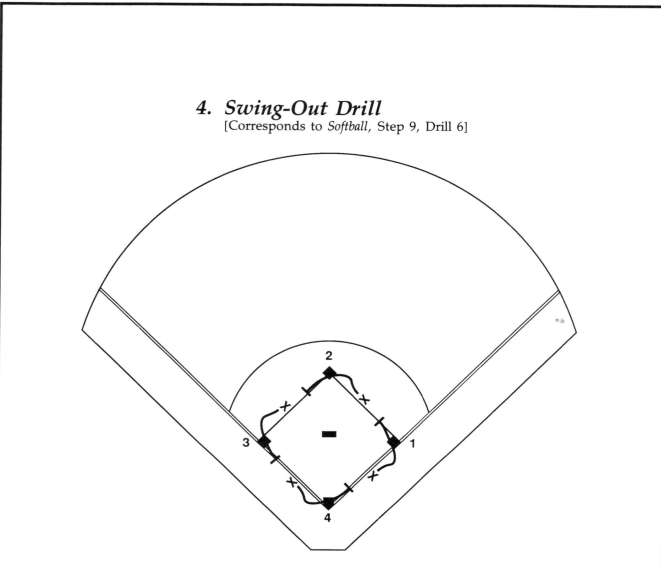

Group Management and Safety Tips

- There is no need to divide students into experience-level groups.
- This drill can be done using the regulation softball bases on the field. To ensure maximum participation with a large class, you can also utilize a combination of the bases on the regulation field and individual bases placed in the outfield area.
- When the drill uses a diamond, one student can begin at each of the four bases. Each student begins about 30 feet past the base and runs toward the next base, rounding it at full speed. The runner slows down 10 feet after the base and jogs toward the next base. At 30 feet past the base, the runner again begins the full-speed run and rounds the next base.

- When the runner who was on third base crosses home plate, a new runner begins the series by advancing to first base. Thus, you can have about six to eight people at the regulation field bases, and none of them has to wait long for a turn.
- Have the runners waiting to go toward first base wait along the first baseline, about 40 feet from first base.
- Repeat until each player has rounded a total of eight bases.
- For those students who are at single bases in the outfield, you can have two persons rounding the base simultaneously. The two students line up on opposite sides of the base, facing the base and about 30 feet from the base. Each runs full speed toward the base and at 15 feet begins the

rounding pattern. They round the base on opposite sides and run 10 feet past the base. They then jog another 20 feet in the same direction, then turn 180 degrees to face the base again. They simultaneously repeat the sequence three more times, bringing them to their original starting positions.

- Be sure that the students are looking where they are going as they round the bases, so that they do not collide with other people.
- Place the individual bases in the outfield at least 40 feet from one another.
- Try to allow each student the opportunity to practice rounding the bases on the regulation field, because baserunning on the grass is more difficult than on the regulation field.

Equipment

- Bases on the regulation field
- Extra individual bases, for every two students of the remainder of the class after placing eight students on the regulation field

Instructions and Cues to Class

- "Run full speed straight at the base until you begin to round the base."
- "Including when you round the base, your baserunning pattern should look like the outer edge of a spoon."
- "Make the arc of your turn small so that you turn 90 degrees in a very short distance. This saves you time so you can get into a direct path to the next base quickly."
- "The arc allows you to change direction with speed, though not full speed. If you didn't arc out on the approach to the base, you would have to stop and pivot 90 degrees. This would be hard on your legs and would mean that you would have to practically stop and reaccelerate as you start toward the next base."
- "As you round the base, be sure to lean into the infield."
- "Hit the base on the inside corner so that you can use it to help push off in the direction of the next base. It is also the part of

the base that makes the path you are running the shortest possible."
- "As soon as you touch the base, lift your head and look for either the base coach or the play being made on the ball. You need to decide whether or not you can advance to the next base."
- "If you have trouble hitting the base as you round it, slow down just a bit and be sure you are heading toward the next base as you pass the one you are rounding."

Student Options

- "Place a marker, such as a glove or a rag, at the place where you begin your arc out of the base path. Place another marker at the outer and top edge of your 'spoon' pattern. Try to make the arc as small as you can while still keeping reasonable speed as you round the base."
- "Get a partner who is about the same speed on the base paths as you are. Each of you begins on a different base and, on a cue, runs to the next base, rounds it, and advances to the subsequent base. Race your partner and see who gets to the final base fastest. The person who can make the smallest arc at the fastest speed will probably be the winner."

Student Success Goal

- 8 bases rounded correctly

To Decrease Difficulty

- Let the runner decrease the speed of the approach to the base. [3]
- Decrease the distance from the base that the player runs in the approach. [4]
- Have the student begin with a relatively large arc and gradually reduce the size of the arc while maintaining medium speed. [4]
- Have the student jog through the entire rounding-the-base pattern. [3]

To Increase Difficulty

- Decrease the allowable arc size. [4]
- Make the runner increase the speed of the approach and the rounding of the base. [3]
- Reduce the length of the jog between bases so that, ultimately, the student is running the length of the entire baseline. [4]

5. Single, Double, Triple, Home Run Drill
[Corresponds to Softball, Step 9, Drill 7]

Group Management and Safety Tips

- Set up two or three stations with all the bases laid out at regulation distance, 60 feet apart.
- You do not need to divide students into groups by experience level.
- Randomly divide your class into as many groups as you have stations.
- Have your students line up behind home plate, facing first base and in line with the first base foul line.
- Have the students "run a single," one right after the other. When one runner gets two thirds of the way to first base, the next person can begin.
- Have each runner, after turning left at the base and looking, jog back to the line at home plate. Have players jog to the third base side of first base as they return to home plate.
- Next, all students run doubles in the same manner, except they round first base (rather than only overrun it) and run full speed to second base, slowing down in time to stop on it. They should not overrun second base.
- The baserunner then comes off the base and jogs back to the end of the line at home plate, jogging on the third base side of second base.
- All students then run triples, rounding first and second base and stopping on third base. Then they jog in foul territory to the line at home plate.
- Finally, all students run out a home run, rounding first, second, and third bases and overrunning home plate.

- On the home run, persons waiting for their turn to start must pay attention to the runner rounding third base. That runner should be allowed to cross home plate before the next runner begins his or her home run baserunning.
- This drill is a good conditioning drill and a good drill for a warm-up. (Be sure to have the students perform milder warm-ups to increase their heart rates, and to stretch out carefully first, though.) Try to be sure that everyone gets a chance to run the drill on the regulation field, because running there is different than running on the grass.
- Have a person with a stopwatch time the people as they cross the base they are overrunning or as they stop on the base they end on. It would probably work best if you had three people timing so that a different one could start when a different runner leaves home plate. Have them simply call off the times for the last three or four strides of the baserunner.
- Make a chart at home plate with each student's name and four lines on which they can write their times for the run from home to first, home to second, home to third, and home to home. Then have them add up their points according to the scoring system given in their textbook.

Equipment

- Bases, 8 or 12
- Home plates, 3, if you have them; otherwise, any bases will be satisfactory
- Stopwatches, up to 3

Instruction and Cues to Class

- ''When you run to first base, run in foul territory, overrun first base, and turn left and look.''
- ''Try to run as fast as you can when running the double, triple, and home run.''
- ''The home run is an inside-the-park home run, so you need to be sure you round the bases, touch each base, then overrun home plate.''
- ''Listen for the time called out by the timer at the base. When you get back to home plate, there will be a chart for you to write your times on.''

Student Option

- None appropriate

Student Success Goals

- To attain the fastest time possible on each distance
- To score the most points possible

To Decrease Difficulty

- Let the student run slower. [3]
- Reduce the distance between bases. [4]

To Increase Difficulty

- Have the student begin each part of the drill with a swing at an imaginary ball. [5, 7]

6. React to Coach Drill

[Corresponds to *Softball*, Step 9, Drill 8]

Group Management and Safety Tips

- This drill requires only a home plate and first base.
- Divide the class into groups of six students.
- Set up as many home-to-first-base stations as are needed for the number of groups in your class.
- Place the two-base fields so that they are oriented in the same direction.
- One player is a base coach at first base, and the other players are batter-baserunners. On the regulation field, you could have second base represent home plate and third base represent first base.

Equipment

- Bases, as many as are needed for the number of two-base stations in your class

Instructions and Cues to Class

- ''When you are the baserunner, swing at an imaginary pitch and run to first base. As you approach first base, the base coach will call either 'round and look for the ball' or 'overrun.' You do what the coach calls.''
- ''Rotate roles after you have run to first so that the baserunner becomes the base coach. Repeat the drill until each of you has run 5 times.''
- ''Run in foul territory and listen for the coach's signal.''
- ''If you overrun the base, remember to turn left and look for the ball. Then return to the base.''
- ''If you round the base, make a small arc and hit the inside corner of the base as you round it. Remember, after you round the base, you need to look for the ball to see whether you should advance or return to first base.''
- The batter-baserunner should focus on listening for the base coach's cue, then react immediately to it.''
- ''As the base coach, you are concentrating on finding the proper time to cue the batter-baserunner. This is an important task because if you are late, the baserunner will be unable to react appropriately.''

Student Option

- None needed

Student Success Goal

- 4 of 5 correct actions at first base in response to the base coach

To Decrease Difficulty

- It would not help to reduce difficulty. A student having difficulty should simply practice more.

To Increase Difficulty

- There is little more to do. Simply proceed to the next drill.

7. Double to the Outfield Drill

[Corresponds to *Softball*, Step 9, Drill 9]

Group Management and Safety Tips

- Students are in groups of 6. It would be helpful if they were also divided according to level of experience. One player is an outfielder playing behind the shortstop position. Another player is a second baseman playing to the first base and the outfield sides of second base. Another is the base coach. Two players are batter-baserunners. One person is the catcher at home.
- Set up as many home, first base, and second base stations as there are six-student groups in your class.
- Orient all the three-base stations in the same direction. Place them far enough apart that a hit could go into the outfield over the shortstop and not interfere with another group.
- At home there is a batting tee, a bucket of balls, and a bat.
- The hitter hits a line drive off the tee to the outfielder beyond the shortstop position. The hitter runs to first base, where the coach tells him or her to ''round and look.'' The outfielder plays the ball and throws it to the second baseman.
- The batter-baserunner rounds first base and decides whether to advance to second or to go back to first base.
- The baserunner should count the number of times he or she makes the correct decision, either staying at first or reaching second base before the ball does.

- The batter-baserunner who has completed his or her baserunning should return to home plate by jogging in the outfield back around first base and outside the coach's box, making sure to stay clear of the next batter-baserunner going to first base.
- The second baseman throws the ball to the catcher, who puts it into the bucket. The second batter-baserunner takes a turn.
- After 5 hits by each batter-baserunner, the players switch positions. The batter-baserunners become outfielder and second baseman. The outfielder and second baseman become base coach and catcher. The base coach and catcher become batter-baserunners.

Equipment

- Bases, 6
- Home plates, 3
- Bats, light and short, 1 per home plate
- Batting tees, 1 per home plate
- Gloves for the students who are fielding and catching the ball
- Bucket of balls at each home plate (at least 8 balls)

Instructions and Cues to Class

- "As batter-baserunner, you hit a line drive to the outfielder. Then run to first base. The base coach will tell you to 'round and look.' You round first base, then look to see whether you should go back to first or whether the outfielder or second baseman has bobbled the ball and you can advance to second base."
- "Baserunners, challenge yourselves if the fielders bobble the ball. See how fast you can round the base, because any bobble might enable you to advance a base."
- "Outfielder, field the ball and use the overhand throw to get the ball to the second baseman."
- "Second baseman, move to the third base side of the base and catch the ball as it comes from the outfielder. Then throw the ball to the catcher after the baserunner has completed his or her run."
- "The object is for the baserunner to make the right decision. Make note of each correct decision, whether it be returning to the base or making it to second base before the ball."

Student Option

- None need be listed, because decision making is the goal of this drill.

Student Success Goal

- 3 correct decisions out of 5 attempts

To Decrease Difficulty

- No reduction of difficulty is necessary in decision making. If the student has difficulty reading the play, then additional practice, with the base coach giving additional cues, might help.

To Increase Difficulty

- Play the Overrun or Round Game (see *Softball*, Step 9, Drill 10). Add a shortstop to and drop the catcher from the Double to the Outfield Drill. The rest of the setup is exactly the same. When the batter hits the ball off the tee, the hit must be a line drive or a grounder that lands anywhere in the infield or outfield in an area between imaginary lines running from home through the shortstop and second base positions.

  The batter hits the ball and runs to first base. If the ball is fielded by the shortstop, the base coach will call "overrun." If the ball is bobbled by the shortstop or goes to the outfield, the base coach will call "round and look."

  The person who fields the ball throws it to the second baseman, who has moved to the third base side of second base.

  The batter-baserunner does as the coach signals and makes the decision about whether to advance or to return to the base.

  The batters take turns. After 5 hits, the outfielder and second baseman change positions, and the base coach and the shortstop change positions. After another 5 hits, these pairs rotate to another pair of positions: Batter-baserunners become the outfielder and second baseman; outfielder and second baseman become shortstop and base coach; and base coach and shortstop become batter-baserunners.

  The goal of the game is for the batter-baserunner pair to get as many doubles as possible. Each double (being safe at second base by getting there before the ball does) counts as one run. See which pair (team) wins the game. [8]

Step 10 Position Play

Several concepts of position play—including position names and numbers, area coverage, and covering and backing-up responsibilities—are presented in the participant's textbook in a single step, Step 10. The concepts are explained with the aid of diagrams and examples to give the student a better understanding of the various elements that go into playing the different softball positions. Reference will be made to other steps where the concepts are applied.

When you teach softball, you probably introduce the concepts of position play more gradually in conjunction with teaching specific skills, such as the force play or the tag play. Drill setups that identify specific positions—like the fungo ground ball drills with a shortstop, a first baseman, a catcher, and a hitter—can also be used to teach areas of coverage for those positions. Game situation drills designed specifically to work on concepts like covering and backing up, such as the "I've Got It" Drill (*Softball*, Step 16, Drill 3), expand the focus of performance beyond skill acquisition.

Your typical softball class is made up of students with varying levels of experience. Whether during skill practice, drill practice, or game play, take advantage of the specific play of your students (both the more experienced and the less experienced) to present or reinforce position and game play concepts.

Rainy days provide a good opportunity to work on position play. The availability of a chalkboard to draw diagrams and the more confined area (the students can hear your comments during game play or drill practice more easily inside than out on the field) make the gymnasium an ideal place to introduce and, later, to reinforce position play concepts.

Following are some examples of activities that could be used in the gymnasium (or on the field with a portable chalkboard) to develop student understanding of the various aspects of position play described in *Softball*, Step 10. Please note that these are examples only. They are intended neither as an all inclusive list *nor* as material to be presented all in a single lesson! Use them individually and in combination with skill material where you deem them appropriate to your lessons. In addition, jot down some of the things you have used in the past that would be appropriate for these categories of position play.

POSITION PLAY INSTRUCTIONAL ACTIVITIES

1. Field Positioning Examples

a. Using a chalkboard, draw a diagram of the regular-depth starting positions, identifying the name, symbol, number, area coverage, and interaction area responsibilities for each position (see *Softball*, Diagram 10.1).

b. Using your more experienced students, place a full team on the "field" and demonstrate positioning. Have the players show the following:

- Regular depth
- "Infield in"
- Shift for a right-handed pull hitter
- Shift for a left-handed pull hitter
- Short fielder assuming position as one of four outfielders in a single arc
- Short fielder in the "Texas leaguer" area, between the other three outfielders and the infield from foul line to foul line

c. Pair up the less experienced students with those in your more experienced demonstration group. Have them go through the above demonstrations together.

d. Ask two of the demonstration players, such as the shortstop and the right fielder, to exchange positions to see whether the players know all the positions.

e. Ask for volunteers from among those students watching the demonstration to name a position and replace that position's player in the field. Involve your less experienced players in a non-threatening, nonembarrassing manner.

2. Covering Examples

Using a handout (see *Softball*, Diagram 10.2) or a chalkboard, explain the base coverage responsibilities for the infielders when the ball is hit to the right (first base) side, up the middle, and to the left (third base) side of the infield. Explain the base coverage by infielders when the ball is hit to the outfield in left, center, and right.

3. Fly Ball Priority System Examples

a. Explain the priority system used when calling for fly balls. Give a handout to the students describing the priority system or refer to the Position Play Keys to Success Checklist (see *Softball*, Step 10).

b. Using the demonstration group, instruct them to use the priority system, call for the ball, and catch it using proper fielding and backing-up techniques. Toss the ball into the following interaction areas:

• Between two infielders
• Between the pitcher and an infielder
• Between two outfielders
• Between an infielder and an outfielder

c. Using a magnet board, give a quiz by placing the ball between two player positions. Instruct the students to identify the positions and to identify who has priority on the fly ball.

4. Backing Up Examples

a. Using handouts (see *Softball*, Diagrams 10.3 and 10.4) or a chalkboard, explain backing-up responsibilities and technique for all fielders.

b. Using the demonstration group, toss the ball to various positions both in the infield and outfield. The players should take the appropriate covering and backing-up positions as if the tossed ball were a hit. The possibilities for your tosses are endless, but be sure to thoroughly cover the infield and the outfield to the right, center (up the middle), and left.

c. Add baserunners to (b) to add difficulty.

d. Use the Position Play Keys to Success Checklist for a summary of covering and backing-up responsibilities (see *Softball*, Step 10) and to evaluate your students' position play during game or modified game situations.

5. Modified Game Example

The game Scrub, described in *Softball*, Step 23, is a modified game specifically designed to give students the opportunity to play all positions. Play it as a whiffleball game in the gymnasium on a rainy day or on the field with a regulation ball. Present the instruction on the position play concepts in addition to or in place of skill concepts.

SUMMARY

The preceding suggestions need not be limited to rainy days or indoor use; they can be implemented outside on a regular field. However, the confined atmosphere of the gymnasium seems more conducive to cerebral activity and to the development of cognitive concepts. It could even prove beneficial to your students to take a nice sunny day and work in the gymnasium on a chalk talk and a demonstration lesson.

Be creative with your students' development of the cognitive aspects of softball. There is no universally ideal way to present these concepts in a softball unit. Your units for classes in different grades should vary because of your students' increasing level of experience as they move through the grades. Sequence the game play concepts, the position play concepts, and the playing rules along with the appropriate skill content in progressive order throughout all the units of softball in the curriculum.

One of the difficulties faced by every teacher is how to deal with the varying levels of experience within a single class. The approach taken in this book is to focus your instruction on two levels, the less experienced and the more experienced. That focus needs to be applied to the development of your students' knowledge of softball as well as skill in softball. Regardless of the level of experience, there are certain fundamental game concepts necessary for any level of play. These concepts, such as position play, need to be presented as new material for your less experienced students and reinforced as review material for your more experienced students.

Step 11   Force Play and Tag Play

The force play is the fundamental defensive game concept in softball. Getting one out at a time and making the play on the lead runner is basic strategy in beginning-level game play. With two outs, making the *sure* out at first base (a force play) is fundamental defensive strategy. With two outs, a runner on first base, and a ground ball hit to either the shortstop or second baseman, the short toss to the player covering at second for the force out is usually the play of choice. That play is even more sure in slow pitch because of the fact that the baserunner must hold at the base until the ball is hit. The play on the baserunner who leaves the base too soon on a fly ball is also a force play.

In many instructional settings, the force play technique is practiced by the first baseman only, when in reality the force play situation arises at all bases. Thus, *all* infielders need to practice the force play at the bases for which they have responsibility. In addition, the force play needs to be executed on throws from the infield and the outfield. Although the actual techniques of ''footing the base'' (putting the correct foot on the base as the ball comes) and catching the ball are the same for throws from both directions, a key factor in proper execution of a force play is for the player to get into position to shorten the distance of the throw.

You need to focus instruction on three aspects of making the force play: movement from the fielding position to the base, footwork at the base, and the stretch to meet the ball with two- or one-handed catching techniques. Your sequence for instruction of the less experienced students could follow that of the game occurrence, or you could focus on the two aspects at the base and then add the movement to the base. Whichever you elect,

it is helpful for the novice player to focus on only one aspect at a time, while patterning the entire sequence.

If you have not been responsible for the previous instruction of your more experienced students, you may need to focus your observation on all three aspects of the force play. However, pay particular attention to their ability to correctly move to the base, because many students fail to get to a position at the base that is on the side of the source of the throw. For example, at times you will see the shortstop at the outfield corner of second base taking a throw from the pitcher for either the single force play on the lead runner or the start of the double play. This positioning only lengthens the distance of the throw. Movement to the base for the first and third basemen in fast-pitch is especially difficult because the base is behind them in most situations. In slow pitch, those players have an easier task moving to the base because the base is in front of them. It is common, in all cases, for the novice player to have great difficulty in simultaneously keeping track of the ball and getting to the base.

Making the tag play at a base involves the same sequence of actions as the force play. That sequence of actions involves moving to the base from the fielding position, getting into position to receive the throw at the base, and catching the ball and making the play on the incoming runner. The tag play, of course, involves the technique of tagging the runner after catching the ball. Again, your more experienced students may be lacking in practice when it comes to moving to the base. They may have always practiced making the tag play while standing over the base. Then, when placed in a game situation and faced with making the tag play, such a fielder is at a loss as to how to get into the proper position at the base, because he or she has not practiced moving from the fielding position to the tagging position at the base.

Another tag play that is often not programmed into the practice setting is the tag of the runner returning to the base. This play occurs in fast pitch as a pick-off play on a runner taking a lead after the pitch. The play seldom, if ever, occurs in slow pitch. However, runners overrunning a base other than first are at risk for the tag play as they attempt to return.

The tag play on the runner between bases is different only in the fact that the runner is standing up while running past the fielder. The emphasis for the fielder on this play is to protect the ball in the glove so that it does not become dislodged. Many students erroneously think that in order for the runner to be tagged out he or she must actually be touched with the ball. Holding the ball in the glove, covering it with the throwing hand, and tagging the runner with the back of the fingers of the glove is a technique that may be foreign to both the less and the more experienced students in your class.

Force play and tag play drills could be used as part of a multiple skills circuit in order to maximize facility utilization. You can set up the infield area for force play and tag plays, and the outfield for fielding fly balls or pitching practice. This makes the orientation for the force and tag play practice much clearer and, thus, easier on the students.

STUDENT KEYS TO SUCCESS

Force Play

- Move to the base prior to throw
- Position self on side of base nearest source of throw
- Place 1 foot on base
- Stretch to meet oncoming thrown ball
- Catch the ball

Tag Play

- Fielder, throw the ball low to the base
- Straddle or stand just to side of the base
- Face the oncoming runner
- Catch the ball
- Bring ball in glove hand down to edge of base
- Let the runner come to the base
- Tag the runner's foot

Force Play and Tag Play Drills

1. Mimetic Footwork Drill
[Corresponds to *Softball*, Step 11, Drill 1]

Group Management and Safety Tips

- Although the footwork drills could be done as single-person practice drills, facility and equipment restrictions usually make practice in small groups more advisable.
- Group students so that at least one more experienced student is in each group.
- Use available lines, such as foul lines or gymnasium floor lines, or mark a line at each practice station. The orientation of the fielding position in relation to the base is greatly facilitated by having a line to put the base on.

- If the use of lines is impossible, use a cone to represent home plate and have the students orient themselves at the base in relation to the cone.
- If class size allows, use the four bases of the regulation field for your practice stations. Use the bases (including home plate) as they are intended; rotate the students around so that they practice at all four. If the class is large and more stations are needed, add stations to the outfield area using the foul lines to orient the bases for practice.
- See *Softball*, Step 11, ''Force Play and Tag Play Practice Situations,'' for a list of practice options.

Equipment

- Loose bases, 1 for each practice station not on the regulation infield, in addition to the regulation four infield bases
- Balls, 1 per student group
- Gloves, 1 per student
- Line marker
- Cones, 1 per station if no lines available

Instructions and Cues to Class

- ''Place the base for your group on the line. Take the appropriate fielding position for the play being practiced. If you are practicing plays at first base, as you face forward the base will be to your left with the line on the left, or outside, edge of the base. If you are practicing plays at third base, the base and line will be to your right. When you are in the shortstop's role, second base will be to your left. When you are second baseman, the base will be to your right. When you are catcher, the base will be about 2 feet directly in front of you.''
- ''Going one at a time, you are to mimetically practice the footwork for the force plays and the tag plays at each base. From your starting fielding position, move into the proper position at the base to receive throws from the infield and from the outfield. Imagine the throw coming from a particular infielder or outfielder and move to the side or corner of the base closest to that fielder. Remember, you want to have

that throw travel the shortest distance possible. You need to get as close to the throwing fielder as you can and still be able either to touch the base for the force play or to bring the gloved ball to the edge of the base so the incoming runner tags himself or herself out.''
- ''If you are in groups, line up one behind the other so that the first person in line is in the appropriate starting fielding position. Go to the end of the line after your turn; the next person in line moves up to the starting position for her or his turn.''
- ''Do 2 repetitions of the footwork practice for force plays, 2 repetitions for off-target throws left and right, and 2 repetitions for tag plays at each of the positions and for each of the throw directions (infield and outfield). Remember, when the throw for the force play is off target to the side, step toward the ball with the foot on that side and tag the base with your other foot. Do not automatically plant one foot on the base every time; if you do, you will end up crossing one leg over the other trying to reach an off-target throw, and you cannot reach as far in that position.''

Student Option

- ''Work with a partner, who observes and gives you feedback on your position at the base, your footwork in making the force play, and your technique in making the tag.''

Student Success Goal

- 40 total successful repetitions (2 force plays, 2 off-target throws right, 2 off-target throws left, and 2 tag plays for each position)

    1b covering first base

    2b covering second base

    SS covering second base

    3b covering third base

    C covering home plate

To Decrease Difficulty

- Decrease the number of successful repetitions needed. [3]

To Increase Difficulty

- Have a feeder softly toss a ball to the covering player (see *Softball*, Step 11, Drill 2, Partner Toss Footwork Drill). [7]

2. *Force Play and Tag Play Without Runners*
[Corresponds to *Softball*, Step 11, Drill 3]

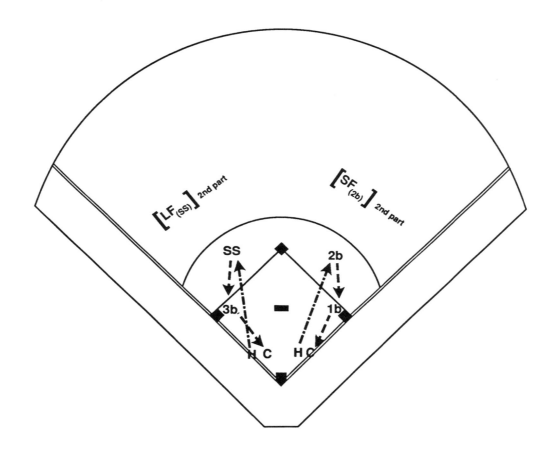

Group Management and Safety Tips

- Group students in fours. One pair of partners is a fungo hitter and a catcher; the other pair is a fielder to whom the ball will be hit and a fielder covering the base and making the force and tag plays.
- This drill adds a hit ball and full throws from regulation distances to the mimetic and tossing footwork drills.

- This drill is very difficult to organize for full class participation. It is probably best combined with practice of some skills that can occur in spaces other than the regulation field, such as pitching or hitting.
- With more experienced students, it is possible to organize two groups practicing on the same field. One group uses third base as the base to be covered by the third

baseman, with the infield throw coming from the shortstop and the outfield throw (shortstop moves to outfield) from the left fielder. The hitter and the catcher stand in front of home plate a few steps toward the shortstop position.

The other group practices at the same time, using first base as the base to be covered by the first baseman, with the infield throw coming from the second baseman and the outfield throw (second baseman moves to outfield) from the short fielder in short right field. The hitter and the catcher stand a few steps in front of the plate toward the second baseman's position.

- The same basic setup can be organized with second base covered by the second baseman and shortstop alternately. They also cover infield throws from each other, and outfield throws from center field position (throwing infielder moves to center). The other group uses home plate, with the catcher covering and infield throws coming from either first or third and outfield throws from left or right (throwing infielder moves to outfield).

Equipment

- Regulation field with tied-down bases
- Balls, 2 or 3 per group
- Extra balls to replace ones lost over fences or under bleachers
- Bats, 2 or 3 of varying weights and lengths per group
- Gloves, 1 per student

Instructions and Cues to Class

- ''This drill is performed almost the same as the mimetic and tossing footwork drills. Now, though, the ball is fungo hit and the throws are made from the regular fielding positions.''
- ''Two groups work on the field at the same time, so be accurate with your throws and watch out for other people in your area of play.''
- ''Do not chase an overthrown ball that goes into the other group's area without first looking to see that your path to the ball is clear.''
- ''The fielder covering a base should get to the ball side of the base quickly, get into the correct position, and look for the throw.''
- ''At each base, do 2 force plays and 2 tag plays with throws coming from the infield and the outfield.''

Student Option

- ''Do the tag play as if a runner had overrun the base and was liable to be tagged out.''

Student Success Goal

- 4 repetitions (2 force plays and 2 tag plays) at each player position

    1b covering first base

    2b covering second base

    SS covering second base

    3b covering third base

    C covering home plate

To Decrease Difficulty

- Have the batter throw the ball, rather then fungo hit, to the fielding player. [3]

To Increase Difficulty

- Add baserunners (see *Softball*, Step 11, Drill 4). [6]

Step 12 Grounders-Only T-Ball

Modified games are designed to give students practice executing specific skills under game-like conditions. Rules are established to ensure as much practice as possible on the skill(s) and game concepts selected for a particular game.

The modified game Grounders-Only T-Ball is fully explained in *Softball*, Step 12. The additional material presented for you in this instructor's book is designed to help you use the game in your class. Suggestions for ways to organize a large group, things to do with the extra students, and the areas on which you can focus instruction make up the content of this step.

INSTRUCTIONAL FOCUS

Your students, to this point, have primarily been developing proficiency in isolated skills. They have had the opportunity to practice some skills together in combinations that typically occur in a game setting, such as fielding a ground ball and making a throw to a base from a game-like distance. The typical task, to date, has been specified in the drill setup. For example, "the shortstop fields the ground ball and throws the ball to first base" has been a specified task.

However, your students have not yet been in a game context, which allows only one opportunity to make each play. They have also not yet been in a situation in which decision making involves on-the-spot play selection from among a variety of options. In modified game play, for example, the fielder has to make a throwing decision based on the number of outs and the placement of the baserunners.

Your role as the instructor is to determine the major skills on which to focus in the modified game, then to control the game setting so that situations calling for the use of those skills do occur. The following list of skills, game concepts, offensive and defensive strategies, and rule applications are those areas that have been presented in previous steps. In the modified game Grounders-Only T-Ball, your students will have opportunities to apply their skills and knowledge in game-like situations.

In the list that follows, the teaching cues and observation pointers are given below the skill or game concept. Use the cues to help the students key in on the techniques or concepts identified as important to their practice.

Skills

Situation a: Hitting stroke using the batting tee

- Emphasize the high-to-low swing path so that the resulting hit will be a ground ball.
- Stress keeping the head down and focusing on the ball.

- Stress good contact on the top rear portion of the ball.
- Help your students adjust position at the tee to place-hit the ball to different locations in the infield. Focus the defensive players' attention on these same points so that they can work on the anticipation skills of reading and reacting.

Situation b: Fielding ground balls and throwing overhand to bases

- Emphasize moving into position to correctly field the ball.
- Stress keeping the head down and watching the ball go into the glove.
- Reinforce the importance of the smooth transition from fielding to throwing.
- Have your students focus on moving their bodies in the direction they throw.

Situation c: Overhand throw

- Stress the overhand delivery; discourage the sidearm throw except where appropriate, such as from the second baseman to first.

Situation d: Baserunning

- Reinforce the idea of running full speed over first base and turning to the left even when returning directly to the base.
- Review what constitutes an attempt to go to second base after overrunning first base.
- Remind the base coaches of their responsibilities and the use of both verbal and visual signals to assist the baserunner.
- Reinforce student use of base-rounding techniques at all bases.
- Cue the baserunner on what to do on a ground ball, a fly ball, and a line drive, even though some of them are outs in this modified game.

Game Concepts

Situation a: Position play

- Help your students define position coverage areas and interaction areas.
- Remind your students about calling for the fly ball even if a certain hit ball is an automatic out in this game.

Situation b: Covering and backing up

- Go over covering and backing-up responsibilities. Use the general principles applying to ground balls hit to the right side and ground balls hit to the left side. Discuss the specifics of base coverage based on the situations that develop.

- Cue the more experienced teams just before the batter hits the ball. However, stop play and set the situation for the less experienced teams if they appear confused.

Defensive and Offensive Strategies

Situation a: Force play (and when it's in effect)

- Discuss how the fielder moves to the covering position on the ball side of the base.
- Review footing the base and stretching for both on- and off-target throws.
- Discuss the lead runner concept with the less experienced teams.
- Discuss the double play with the more experienced teams (see *Softball*, Step 21).
- Review all base coverage responsibilities.

Situation b: Tag play (and when it's in effect)

- Discuss how the fielder moves to the covering position at the base.
- Review how positioning at the base is based upon the path of the runner and the thrown ball.
- Stress the concept of the fielder's letting the runner tag him- or herself out, then sweeping the glove and ball out of the way.

Situation c: Baserunning

- Emphasize the concept of being forced to advance to the next base.
- Review the concept of tagging up on a fly ball (even though it's not applicable in this game).
- Remind the runners to watch the base coach for signals.

Situation d: Place hitting

- Discuss the concept of hitting behind the runner.
- Emphasize the concept of reading the defense and taking advantage of open spaces into which to hit (only in the infield area in this game).

Rule Application Situations

a. Fair and foul territory
b. In-play and out-of-play territory
c. Fair and foul ball
   - in the infield
   - in the outfield (even though ball is out of play)
d. Baserunner legally leaving the base as the ball is hit
e. Baserunner forced to run
f. Baserunner advancing at own risk
g. Baserunner overrunning first base being liable to be tagged out
h. Tagging up on a fly ball
i. Batting order
j. Position numbers
k. Error
l. Fielder's choice

PRACTICE FOCUS

As indicated in the participant's book, the purpose of the modified game is to work on game concepts and the execution of skills under game-like conditions. Scoring, if it is desired, is based on performance points, not on runs scored. If you have extra people in the class, they should use the player scoresheet from the participant's book and provide feedback on performance for the students who are playing. The completed sheets might be helpful to you as a checklist type of evaluation.

Group Management and Safety Tips

- Group your class by ability into four teams of six players each; make two equal less experienced teams and two equal more experienced. Make sure, for instance, that the very least experienced and the very most experienced students are divided equally between the two less experienced teams and the two more experienced teams, respectively.
- Use extra students not able to participate actively to keep the player scoresheets. Extras who can be active can act as umpires, base coaches, and an outfielder or two per team. Let the outfielders hit as part of the batting order when the team is up to bat; however, they do not make

defensive plays from the outfield, because balls hit there are out of play. Rotate these active extras into the six playing positions.

- Don't take yourself out of the teaching role by keeping score or acting as an umpire. Use students for those roles.
- Set up two fields, one for the less experienced game and the other for the more experienced teams. Arrange the fields so that you can easily observe the play of both games. If the field space is available, use the regular diamond as one field and establish another on the other side of the backstop so that the catchers are back to back. The teams are thus protected by the backstop from errant throws to home.
- Catchers must wear face masks.
- Use an IncrediBall® for play in the less experienced game.
- If using a regulation ball in the more experienced game, be sure the students in the pitching position are skillful fielders with good reactions to balls coming off the tee. When a less skilled student is in the pitcher's position, have him or her stand behind the pitching rubber for the starting fielding position, or use the IncrediBall® with this group, also.
- Place the batting tee to the rear of home plate. Instruct the baserunners to run across the regular home plate, *not* the tee. Another option is to instruct the catcher to remove the tee after the batter hits the ball when there is a runner on or rounding third base.
- If the majority of the batters are right-handed, place the "bench" for the team at bat on the first-base side of the field,

well back from the foul line. Put the bench behind the side fence on either the first- or third-base side if easy access to the field remains available.

- Use the time before the start of an inning or a half-inning to focus group instruction on offensive or defensive play.
- With the less experienced teams, especially, cue the defensive team on what the situation is and what the anticipated play should be. Conduct the game as a "controlled scrimmage" by stopping play and explaining situations.

Equipment

- Batting tees, 1 for each playing field (if one is adjustable for inside and outside "pitches," use it for the more experienced group)
- Catcher's masks, 1 for each group (if head straps are difficult to adjust, have different sizes available)
- Bats, 3 or 4 of different weights, lengths, and grip sizes (be sure to have light bats available, especially for the less experienced teams)
- Gloves, at least 6 per game (1 can be left by the player at each defensive position when teams change from defense to offense)
- Balls, 1 per 2 people (for pregame warm-up)
- IncrediBalls®, at least 6 for the less experienced game
- Bases, 1 set for each field
- Cones, 2 to mark the outfield ends of the foul lines on the second field

Step 13   Fielding a Fly Ball

Fielding fly balls is a skill that both infielders and outfielders use often in a game. The techniques involved in fly ball fielding are nearly identical to those used in fielding a ground ball and catching. The main difference is that the outfielder must often throw the ball a great distance after making the catch. Consequently, body position when making the catch is changed slightly in order to facilitate the throw that follows the catch.

As you instruct your students on catching fly balls, focus on the body position that must be attained prior to the catch. The student fielding the fly ball should get into position under and behind the ball. However, rather than facing forward, the fielder should stand with the glove-side shoulder turned slightly toward the target. He or she should catch the ball while moving forward and make the catch in front of the throwing-arm shoulder. Then it is easy to move the ball into throwing position, crow-hop (step toward the target on the glove-side foot, hop on the throwing-side foot as it closes to the glove-side foot, then step on the glove-side foot as the ball is released), and throw the ball to the target.

A less experienced player tends to face the dropping ball in a square position and reach out with the glove hand to try to make the catch with one hand. This player also has difficulty reading the direction and depth of the ball as it comes off the bat (or toss). You can help him or her get into proper fly ball fielding position by gradually increasing the height of the toss while he or she stands in a stationary fielding position. Then toss the ball to the fielder's throwing-hand side so that he or she has to turn the body to get the glove to the spot where the ball is descending. Continually cue the fielder to "catch with both hands ahead of and above the throwing shoulder." Check to make sure that the fielder is watching the ball all the way into the glove.

A more experienced fly ball fielder needs encouragement and feedback concerning the more advanced technique of moving in toward the target while getting into position to catch the descending ball. When catching the ball, the fielder should crow-hop and throw the ball to the target with a full overhand throw. Watch carefully to make certain that the throwing arm is coming high over the shoulder and the follow-through is all the way down and across the body. A sidearm throw from the outfield would cause the ball to curve as it comes into the target, decreasing the likelihood of getting the advancing baserunner out.

STUDENT KEYS TO SUCCESS

- Feet in stagger stride, glove-side foot ahead
- Glove-side shoulder turned toward target
- Move slightly in direction of target as ball is caught
- Catch ball with two hands high, in front of throwing-side shoulder
- Bring ball to throwing position
- Use full overhand throw to target

Fielding a Fly Ball Rating

CHECKPOINT	LESS EXPERIENCED	MORE EXPERIENCED
Preparation		
Stance	• Square to ball	• Glove-side foot ahead
Body Position	• Square to ball	• Glove-side shoulder turned to target
Hand Position	• Glove hand extended	• Glove hand extended, throwing hand behind and slightly under glove
Execution		
Focus	• Averts eyes as ball descends	• Watches ball into glove
Hand Position	• One-handed catch	• Two-handed catch
Movement	• Stationary	• Moves slightly toward target
Follow-Through to Throw		
Body Position	• Square to target	• Glove side turned toward target
Throwing Movement	• Turning toward target	• Crow-hops toward target
Throwing Action	• Overhand but weak	• Full overhand throw
End Position	• Erect	• Bent at waist, arm down and across body

Error Detection and Correction for Fly Ball Fielding

The errors you will see in your less experienced students are often associated with the fear of being hit by the descending ball. You can use a softer ball to alleviate some of that fear. It is also helpful to gradually increase the height of the ball so that these students will become accustomed to catching it and feel confident about their ability to be successful. Proper position and catching with two hands will help them succeed.

The more experienced students need to work on getting their bodies into the correct throwing position, with the glove side turned toward the target and moving forward as they make the catch. You can explain to them that the correct body position and movement will make their throws easier and more accurate. Sometimes it is helpful to have them try to explain to you why the correct body position and movement in on the ball are necessary. It is also important that you watch to see whether the more experienced players track the ball from the moment it comes off the bat (or is thrown). Directing their attention to the direction and height of the ball as it is hit (or thrown) often enables them to get into position behind the ball more quickly.

ERROR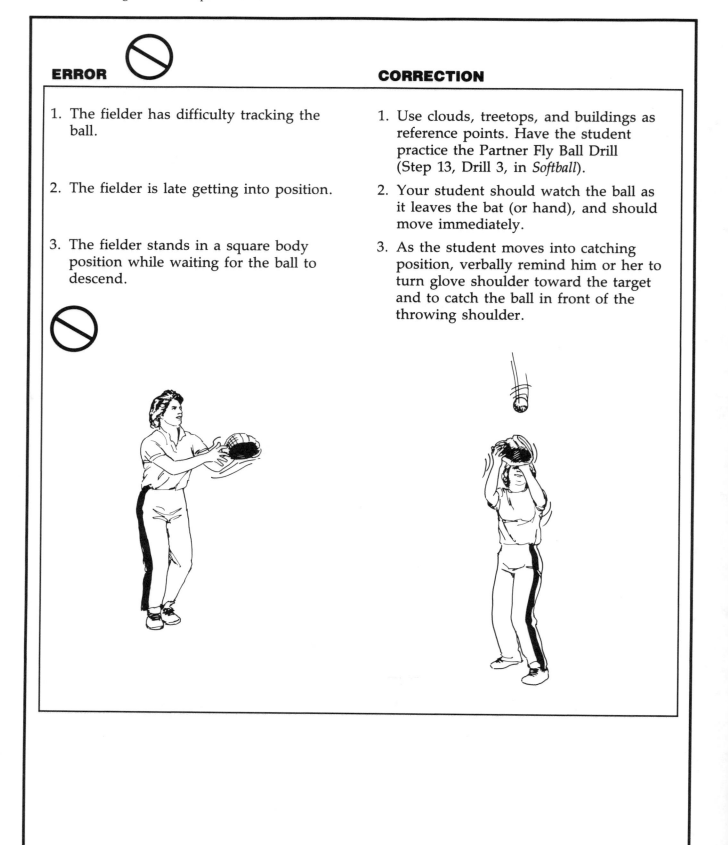

CORRECTION

1. The fielder has difficulty tracking the ball.

2. The fielder is late getting into position.

3. The fielder stands in a square body position while waiting for the ball to descend.

1. Use clouds, treetops, and buildings as reference points. Have the student practice the Partner Fly Ball Drill (Step 13, Drill 3, in *Softball*).

2. Your student should watch the ball as it leaves the bat (or hand), and should move immediately.

3. As the student moves into catching position, verbally remind him or her to turn glove shoulder toward the target and to catch the ball in front of the throwing shoulder.

ERROR   **CORRECTION**

4. The fielder uses a sidearm throw.

4. Have the student exaggerate the overhand throwing action, particularly in moving the elbow up and the ball and the hand overhead.

Fly Ball Fielding Drills

1. *Fly Ball Wall Drill*
[Corresponds to *Softball*, Step 13, Drill 2]

Group Management and Safety Tips

- Only less experienced students need to do this drill. The more experienced should begin with the Partner Fly Ball Drill (Drill 2).
- Divide the class into two groups: less experienced students and more experienced.
- If you are in a gymnasium, the less experienced students will do this drill at the walls, and the more experienced students will simultaneously do the next drill in the center of the gym.

- If you are outside, the less experienced students can work at a wall of the school building (preferably one with no windows and two stories high). The more experienced can do the Partner Fly Ball Drill at any location on the playing field.
- If this drill is being done on the gymnasium wall, use Rag Balls® or IncrediBalls®. If this drill is being done on an outside wall, use old, "mushy," scuffed softballs.
- Place a line (or cones) about 10 feet from the wall. The students do this drill from this line.

- Have your students stand on the line facing the wall. Make sure that they are spaced about 12 feet away from students on either side of them.
- Cones (or other markers) could be used to establish the 12-foot areas. Then the students could throw to the wall and try to catch the ball in the 12-foot area to their right or left (whatever direction is being practiced).
- As your students do this drill, make sure that you give the cue for tossing the ball to the right or to the left so that they don't get in one another's way. Make sure they are moving in the same direction at the same time.
- Put all left-handers at one end of the line.

Equipment

- Gloves, 1 per student
- Old balls, 1 per student
- Line markers such as cones or scrimmage vests

Instructions to Class

- ''Throw the ball overhand high and straight ahead on the wall. Move into position and catch the ball above and in front of your head.''
- ''Continue until I give you the cue to throw the ball against the wall either to your right (throwing side) or to your left (glove side).''
- ''Practice getting into correct position, catching the ball, and moving continuously into throwing position. This is the same as in fielding a ground ball except that you are coming from a high catching position rather than a low catching position.''
- ''Count the number of catches you make when you throw the ball directly ahead, to your glove side, and to your throwing arm side. Remember, you throw to the right or the left only when I give the cue.''

Cues to Class

- ''Be sure that you move quickly to the spot where the ball is going to come down. Be waiting for the ball, not diving for it.''

- ''Watch the ball all the way from the top of the wall and into the glove.''
- ''Remember that your waiting position under the ball should be with your glove-side foot and shoulder turned in the direction of the target.''
- ''Catch the ball with two hands in front of your throwing shoulder. Then you are in position to throw the ball to the target.''

Student Options

- ''Have a partner watch you catch the ball and give you feedback on your body position. Is your glove side toward the wall? Did you catch the ball above and in front of your throwing shoulder?''
- ''If this is easy and you are consistently catching the ball, have your partner throw the ball to the wall. Watch where it is going and move into position to catch the ball as it rebounds.''

Student Success Goal

- 24 of 30 total successful catches

  9 of 10 catches directly in front

  8 of 10 catches moving to left (glove side)

  7 of 10 catches moving to right (throwing side)

To Decrease Difficulty

- Move the fly ball catcher closer to the wall. [4]
- Let the student use a softer ball (an old IncrediBall®). [2]
- Have the student throw the ball higher so there's more time to track it. [3]
- The student could practice the Self-Toss Drill (*Softball*, Step 13, Drill 1). [5]

To Increase Difficulty

- Have your student throw the ball with greater force. [3]
- Make the student throw the ball farther to the left and the right. [4]
- Have a partner throw the ball to the wall. [1]

2. *Partner Fly Ball Drill*
[Corresponds to *Softball*, Step 13, Drill 3]

Group Management and Safety Tips

- More experienced players should begin this step with this drill.
- Each student should get a partner from the same experience-level group.
- The partners locate themselves 60 feet away from one another, facing one another. Be sure that all pairs are oriented in the same direction. Be sure that neither partner is looking into the sun.
- Mark the 60-foot distance with a marker from one or both of the foul lines (in the outfield). Make certain that if you use both foul lines, the pairs near the home corner are not so close to one another as to get into each other's way.
- If you have a soccer or football field, you could use the sidelines for locating the pairs. Then there would be plenty of room for all players to move.
- Locate each pair at least 25 feet from the other pairs. They will be moving to the right and the left, and there needs to be sufficient room for them to move without colliding.
- Caution the thrower that he or she is responsible for the safety of the fielder. The thrower must look to the pairs on both sides to see where they are, then direct his or her throw accordingly.
- Have the less experienced begin with a softer ball. When they feel ready, have them switch to a regulation softball.
- If possible, put all left-handers on a separate line so that when they move to the glove and throwing side, they do not collide with the right-handers.

Equipment

- Gloves, 1 per student
- Softballs, 1 per student
- Extra softballs: regulation, Rag Balls®, IncrediBalls®
- Line markers, such as cones

Instructions to Class

- ''The throwers first throw 10 high fly balls directly to the fielder so that he or she does not have to move right or left to catch the balls.''
- ''Fielders, you get into the catching position under and behind the ball and catch the ball. Then, in one motion, throw the ball overhand to the thrower, aiming for his or her chest.''
- ''After 10 throws, change roles and repeat the drill.''
- ''Next you throw fly balls to the glove side of the fielder. Do 10 just as you did before, the fielder moving under and behind the ball, catching it, then throwing it back to the thrower.''
- ''Next throw to the throwing-arm side. Then throw behind the fielder so that he or she has to move backward to get into position to make the catch.''
- ''Throwers, start with throws that are easy for the fielder to catch. When you know they are ready to be challenged, make the throws harder to catch. You can do this by making the fielder move farther to catch the ball or by changing the height of the throw.''
- ''Finally, mix up the throws so that some go to the right, some to the left, some straight ahead, and some behind.''
- ''Count the number of catches and on-target throws you make in each segment of the drill.''

Cues to Class

- "Fielders, move as soon as you see the ball released by the thrower. You need to practice reacting immediately so that you can get into a position behind and under the ball and be moving toward the target as you catch the ball. This will help you throw more accurately and quickly."
- "Diving after the ball is spectacular, but it usually means that you were late moving to the ball or that you tracked it improperly."
- "Fielders, turn your glove side toward the target so that your throw can flow continuously from your catch of the ball. You need to be able to get a throw off quickly from the outfield because the ball has a long distance to travel to beat a runner advancing to a base."
- "Catch the ball in front of your throwing-arm shoulder."
- "Shade your eyes from the sun with your glove."
- "When you catch the ball while moving forward, do the crow-hop as you bring the ball to the throwing position. The crow-hop consists of stepping on your glove-side foot as you catch the ball, hopping forward on your throwing-side foot to a point beside your glove-side foot, then stepping toward the target with your glove-side foot as you throw the ball to the target."
- "Exaggerate the throwing action as you throw back to the target. Be sure that your arm goes high over your throwing shoulder, reach out to the target with your throwing hand, and follow through down and across your body. Bend at the waist and make your throwing hand touch your glove-side knee."

Student Options

- "Fielders, call out the direction you want the ball to go so that you can get a jump on the ball. Be sure that you focus on the height and direction of the ball so that your tracking skill improves."
- "Make the drill a game by scoring points for a throw that is just barely catchable and for a successful catch and throw. The object of the game is for the pair of you to score as many points as you can without making an error on the throw or the catch. If you make an error, start your point tally again at one. See how high your point total can go. Points are important, but not if you don't challenge one another. You are helping one another improve."

Student Success Goal

- 38 of 50 total catches and on-target throws

  9 of 10 catches directly in front

  8 of 10 catches to glove side

  8 of 10 catches to throwing side

  6 of 10 catches on throws behind fielder

  7 of 10 catches to random directions

To Decrease Difficulty

- Have the thrower throw the ball higher so there is longer tracking time. [3]
- Let the pair use a softer ball. [2]
- Have the thrower decrease the lateral distance the fielder moves to get under the ball. [4]
- Have the fielder catch the ball, get into position to throw, but not actually make the throw. [5]
- Have the thrower, when throwing randomly, cue the fielder as to the direction the throw will go. [1, 8]

To Increase Difficulty

- Have the thrower vary the height of the throw. [3]
- The thrower could increase the lateral distance the fielder has to move to get to the ball. [4]
- Make the thrower vary the height, lateral distance, and depth to which the ball is thrown. [4, 8]
- Require the fielder to throw to different distances after the catch. [4, 8]
- Increase the speed of the drill by using two balls. As soon as the first ball is caught, the thrower throws the second ball in a different direction. [3]
- Vary the direction of the target for the fielder as specified in *Softball*, Step 13, Drill 4. A third partner is added to the above drill and this partner is farther away (100 feet) than the tosser (60 feet). The target catcher needs an empty bucket into which to drop the thrown balls he or she catches. The target catcher moves according to the chart given in the textbook. The target catcher calls out to the fly ball fielder the direction that the throw is to go. [3, 6, 8]

3. *Catcher's Pop-Up Drill*
[Corresponds to *Softball*, Step 13, Drill 5]

Group Management and Safety Tips

- The class can be divided either according to ability or randomly.
- Every class member must have a partner.
- The student pairs may be located anywhere on the playing area, but need to have a 15-foot-square area in which to drill.
- Orient all pairs so that all the catchers are facing the same direction.
- Caution all students to make their tosses within their 15-foot-square area.
- It is the tosser's responsibility to make certain that the catcher is not going to collide with another catcher.

Equipment

- Gloves, 1 per student
- Balls, 1 per student pair
- Softer balls
- Catcher's masks for the more experienced (in an increased difficulty option)

Instructions and Cues to Class

- "Fielder, you are going to crouch like a catcher, then stand up to catch pop-ups (fly balls above and in catcher's range)."
- "Tosser, you should stand to the side and slightly behind the catcher so that you can toss a pop-up without getting in the catcher's way."
- "Tosser, you will toss the ball straight up into the air, then call to the catcher, 'up and over your head.' This is what the infielders do in a game situation so that the catcher knows what direction to move when the ball is a pop-up."
- "Catcher, wait for the tosser to call the direction of the ball, then stand up and take your first step with the foot on the side you are to move to. Look up for the ball immediately so that you can move under it and make the catch."

- "After 10 tosses, switch roles. Then repeat the drill by tossing the ball so that the catcher must move to the glove side, the throwing-hand side, then any side, any height, and any distance."
- "As always, tosser, you are responsible for the safety of the catcher. Be sure that when you throw the ball, no one is moving in the path of the catcher."
- "Tosser, you are responsible for making the catcher work hard and get better at catching pop-ups. Challenge the catcher."

Student Option

- "Have the catcher wear a mask and flip it off as he or she jumps up and moves under the ball."

Student Success Goal

- 26 of 40 catches

    7 of 10 catches overhead

    7 of 10 catches to glove side

    6 of 10 catches to throwing side

    6 of 10 catches in random directions

To Decrease Difficulty

- Let the pair use softer ball. [2]
- Have the tosser throw the ball higher so the catcher has longer to get under it. [3]
- Have the tosser throw the ball higher and laterally, so the catcher has longer to get under it. [4]
- Before the ball toss, the tosser could cue the catcher as to the toss direction. [1]
- Have the catcher begin from a standing position. [5]

To Increase Difficulty

- Have the tosser randomly toss the ball to various heights. [8]
- Have the tosser throw the ball in various directions and to varying heights. [8]
- Have the tosser throw the ball to varying distances, directions, and heights. [8]
- Have the catcher wear a mask that must be flipped off as he or she stands up. [7]
- Have the tosser throw lower pop-ups so there is less tracking time. [3]

4. Drop-Step Drill

[Corresponds to *Softball*, Step 13, Drill 6]

Group Management and Safety Tips

- Each class member gets a partner of any experience level.
- The partners stand facing one another, 10 feet apart. Have the throwing partner stand on a foul line (or a sideline) and the fielding partner stand 10 feet away.
- Each pair needs about 30 feet of lateral space for this drill, so space the pairs accordingly. The fielder will move no more than 15 feet laterally and no more than 25 feet beyond the starting point. Thus, you can probably have two lines of

partners, one behind the other. One pair can start on the foul line, a second pair can start at least 70 feet from the foul line.
- Make sure that all throwers are facing the same direction.
- Try to mark the 30 feet of lateral space in some way so that a pair of partners stays in their area while doing the drill.

Equipment

- Gloves, 1 per student
- Balls, 1 per student
- Line and lateral area markers, such as cones, flags, or pinnies

Instructions to Class

- "Fielder, stand in the fielding position facing the thrower. The thrower will fake a throw to one side of you. On that fake, you should start running back for a fly ball in that direction. Take your first step with the foot on the side that the fake throw seems to be going to. This is called the *drop step*."
- "Thrower, toss the ball to the side you originally indicated. Throw it high and far enough that the fielder has to keep moving to catch the ball."
- "Thrower, aim the ball for a spot at least 5 feet inside the 30-foot boundary so that the fielder does not collide with another fielder."
- "Fielder, after you catch the ball, slow down by bending your knees, and bring the ball to throwing position. Now you have to get your body turned for the throw back to the original set-up thrower. After you catch the ball, turn your head immediately and look for the target; this helps you make an accurate throw."
- "Do this 5 times, then switch roles."
- "Challenge your partner. Fake and throw right 2 times, followed by a perfect throw to catch. Then fake and throw right 3 times and vary the distance the fielder has to move to make the catch. Also do the same thing to the left."

Cues to Class

- "Fielder, keep your eye on the ball in the thrower's hand. This will help you time your run and help you get to the ball's path when the ball is actually thrown. This drill helps you catch fly balls on the run."
- "Fielder, watch the ball all the way from the toss (hit) into your glove. Be sure to take the drop step with the foot on the side you are moving toward so you can move quickly to the fly ball."
- "Fielder, don't run around in an arc after you catch the ball. Slow and stop by bending your knees. Then make a pivot to get into position to throw the ball back to the thrower."

Student Option

- "Discuss with your partner any problem you both seem be to having. Set up a drill so that you get repeated practice of your common problem."

Student Success Goal

- 9 of 15 total catches

    3 of 5 catches moving to right

    3 of 5 catches moving to left

    3 of 5 catches moving in random directions

To Decrease Difficulty

- The tosser should not vary distance of the throws. [3]
- Let the pair use a softer ball. [2]
- Have the tosser arc the ball higher so there is more tracking time. [3]
- Have the tosser decrease the distance the fielder has to run. [4]
- The tosser could increase the lateral distance so the fielder has a better view of ball. [4]

To Increase Difficulty

- Have the tosser vary the height of the ball as well as its distance. [8]
- Have the tosser reduce the arc of the ball flight so there is less time to track it. [3]
- The tosser could toss the ball closer to the fielder so that the fielder must turn more as he or she is running back. [4]

5. *Where Is It? Drill*

[Corresponds to *Softball*, Step 13, Drill 7]

Group Management and Safety Tips

- Students should be divided into less experienced and more experienced groups. Within each group have them pair up.
- Partners stand 20 feet apart, facing the same direction. The thrower is on a foul line (or sideline), and the fielder is 20 feet out into the field.
- The pairs need about 30 feet of room laterally and about 20 feet beyond the position of the fielder, so two lines of partners could be used just as in the previous drill.
- The thrower must be responsible for the fielder's safety, for preventing collisions.

Equipment

- Gloves, 1 per student
- Balls, 1 per student pair

Instructions and Cues to Class

- "This drill helps you develop your ability to find the ball quickly and move into position to catch it while tracking its flight."
- "Thrower, you throw the ball into the air in any direction and to any catchable distance. First make the throws easy to catch; then make them harder to catch."
- "Thrower, be sure you shout 'Turn!' as you release the ball. Otherwise, it isn't fair to the fielder."
- "Fielder, when the thrower releases the ball, he or she will shout 'Turn.' You should immediately turn and look up for the ball. Then move as quickly as you can into position to field the ball. Try to get under the ball and face in the direction of the thrower as you catch. This is what you will do in a game, and you can make your throw sooner."

- "Look for the ball and move to the catching position. Catch the ball and bring it in one motion to the throwing position. Do not throw the ball."
- "After each throw, switch roles. Continue until you have each had 10 fly balls to catch."
- "Count your catches. Each catch is worth 1 point. If the throw is not catchable, subtract a point from the thrower's total. See who can get the most points in 10 tries."

Student Options

- "Have the thrower call out 'Turn right!' or 'Turn left!' "
- "Get a third partner to be a target for the fielder to throw to after making the catch. After 5 catches, switch positions. Keep track of your score. Points are scored in the same way except that if the fielder's throw is catchable by the third partner (who moves no more than 2 steps in any direction), the fielder gets an extra point. If the throw is off target, subtract a point from the fielder's total. Points can be scored only by the fielder."

Student Success Goals

- 5 of 10 catches
- Score more points than your partner

To Decrease Difficulty

- Have the thrower call out the direction just before releasing the ball. [1]
- Let the pair use a softer ball. [2]
- Have the thrower make the throws easily catchable by throwing them higher, allowing the fielder more time to find and track the ball. [3]
- Have the thrower decrease the distance to be traveled by the fielder to get into position to catch the ball (the throw must still be high). [4]

To Increase Difficulty

- Have the thrower make the fielder move farther to make the catch. [4]
- Have the thrower reduce the height of the throw. [3]
- Have the thrower call the wrong direction just before releasing the throw. [8]
- Add a target for the fielder to throw to after the catch. [3]
- Have the thrower vary the height, distance, and direction of the throw. [8]

Step 14   Hitting a Soft Toss

Soft-toss drills (called "ball-toss drills" by some) have been used for years in competitive-level play as a hitting warm-up before a game. Teams use soft-toss drills to increase the number of swings hitters get in practice. Although not comparable to hitting off a pitcher, hitting the soft toss does require the batter to make some timing judgments during the swing in order to contact the ball. Therefore, in terms of the overall skill progression, soft-toss hitting is more difficult than the forms of hitting presented for use with your classes so far.

The stroke used to hit the soft toss is the same as that explained and used in all the previous steps focused upon hitting. Your students, at this point, should feel comfortable with things like the grip, the stance, the gross movement of the arm swing, and the follow-through. There should be few noticeable differences between your students on those aspects of hitting.

Your cues for the hitter should now begin to focus on the finer points of the swing and on timing the swing with the soft toss. Focus your cues for the majority of your students on points such as the open position of the front foot on the stride so that the hips can be fully open at the point of contact, and the head position being down and steady with the eyes following the ball from the time it leaves the tosser's hand until the point of contact. Most of all, now is the time for you to carefully observe the hitter at the point of contact. Direct your feedback toward the hitter's body position and action as the bat meets the ball. If the contact position is incorrect, work backward in your observation to those actions that bring the hitter to the contact position. The foot position in the stride step, the initiation of the swing with the hip turn, and the pivot on the feet are key points to look for in determining why the hitter does not assume the correct contact position.

The new skill in this step, and an extremely important one to focus on because of the safety factors involved, is the soft toss itself. For the less experienced students, especially, treat the skill of tossing the ball for the soft-toss drills as a separate skill. In this case, "less experienced" includes anyone who has not executed the soft toss before. Some of your otherwise more experienced students may be unfamiliar with the proper technique for the soft toss, so consider them less experienced here.

Most of your students have had experience using an underhand motion to toss a ball a short distance. They have used the gross movement in many prior drills. Tossing from a kneeling position should not pose a problem; kneeling on the tossing-side knee provides freedom of movement for the tossing arm. The major factor for you to stress with the tosser is the point of aim. The ball *must* be tossed to come down opposite the front foot of the hitter.

Tossing the ball toward the hitter's belt buckle could result in the ball being hit back at the tosser. If you have doubt about any of your students' ability to toss the ball to the proper spot, have them practice the toss with a batter standing in position to hit, but do not allow the batter to swing at the ball. Place an empty bucket in the area where the ball should drop (by the hitter's front foot); have the tosser practice tossing balls to land in the bucket after passing through the hitter's contact zone.

Carefully go over all the Keys to Success for the tosser (see Figure 14.2 in the participant's book) with your class as part of their introduction to the soft-toss drills. In addition, place some responsibility on the hitters by instructing everyone not to swing at any ball that is tossed into an incorrect contact zone.

The differences between your less experienced students and your more experienced students in hitting the soft toss are about the same as for hitting the ball off the tee. As discussed previously, there should be little difference now between the two experience levels in the preparation phase, the gross arm swing, and the follow-through. The less experienced hitters will be obvious to you when you observe the execution phase, though. They will still tend to swing with the arms and fail to use the hips and legs to develop force for the hit. The important consideration is to give sufficient practice for the less experienced tossers so that the drills can be conducted safely.

STUDENT KEYS TO SUCCESS FOR THE TOSSER

- Take tossing position opposite hitter's back foot
- Toss ball so hitter makes contact ahead of front foot
- Toss ball so hitter contacts ball with arms extended
- Watch hitter hit ball
- Give feedback to hitter on contact and follow-through of swing

STUDENT KEYS TO SUCCESS FOR THE HITTER

- Time the start of swing so step and beginning hip turn occur before ball approaches contact zone
- Step into open position with front foot
- Pivot into contact position on ball of back foot and heel of front
- Contact ball off front foot, hips square to line of direction, arms fully extended
- Swing through ball, wrapping bat around body

Soft Toss Rating

CHECKPOINT	LESS EXPERIENCED	MORE EXPERIENCED
Preparation Knee Down	• Glove-side knee	• Tossing-side knee
Kneeling Position	• Opposite midline of hitter	• Opposite hitter's back foot
Focus Point	• Hitter's midline	• Spot ahead of hitter's front foot
Tossing-Hand Position	• Above waist	• Well below waist
Execution Release Point	• Inconsistent	• Consistent
Direction of Arm Swing	• Inconsistent	• Consistent
Focus Point	• Diffused	• On contact target zone
Follow-Through Arm Position	• Low	• High, by head

Error Detection and Correction for Soft-Toss Hitting

Your observation of this combination skill should be directed first at the tosser. An improper toss is the cause of most errors by hitters. A ball tossed too low, too high, or too close to the hitter or toward the midline of the body makes the hitter's task impossible. Focus your cues for the tosser on the direction of the arm swing, the point of release, and the force of the toss. Emphasize the fact that the toss is a *finesse* move, not a gross motor action.

In observing the hitter, you should concentrate on the contact zone. Extended arms, open hips with feet pivoted, front leg straight, back leg bent, and weight centered under the back knee are your checkpoints at contact. In order to correct the hitter's contact-point errors, you may also have to make corrections on actions the hitter takes getting to that point.

ERROR    **CORRECTION**

For Tosser

1. The ball goes in a straight line and ends up too close to the hitter.

1. Check that the toss is made with a down-and-up motion, not back and forward. The ball must traverse an arc to get to the target spot.

ERROR   **CORRECTION**

2. The ball goes toward the hitter's mid-section.

2. Have the tosser direct the arm swing toward the hitter's front foot. Have the tosser kneel facing the hitter's front foot.

For Hitter

1. The hitter misses the ball completely.

1. Cue the hitter's focus to the ball: ''See the ball being hit.''

2. The hitter tips the ball up or down to the ground.

2. Instruct the hitter to try to contact the middle of the ball.

3. The hitter swings too early or too late.

3. Have the hitter start the swing as the ball begins to drop into the contact zone. Verbally cue a later or earlier initation of the swing.

Soft-Toss Hitting Drills

As with the batting tee drills in Step 5, the "Group Management and Safety Tips" and "Equipment" sections are now presented prior to the listing of individual drills because they are basically the same for both drills.

Group Management and Safety Tips

- The basic physical setup for the drills in this step will be the same. Students work in pairs, taking turns in the hitter and tosser roles. Each pair should have a bucket of at least 10 balls. Balls are hit into a net, a modified fence (same as for the batting tee drills), or an open and unobstructed area with students as ball retrievers.
- General management concerns are the same as those for the batting tee drills, especially regarding use of the drills as stations in either a hitting circuit or a general skills circuit, in order to maximize the use of facilities and equipment.
- Grouping by experience levels is not necessary for these drills. However, more experienced hitters working with less experienced tossers must use extreme care and not swing at improperly tossed balls, especially if they are tossed toward the hitter's back foot.

Equipment

- Bucket of 10 fleece balls, IncrediBalls®, or regular softballs per pair of students or per station (for the more experienced hitters, have 10 to 20 old tennis balls, baseballs, or 11-inch IncrediBalls® or regular softballs; these smaller balls are more difficult to track and hit [be sure the hole size in the net will restrict the smaller balls before using them])
- Whiffle golf balls, 15 to 20 for Drill 1
- Bats, 2 to 3 of different weights, lengths, and grip size per station
- Wooden wands or broom handles cut to bat length (they *must* have some form of cloth-tape grip so that they do not slip out of the batter's hands)
- Gloves, 1 per student if combining the hitting drill with fielding practice

1. Soft-Toss Net Drill
[Corresponds to *Softball*, Step 14, Drill 1]

Instructions and Cues to Class

- ''Tosser, be sure to toss the ball so that the hitter can make contact with the ball ahead of his or her front foot. Toss the ball in an arc so that the hitter can judge the path of the ball and get the bat to the contact point in the time it takes the ball to arrive.''
- ''Hitter, do not swing at the ball unless it is going into the contact zone ahead of your front foot. You must help protect the tosser from being hit with your batted ball.''
- ''Using a controlled swing, take a good turn on the ball (rotate hips toward front of plate), hit the middle of the ball, and send it into the net.''
- ''Swing through the ball. Roll your wrists and follow through by wrapping the bat and hands around your body.''
- ''Concentrate on your position at the point of contact. As you make contact with the ball, your hips should be square to the net, your arms fully extended, and your head down and steady with your eyes focused on the ball.''
- ''Your rear shoulder should be at your chin at the end of the swing.''

Student Option

- ''Have the tosser watch your contact point and follow-through. Ask your partner to give you feedback on those two portions of your swing. Remember, though, it is difficult for the tosser to watch the beginning of your swing because he or she is concentrating on the spot ahead of your front foot where the ball toss must go.''

Student Success Goals

- 20 on-target tosses
- 17 of 20 hits (on good tosses) that go directly into net

To Decrease Difficulty

- Let the pair use a larger ball. [2]

To Increase Difficulty

- Make the pair use a wooden wand or a stickball bat with whiffle golf balls (see *Softball*, Step 14, Drill 2). [2]

2. High-Ball and Low-Ball Hit Drill

[Corresponds to *Softball*, Step 14, Drill 3]

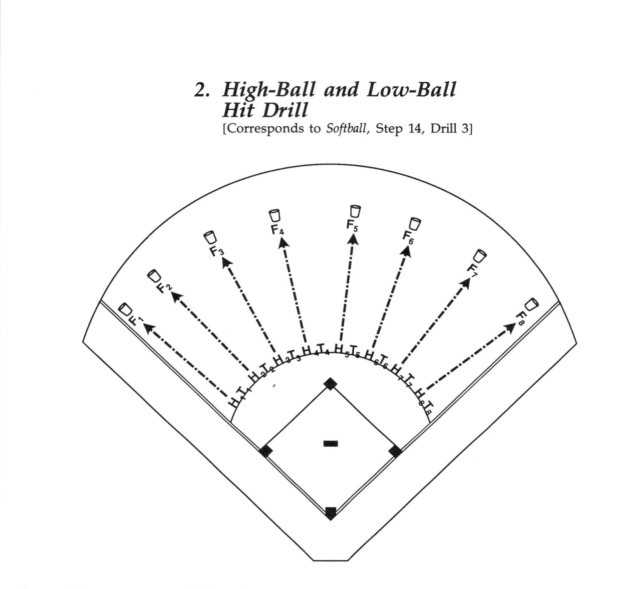

Group Management and Safety Tips

- Read all the tips mentioned before the first drill.
- Students are grouped in threes: a hitter, a tosser, and a fielder.
- The groups must be placed so that all hits are going in the same general direction. The groups need to be spread far enough apart so that the fielders are not in danger of being hit by balls from other groups. When practicing the high-to-low swing, which produces ground balls, the hitters and tossers can be positioned around the outfield edge of the infield, with the fielders in the outfield. More space is needed to practice hitting fly balls; therefore, using this drill as a station in a circuit is recommended.
- The fielder leaves the 10 balls with the tosser and takes the empty bucket out into the fielding position. The balls are deposited in the bucket after being fielded. The balls are brought in by the fielder, when rotating into the hitter or tosser role.

Instructions and Cues to Class

- The instructions to the tosser and the hitter are basically the same as for Drill 1. Add the following cues to the hitter regarding the desired swing path and to the tosser regarding the point of aim for the toss for each of the swing paths:
  a. "Hitter, a high-to-low swing path produces a ground ball; a low-to-high swing path produces a fly ball."
  b. "Tosser, when the hitter is attempting to hit a ground ball, toss the ball low in the contact zone so the hitter can swing down on the ball. Toss the ball high so the hitter can swing up to make contact at shoulder height when he or she is trying to hit a fly ball."
- "Fielders, field the ball using the correct technique and place the ball in the bucket. Remember to move into position so that you can field the ball in front of your body, not off to the side."
- "Even though you are not going to make a throw, practice fielding and bringing the ball to the throwing position all in one smooth, continuous motion. Then drop the ball in the bucket."

Student Option

- "You and your partner may set imaginary situations in which fly balls or grounders are called for; write them on individual cards. Before each toss, draw a card. The tosser tries to toss appropriately, and the batter hits according to the toss. Make up a scoring system for you and your partner to use."

Student Success Goal

- 20 of 30 correct hits (fly ball or grounder, as indicated by the swing path)

To Decrease Difficulty

- Have the batter hit only to high or low targets on a net. [3]
- Let the pair use a larger ball. [2]

To Increase Difficulty

- Have the batter hit fly balls or grounders, as appropriate, on random high or low tosses. [8]

Step 15 Fungo Hitting a Fly Ball

The skill of fungo hitting fly balls is one that has limited applicability to a student's development of hitting skill. Rather, it is a utilitarian skill a student should learn in order to help other students practice fielding fly balls. As in fungo hitting ground balls, bat control and eye-hand coordination are reinforced. Additionally, the swing path of the fungo-hit fly ball has carryover to the batting stroke in slow pitch. The tossed ball is descending, so the batter must swing slightly upward to make good contact and for the ball to come off the bat as a fly ball.

As you observe the students practicing this skill, key in on their swing path and their focus on the ball. The swing path must be from low to high. In order to swing low to high, the hitter must begin the swing with the bat down below the rear shoulder. Then the weight must be shifted to the back foot, and the rear shoulder must be dropped. The ball should be tossed higher than when fungo hitting ground balls, and contact on the swing should be at about shoulder height.

Many students fail to shift the weight back and drop the rear shoulder. Others do not toss the ball high enough, and the contact of the ball will then be low and the swing path of the bat relatively level. Students who miss the ball consistently are undoubtedly not watching the ball throughout the entire toss and descent. They probably look out to the target rather than see the bat hit the ball.

STUDENT KEYS TO SUCCESS

- Bat held in top hand and below rear shoulder
- Ball toss high
- Step toward target with front foot
- Weight shifts back, rear shoulder is dropped
- Swing path of bat low to high, ball contact at shoulder height
- Bat at front shoulder height on follow-through
- Watch ball through toss and contact

Fungo Hitting a Fly Ball Rating

CHECKPOINT	LESS EXPERIENCED	MORE EXPERIENCED
Preparation **Stance** **Bat Position** **Ball Position**	• Open • Even with rear shoulder • Midline of body at waist	• Square • Below rear shoulder • Toward target, over front foot
Execution **Ball Toss** **Front Foot** **Body Position** **Swing Path** **Contact Point**	• Low, only slightly above head • Stays planted • Erect • Low to level • Below shoulder	• High, far above head • Steps in direction of hit • Rear shoulder dropped • Low to high • Front shoulder level

CHECKPOINT	LESS EXPERIENCED	MORE EXPERIENCED
Follow-Through **Body Position** **Bat Position**	• Leaning forward • Wrapped around at waist height	• Weight back • Wrapped around at shoulder height

Error Detection and Correction for Fungo Hitting a Fly Ball

Most errors here are caused by a poor toss or an incorrect swing path. The common errors and correction suggestions are listed below. Remember, this skill is used only in practice; consequently, you must identify its utilitarian nature for your students.

ERROR

CORRECTION

1. Ground balls are hit.

1. Have the batter do one or more of the following: toss the ball higher; drop the rear shoulder and swing up at the ball; contact the ball at front shoulder height; or follow through up toward the sky.

CORRECTION

2. The hit does not go to the target.

2. Have your student step with the forward foot toward the target, and start with the glove side of the body toward the target.

3. The ball is always hit to the throwing-hand side.

3. The toss must be toward target, and at the front foot location.

ERROR	CORRECTION
4. The batter misses the ball completely.	4. The batter should watch the ball and see the bat make contact with it.

Fungo Hitting Fly Ball Drills

1. *Obstacle Drill*
[Corresponds to *Softball*, Step 15, Drill 1]

Group Management and Safety Tips

- An entire class cannot do this drill simultaneously. Use this drill as a station in a skill circuit with fielding, pitching, batting tee, or fungo hitting ground ball work.
- Obstacles that can be used for this drill include the softball or baseball backstops, soccer goals, football uprights, bleachers, field hockey goals, or fences around a tennis court.
- You would probably want students who are of the same experience level to practice together.
- Students need to be in pairs, the partners about 30 to 50 feet apart on opposite sides of the obstacle.

- Some obstacles will require that when the fly-ball fungo-hitter hits a bucket of balls, the partner must retrieve them. Then partners will switch roles and positions. Some obstacles are located so that partners can stay put and hit the ball over and back to one another.
- Be certain that the drill area is free of breakable things, such as windows.
- Space the pairs so that they are not hitting the ball into spaces occupied by another pair.

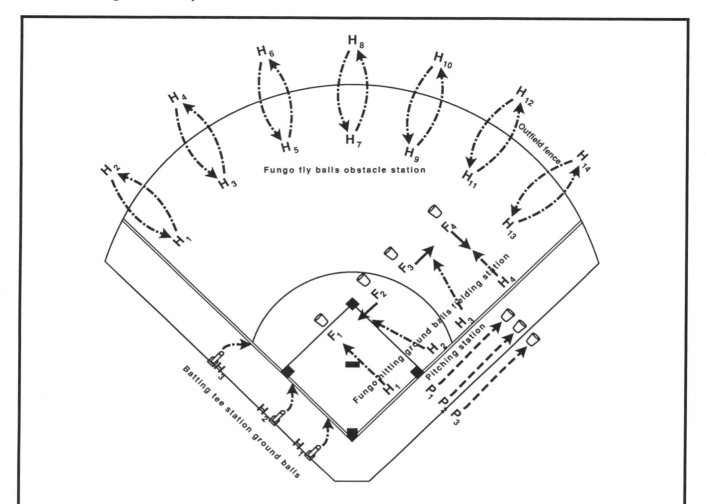

Equipment

- Bats, 1 per student (lightweight and short)
- Balls, 1 per student, or a container of 5 balls per student pair
- Markers to establish distances of players from partners and other pairs

Instructions to Class

- "Fungo hit the ball over the obstacle to your partner. Your partner will fungo hit the ball over the obstacle back to you."
- "You are trying to make 10 fungo hits that clear the obstacle. Count the number of tries it takes for you to get 10 over the obstacle."

Cues to Class

- "Toss the ball higher than you do when you are fungo hitting ground balls. Contact the ball at the height of your front shoulder."
- "Start with the bat low: Drop it below your rear shoulder. Then, if your toss is high enough, you can swing up at the ball. This will make the hit go up into the air."
- "Try dropping your rear shoulder down as you toss the ball up."
- "Step in the direction you want your hit to go. If you can't seem to step forward, maybe your toss is too much toward the centerline of your body. Move the toss more toward the target, so if it were to land without being hit, it would land by your front foot."
- "See the ball as the bat contacts it."
- "Bend your rear knee as you hit the ball. Swing up and through the ball."
- "Remember, both feet should be pointing toward the target when you make contact with the ball. Rotate your hips toward the target."
- "Reach for the clouds on your follow-through."

Student Options

- ''Have your partner watch you as you hit the ball. Your partner should focus on the swing path. If it is not low to high, together try to figure out what the problem is. Use the Keys to Success Checklist in *Softball*, Step 15.''
- ''Play a game with your partner. Each fungo hit that clears the obstacle is worth 1 point. Every time you swing and miss the ball completely you must subtract 1 point from your total. See how many points each of you can get in 10 attempts. Who won?''

Student Success Goal

- 10 hits that clear the obstacle in less than 15 attempts

To Decrease Difficulty

- Let the pair use a lower obstacle. [2]
- Lower the Success Goal. [3]

To Increase Difficulty

- Make the pair use a higher obstacle. [2]
- Move the hitter closer to the obstacle so the hit must be directed up quickly. [4]
- Set a goal of 5 consecutive fungo-hit fly balls that clear the obstacle. [1]
- Move the hitter farther away from the obstacle so the hit must travel a longer distance. [4]

2. *Accuracy Drill*
[Corresponds to *Softball*, Step 15, Drill 2]

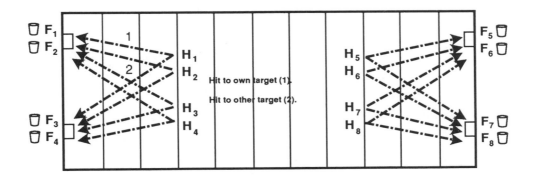

Group Management and Safety Tips

- This drill cannot be done by an entire class simultaneously. It should be included as a part of a skill circuit. It could actually be done with fielders rather than targets so that some students can practice fielding fly balls.
- There is no need to group students according to experience level.
- Students need to practice this drill in pairs or trios.
- It would be easy to set up this drill on an adjacent football, soccer, or field hockey field because distances are already marked on such fields. In addition, you could set up four stations. For each fungo hitter, there should be two 10-foot square targets per goal line, set even with what would be the hash marks on a football field. The fungo hitters hit from a point 100 feet away from the target toward the center of the field. Have two hitters on the hash marks so that they are at least 10 yards apart. The hitters' partners will be at the targets 100 feet away.

- The fungo hitters should have at least 5 balls at the hitting location.
- The fielding partners should each have a container into which they can drop the balls after they have collected them. When they switch roles with the hitter, they bring the bucket of balls to the hitting site, dump it, and give the container to the person going from hitting to fielding.
- The fielders need to be alert to both students fungo hitting toward the end line targets. Also, they must let the balls land before they attempt to field them.

Equipment

- Markers for targets, such as cones, loose bases, flags, and scrimmage vests
- Bats, 2 per student pair (students' choice of length and weight)
- Containers for collecting balls, 1 per student pair
- Balls, at least 5 per student pair

Instructions to Class

- "Hitters, fungo hit fly balls to the target. You are trying to get the ball to land in the target on the fly."
- "Each ball that lands in the target is worth 1 point. Fielders, you should keep score for your partner."
- "Remember, these are fly balls, so you want to have them go high into the air. They should be at least the height of the obstacle you hit over when you practiced the Obstacle Drill."
- "After the 5 balls are fungo hit, switch roles. Hitter, get the emptied container from your partner so you can collect the balls."
- "Repeat the drill until each of you has hit 20 fly balls."
- "Fielders, be aware that two people are hitting toward the end line that you are on. Don't field the ball on the fly; field it after it has landed."

Cues to Class

- "Step toward the target. If you miss the target, be sure that your toss is at the position of your front foot. Then step toward the target."
- "Swing low to high and contact the ball at shoulder height."
- "Watch the ball until the bat hits it. Look at the target first, then concentrate on your swing and contact with the ball. The target is not going to move, so don't look for it as you swing."

Student Option

- None: This skill is intended primarily to give fielding practice.

Student Success Goal

- 15 points in 20 attempts

To Decrease Difficulty

- Increase the size of the target. [4]
- Let the hitter stand closer to the target. [4]
- Let the hitter use a batting tee. [5]

To Increase Difficulty

- Decrease the size of the target. [4]
- Make hitter stand farther from the target (see *Softball*, Step 15, Drill 3). Put markers at 130 feet, 160 feet, and 190 feet. Have the students hit 5 balls from each distance and keep score according to the chart in their books. Do this drill on a different day due to increased management time. [4]
- Vary the direction of the hit (see *Softball*, Step 15, Drill 4). Put another target between the two existing end-line targets. Have the hitter now position him- or herself between the original target and the new center target. From the 130- or 160-foot mark, the student hits 5 balls first to the target to the right, then switches roles with the partner. Then partners switch again, and the hitter hits 5 balls to the target to the left. Have the students count the number of on-target hits at each target. In this drill it is important that the hitter's initial stance is square to a point directly between the two targets at which he or she hits. Do this drill on a different day as part of a progression. [3]

Step 16 Combining Fly Ball Fielding and Hitting

In this step your students practice fielding a fly ball off a hit. In the outfielder's role they move under fly balls, catch them, and in a continuous motion throw at distances and in directions that would occur in softball games.

Your cues should be focused on the actions used in combining fielding and throwing into one motion. Here your students need to work on getting behind and under the descending ball so that they are in position to immediately make a throw. Also, your students need to work on the defensive strategies inherent in outfield play. They must first think about where the throw is to go; this is done prior to the hit. Then they must move into position in order to field the ball while moving slightly in the direction of the throwing target. They must make an accurate throw (on the fly or a one-bounce throw) to the target. Your cues should direct the students to read the ball as it comes off the bat. The quicker they react to

the direction of the hit ball, the more likely they are to get into correct position to field it and to throw it to the proper location.

The outfielder is going to have to make the catch, then make a throw to stop a runner from scoring or advancing a base. You should explain this to the students and emphasize that this is the reason they must always think about where the runners are and about what base the ball must be thrown to.

STUDENT KEYS TO SUCCESS

- Think about where the throw is to go before the ball is hit
- Get quickly into position under and behind ball
- See ball go off the bat; react immediately by moving to spot where ball will descend
- Catch and throw in one motion

Combination Fly Ball and Overhand Throw Drills

1. Basic Fly Ball Drill
[Corresponds to *Softball*, Step 16, Drill 1]

Group Management and Safety Tips

- Although your students do not have to be grouped according to experience level to do this drill, it would probably be better if they were.
- Divide students into groups of three: a hitter, a catcher (and soft tosser, if so desired), and an outfielder.

- There is probably not sufficient space for all students in a large class to do this drill simultaneously on a softball diamond. However, if an adjacent field (football, soccer, field hockey) is available, several groups of three could practice there.

- The fielder is 130 to 150 feet away from the hitter and catcher. If the hitter or fielder is less experienced, move the fielder closer to the hitter. If the hitter and fielder are more experienced, you can move the fielder farther away from the hitter so that the throw is longer.
- The fielder must be aware of other outfielders going after fly balls. The hitter's responsibility is to protect the fielder by hitting the ball directly to him or her. The catcher should call to the fielder if there is any danger of a collision.
- The hitter hits (a fungo hit or from a soft toss—the hitter's choice) a fly ball to the fielder, who fields it and throws it overhand to the catcher at home. It should be a one-bounce throw to the catcher.

Equipment

- Gloves, 1 for each player
- Bats for each hitting location, choice of length and weight
- Balls, 1 per student (3 per group)
- Home plate, 1, or a loose base to represent home plate

Instructions and Cues to Class

- "Hitter, you hit a fly ball to the fielder. You must try to hit the ball close to the fielder so that he or she does not have to move into the path of other fielders."
- "Fielder, see the ball as it comes off the bat. Move into position under and behind it so that you can catch it while moving toward the catcher at home plate. Then, throw a full overhand throw that bounces once before it reaches the catcher."
- "React quickly to the hit so that you can move into position to make the catch and throw all in the same motion."
- "Use the crow-hop, if you need to, after the catch."
- "The one-bounce throw should be like a line drive rather than a fly ball. It takes less time if the ball is thrown so that it would hit the shoulder of a fielder who is standing in the line of fire than if it would loop well over the head of such an infielder."
- "Catcher, call out 'Home, home!' as the fielder is making the catch. This helps the

fielder know where to throw the ball. This is always done in a game."
- "Hitter, hit 10 fly balls to the fielder. Each of you needs to keep track of the number of catchable hits you make, the number of catches and on-target throws, and the number of catches at home."
- "After 10 hits, rotate positions. You decide the rotation order."

Student Options

- "You can either fungo hit the fly balls or have the catcher give you the soft toss."
- "You can move the fielder closer or farther away, if you think you are ready for that."

Student Success Goals

- 8 of 10 on-target fly balls
- 8 of 10 fielding and on-target throwing combinations
- 8 of 10 catches at home

To Decrease Difficulty

- Decrease the distance of the hit (and the throw). [4]
- Let the group use a softer ball, such as an IncrediBall®. [2]

To Increase Difficulty

- Increase the distance of the hit (and the throw). [4]
- Have the hitter vary the direction of the hit so the fielder has to move farther. [8]
- Have the hitter vary the distance and direction of the hit and the subsequent throw. [8]
- Have the group do the Back to the Fence Drill (see *Softball*, Step 16, Drill 5). The setup is the same except that the hitter and catcher line up about 130 feet from the outfield fence. The fielder stands 30 feet from the fence. The hitter hits a fly ball close to the fence. The fielder does the drop step, retreats toward the fence, and makes the catch. The fielder must first use peripheral vision to sight the fence, then slow his or her run to go right up to the fence. Then the fielder comes back to field the ball and throws home to the catcher. [7]

2. Lateral Drill
[Corresponds to *Softball*, Step 16, Drill 2]

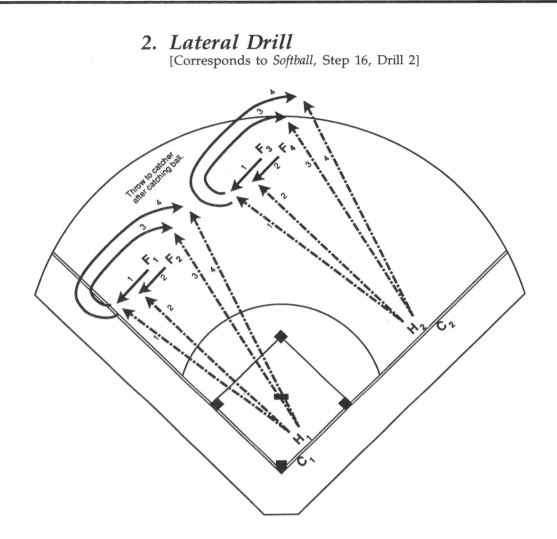

Group Management and Safety Tips

- This drill is best done with your students grouped according to experience level.
- Once again, this drill cannot be simultaneously done by all your students on one softball diamond. Use an adjacent field if it is available. Otherwise, put more people in the outfield positions.
- The students in each group form pairs. Two pairs work together. One pair is the hitter and catcher, positioned as at home plate. The other pair are outfielders, positioned as in center field. If you must put more students in each setup, have two pairs of students in the outfield. All four students will be located together in center field.
- The hitter hits a fly ball that travels to the left of the fielders so that the first fielder has to run laterally 60 feet to get into po-

sition to make the catch. The fielder catches the ball, stops, and makes an overhand throw to the catcher. Then the fielder continues 10 feet farther left and waits for the other fielders to take turns running toward him or her to field flies.
- When all the fielders have had their turns and are together again, the hitter hits balls that the fielders have to run 60 feet to the right to catch. Then the previous sequence of turns is repeated to the opposite side.
- After each fielder has fielded two hits to the left and two hits to the right, the catcher and the hitter change roles. The new hitter also hits two balls to the left and two balls to the right for each fielder.
- Then the pair at home switches roles with the pair in the outfield.
- Once again, safety is the responsibility of the hitter and catcher.

Equipment

- Gloves, 1 per student
- Balls, 1 per student pair
- Bats at each station, a choice of lengths and weights
- Loose bases or other markers for home plates

Instructions to Class

- "Hitters, hit a fly ball that makes the outfielder run at least 60 feet to the left to make the catch. Do the same for each of the fielders. Then hit fly balls at least 60 feet to the right of the fielders in their new location."
- "Fielders, you start in a line, and one of you at a time fields a fly ball. After you field the ball, throw it overhand to the catcher. Then move at least 10 feet more in the direction you were running before. Wait there while the other fielders get their turns to field balls."
- "Fielders, react to the ball off the bat. Run as hard as you can to get to the ball. Catch it and stop your lateral movement. From your stopped position, turn, step or crow-hop, and throw the ball to the catcher."
- "Catcher, call out 'Home, home!' as the fielder is catching the ball. Make a big, clear target with your glove for the fielder to throw at."
- "Hitter, be sure you get out of the way of the catcher while he or she is catching the fielder's throw."
- "Keep track of the number of catchable hits, fly ball catches, on-target throws, and catches at home you make."
- "Hitter and catcher, change roles after each fielder has had two fly balls to the left and two to the right. Repeat the drill. Then change positions with the outfielders."

Cues to Class

- "Fielders, stop as soon as possible after the catch. You want to make the throw home as soon as you can."
- "Do not throw sidearm. Concentrate on the full overhand throw so that the ball does not curve as it travels in to the catcher."

Student Options

- "Compare your scores as a hitter, a catcher, and a fielder. Determine where you need the most practice. Figure out a way you can practice your weakness either at home or the next time you get a chance to have a choice of practice tasks."
- "Hit the ball both from the ball toss and as fungo hitting."

Student Success Goals

- 5 of 8 on-target hits
- 5 of 8 error-free fielding and throwing combinations
- 6 of 8 error-free catches at home

To Decrease Difficulty

- Decrease the distance the fielder has to run to catch the ball. [4]
- Decrease the distance the fielder has to throw the ball. [4]
- Decrease the distance the hitter has to hit the ball. [4]
- Let the group use any type of softer ball. [2]

To Increase Difficulty

- Increase the distance the fielder has to run to catch the ball. [4]
- Increase the distance the fielder has to throw the ball. [4]
- Vary the distance the fielder has to run to catch the ball. [8]
- Vary the distance the fielder has to throw the ball. [8]
- Have the students do the "I've Got It" Drill (see *Softball*, Step 16, Drill 3). The setup is virtually the same, except that the pairs in the outfield are not in the same location but are located as if one is in center field and the other is in left field. The hitter hits a fly ball between the two fielders. Both fielders run to catch the ball; the fielder who gets there first yells "I've got it!" and catches the ball. The other outfielder has assumed a backing-up position. An overhand, one-bounce throw is made to the catcher. The fielders exchange positions and the drill is repeated. Then the pairs switch positions. [6]

3. In the Air Drill
[Corresponds to *Softball*, Step 16, Drill 4]

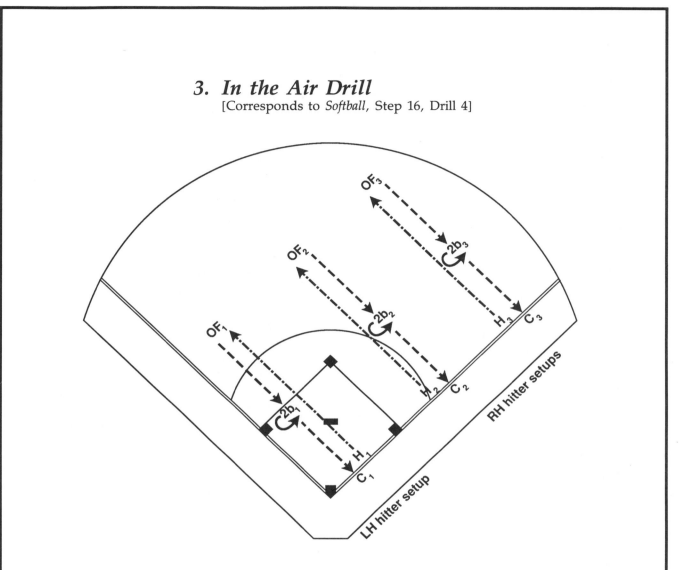

Group Management and Safety Tips
- The group setup is almost the same for this drill as for the previous drill.
- One fielder is positioned in center field, and the other is at second base.
- The hitter hits a fly ball to the outfielder in center field. The outfielder makes the catch and throws an overhand throw to the player at second base. The player at second base pivots and makes an overhand throw to the catcher.

Equipment
- Gloves, 1 per student
- Balls, 1 per student pair
- Bats, a choice at each hitting location
- Loose bases or markers, 1 to represent home plate at each station

Instructions and Cues to Class
- "Hitters, hit 10 fly balls to the outfielders. Then switch roles with your partner. The fielders do the same. After the next 10 hits, you and your partner switch positions with the two fielders."
- "Outfielder, make sure that your throws are overhand. The throws are short enough for you to throw the ball in a straight line in the air to the fielder covering second base. You are practicing a relatively short overhand throw; do not use a one-bounce throw. In a game, you are responsible for getting the ball to the fielder in a catchable manner."
- "Keep track of the number of successes you have in each role."

- "Second baseman, as you gain confidence in your throw, gradually throw with greater force to home. After receiving a throw from the outfield, if you have to throw home, it is because a runner is attempting to score. Your throw must be accurate and low to catch a sliding baserunner. Aim your throw for the catcher's knees."

Student Options

- "Hitter, when you feel the outfielder is ready, you can make him or her move a bit to the right or left to catch the ball. You can also make him or her move in or back to make the initial catch."
- "Make up a game using the skills in this drill. Set up the game so that one pair is competing against the other. Don't make it too complicated. Focus the game on correct use of the skills."

Student Success Goals

- 8 of 10 catchable hits
- 8 of 10 outfield catches and on-target throws
- 9 of 10 catches at second base and on-target throws
- 9 of 10 catches at home plate

To Decrease Difficulty

- Let the group use any type of softer ball. [2]
- Change the distance of the throw to second base so that it is easy for the outfielder to make a throw on the fly to the second baseman. [4]
- Change the distance of the throw toward home so that it is easier for the second baseman to make an accurate throw. [4]

To Increase Difficulty

- Lengthen the distance between the outfielder and the second baseman. [4]
- Have the hitter vary the distance of the fly balls so that the outfielder has to move to the ball and throw different distances to second base. [4, 8]
- Have the hitter vary the direction of the fly ball so that the outfielder has to move to get into position to make the throw and has to throw to second base from various locations. [8]
- Have the hitter randomly vary the direction and distance of the fly ball so that the outfielder has to react to the ball off the bat, then adjust the throw to second base according to direction and distance. [8]

Step 17   Position-Play Half-Field Games

Your students have practiced a sufficient number of skills to apply them in games. It is not yet time for them to play the full softball game because there are still more skills they must practice. It is also important for the students to use the skills they have acquired in situations where the game options are reduced in complexity.

The key to the modified game in this step is practice while playing the games. Consequently, it is essential that you, the teacher, do not simply let your students play. This would detract from the students' development as knowledgeable and effective players of the game. Help the students recognize the defensive situations as they arise by calling their attention to the runners on base, the number of outs, the base to which the throw should go, and the nature of the base coverage and backing-up responsibilities. You can help the students develop their offensive decision-making skills by asking questions regarding where the ball should be hit when runners are on base with whatever number of outs. The baserunners need to learn to judge when to advance a base and when to hold the base they have attained.

You should stop play before each new batter and tell the students the new situation that has developed. Then ask them what the offensive options and defensive responsibilities are in this situation. This approach is usually the best one to use with your less experienced students.

With your more experienced students, however, as the games progress, you can gradually shift the situation analysis to the students. Ask them questions about the situation and what the options and responsibilities of the opposite team would be. If the offensive hitters and baserunners can tell you what the defense is supposed to do in a situation, then they surely will be able to adjust their offensive skills to counter the defense. Similarly, if the defensive players can determine the best offensive option for the situation at hand, they surely will be ready to react to the play that develops. Another role for your more experienced students would be to have them serve as coaches for the less experienced ones. They can analyze the situation and ask the questions that will help the less experienced players develop game strategy and experience success in the anticipation and decision making required to apply their offensive and defensive skills strategically and correctly.

Your students will undoubtedly want simply to play. It is important that you resist the temptation to allow them to do so. Try to impress upon them that softball is a game in which there must be significant analysis of the plays and situations. The modified game will help the students learn to use the skills they have acquired in ways called for by the full game. This will make them more effective players in the long run.

It is also likely that each student will select a single position in which he or she feels comfortable, then stick to it. Encourage the students to try playing more than one position.

These learning activities are not designed for the students to show they are perfect; rather, they are opportunities for the students to improve their skills and decision making. Errors and mental lapses are to be expected; all athletes and ballplayers learn from their mistakes. Let your students know that now, in these games, is the time to make the mistakes. They will discover what they have yet to learn and what they need to work on in order to become more knowledgeable and proficient softball players. You are vital to your students' acceptance of this premise. Try to establish a climate in which it is okay to make errors. Let your students know that no one is perfect and that no one has the right to belittle anyone for a lack of exposure or experience in playing these games. These games are not ''for blood''— they are for practice!

Warm-Up Drills and Half-Field Games

The activities of this step are explained in great detail in *Softball*, Step 17. Consequently, this book presents only the ''Group Management and Safety Tips,'' ''Equipment,'' ''To Decrease Difficulty,'' and ''To Increase Difficulty'' sections. Additionally, where appropriate, some teaching cues or situation options will be identified.

1. Warm-Up Before the Game Drills

[Corresponds to *Softball*, Step 17, Warm-Up Before the Game Drills]

Group Management and Safety Tips

- This drill can be done by all students. It will be done more efficiently if your students are divided by experience level. The grouping also should be done for this drill because the next drill, Half-Field Modified Games, requires such for liability reasons.
- The directions in the participant's book specify that this drill can be repeated each inning. This may take away too much game time. However, this drill can be practiced each day of class. It provides an excellent warm-up and a practice of the fielding and throwing options that are called for in softball games. In addition, the drill forces students to show position-play knowledge because the defensive responsibilities of covering and backing-up are inherent in the drill.

- Encourage your students to play a different position each time the drill is used. This is a nonthreatening way for them to practice the skills and coverage responsibilities of each position.
- On the day that this drill is taught, it would be helpful to remind your students to bring their textbooks so that they can review the Position Play Keys to Success Checklist for covering and backing-up responsibilities, found in Step 10.
- It would be very helpful for you to make three large posters of the sequences used in this warm-up drill. One poster for the order of outfield catches and throws can be made by copying the chart in the textbook. A second poster of the infield portion of the drill can also be made by copying the appropriate chart in the

textbook. Finally, a third poster showing the infield warm-up return throws should be made. Be certain to put these posters on substantial paper and either laminate them or cover them with plastic wrap to make them windproof and rainproof.

- One way of teaching this warm-up drill (which, incidentally, is a form of the warm-up traditionally used by most softball and baseball teams) is to do one section of the drill each day. On Day 1 you can focus on the outfield portion of the drill. Have the students do the outfield portion, then rotate the outfielders to the infield positions. This rotation will have to be made twice so that all 11 students will have the opportunity to practice the outfield portion of the drill. On Day 2 you can focus on the infield portion of the drill. On Day 3 you can teach the return-throw portion of the drill. After that point, you can use the drill as a whole as a warm-up for the class and for game play.

- A diamond needs to be set up for each group of 11 students. One can be set up on the softball field and the other on a grass field. It is probably best to have your less experienced players play on the regulation field because the ball is likely to take truer bounces there.

- Extra players can rotate into the drill by simply standing off the field of play on the sideline closest to the position into which they will rotate. After the first person has completed a turn at a position, the extra player will take his or her place. The person who goes to the sideline will stay out for one rotation of the drill, then exchange places with a player in a different position on the field. This way, no one player remains out of the action for very long, and the students must play a variety of positions.

- Be sure that you are not the fungo hitter for the warm-up drill. You may have to be the hitter the first time teaching the drill, but if it is possible for you to have a student do the fungo hitting, do so. The large posters should make it possible for the students to follow the order of the drill. Then you can move between the two

stations and give the supervision and help that is needed.

- Ask the players who are sitting out or waiting their turn to read the order of the drill from the chart to the students on the field.

- Have the student who is doing the fungo hitting (this can be a more experienced player on the less experienced field) begin slowly. It is helpful to hit two consecutive balls to each player so that there is some reinforcement of the actions that occur.

- Your attention and cuing should focus on the covering and backing-up responsibilities of the players. Every player should be moving on every play. If a player is having technical skill difficulties, do not take time in this warm-up drill to work on that. Rather, make a note of the problem and talk with the student later about a way to practice that problem skill.

Equipment

- Gloves, 1 per student
- Three bases and a home plate, 1 set per diamond
- Buckets of balls (IncrediBalls® and soft regulation balls), 1 at each field
- Posters of the drill order
- Bats of varying lengths and weights at each station

To Decrease Difficulty

- Slow down the drill. [3]
- Use softer balls. [2]
- Remind everyone before each hit where they are to go and how the action is to progress. [1]
- Have the fungo hitter hit directly to the fielders. [4]

To Increase Difficulty

- Have the students make the throws for tag plays and for force plays in accordance with the fungo hitter's call. [8]
- Have the fungo hitter challenge the fielders by moving them greater distances to field the ball. [4]
- Have the fungo hitter vary the force at which the ball is hit. [8]

2. Half-Field Games

[Corresponds to *Softball*, Step 17, Half-Field Games]

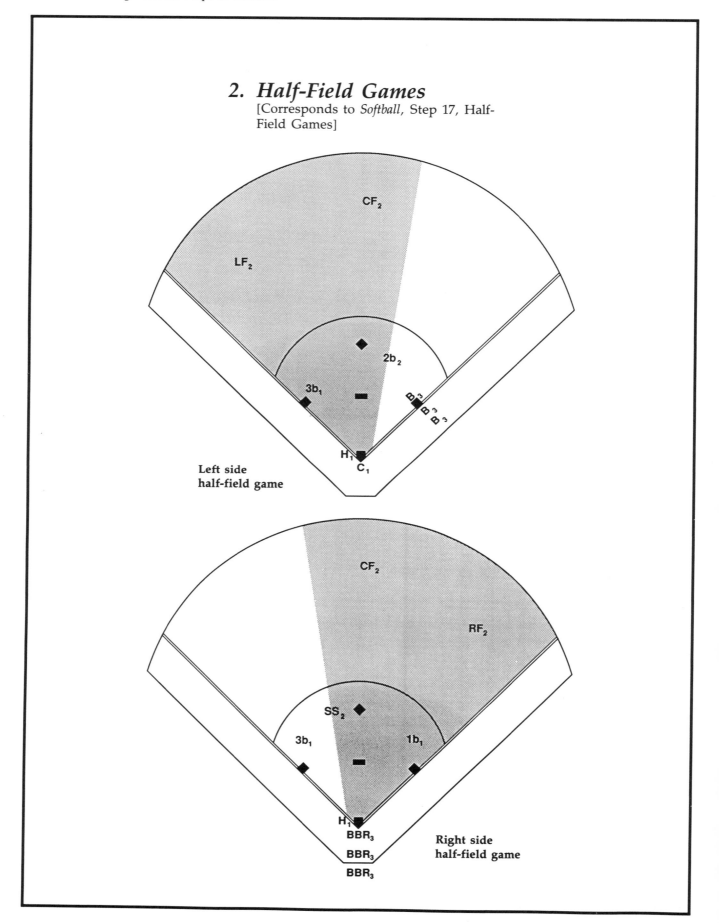

**Left side
half-field game**

**Right side
half-field game**

Group Management and Safety Tips

- The tips are the same for both half-field modified games.
- The students should be grouped by experience level.
- The games require only nine players each, but extra students can serve as base coaches, umpires, and scorekeepers. Simply group the extras into threesomes to rotate into the game as a unit. When there are extras, the inning is complete when each group of 3 has batted. With each three-out rotation, have the extra group rotate in as baserunners; have the hitter, the catcher, and the third baseman (or second baseman, depending upon the game) rotate out to become base coaches and umpire.
- Have the students read the rules to the game before they come to class.
- Be sure that you have two copies of the student textbook with you so that one can be put at each field. They are then available for the students to check on rules when you are not at that diamond.
- As in the previous drill, this game can be set up on the regulation field and on an adjacent grass field (or the baseball diamond, if available). Once again, the less experienced should probably be on the diamond unless the infield is skinned. A grass infield slows the ground balls and would be helpful for the less experienced players.
- It is a temptation to combine both levels of players in one group. However, to do that is to increase your legal liability vulnerability. It is important to have students of like skill playing the games together as a unit.
- If there are extra more experienced players, one way to use them would be to have them serve as coaches for the less experienced game. They could set the situation before each fungo hit, then ask questions of the players as to what their responsibilities will be on the play that follows. They can then give feedback on the actual execution of the play as it occurred. Be sure to tell your more experienced students to coach the position play, backing-up, hitting, and baserunning strategies rather than give skill execution feedback. Remind the more experienced players serving as coaches to be very positive as they work with the less experienced players. Stress that this is a learning game and that the students need to feel it is okay to make mistakes.
- In these games it is critical that the fungo hitter play on the side of the baserunners. It would otherwise be possible for the fungo hitter to play for his or her group of three and hit balls so that the baserunners are likely to be put out. Remind the students that these games are for practice, and practice will occur only if people do what is called for by the situation in each position that they play.

Equipment

- Gloves, 1 per student
- Bats of various lengths and weights at each station
- Buckets of balls (IncrediBalls® and soft regulation balls) at each station
- Three bases and home plate, 1 set on each field

To Decrease Difficulty

- Let the students use a softer ball. [2]
- Have the fungo hitter throw the ball rather than fungo hit it. [3]

To Increase Difficulty

- The fungo hitter should be reminded to really challenge the fielders. [8]
- Have the more experienced players use a regulation ball. [2]

Step 18 Hitting a Pitched Ball

This final step on hitting appears late in the participant's textbook because the progression is developed with the less experienced student in mind. In reality, drills from this step would be incorporated for your more experienced students earlier in a unit of softball. Refer to Step 5 in *Softball* for the detailed explanation of hitting. The Student Keys to Success listed on p. 155 are the major points on which to focus your observations and around which to develop your teaching cues. However, the three phases of the Keys to Success and the Keys to Success Checklist in Step 5 of the participant's textbook will provide you with more complete lists for cuing.

The skill-station, skill-circuit, and task-lesson concepts are continually recommended to you as options for teaching softball skills because they maximize facility and equipment use and address the problem of different experience levels typically found in the class situation. In focusing a lesson on hitting, it makes little sense to have students of different experience levels all performing the same batting tee drill when stations using the batting tee, fungo hitting, the soft toss, and the pitched ball would better meet their needs. Both groups need not rotate through each station as in a true circuit. Rather, groups can be assigned to practice stations matching their experience level; then they rotate through only those stations with tasks at their level.

As previously mentioned, your more experienced students can benefit from practice time on the tee, fungo hitting, and the soft toss. However, they will need to move more quick-

ly to practice situations using a pitched ball than will the less experienced students. The more experienced student's motivation to practice hitting in conditions other than using a pitched ball is increased when the practice situations are combined with fielding practice, modified games, and so forth.

Most of all, your more experienced students (or all students for that matter) simply want to play the game. In a class-situation full game, though, a student might come to bat once or twice and could get as few as two swings at a pitched ball. Skill in hitting is not developed very quickly when "practice" consists of two swings two or three times a week. Drills for hitting a pitched ball that are challenging to the student will help develop hitters more efficiently and effectively than will regulation game play. Motivation is a factor affecting learning in any practice setting. Your less experienced students need to move through the other progressive hitting steps to experience hitting the pitched ball even before the overall hitting technique is perfected. They can then move back and forth to hitting-drill situations of lesser and greater difficulty.

For the less experienced student, the major challenges in hitting a pitched ball are to predict the flight of the pitched ball and to time the swing to make contact with the ball in the hitting contact zone. Direct your cuing to their swing timing. The inexperienced hitter faced with hitting a pitched ball for the first time tends to revert back to the arm swing alone. Technique takes a back seat to the desire to hit the ball by making contact in any way possible. You continually need to reinforce correct technique, especially the hitter's focus on the ball, the hip turn, and the pivot on the feet.

For the more experienced players, in addition to giving technique reminders, you need to begin to focus on their ability to meet the situational demands of hitting in a game. The ability to place-hit the ball has been mentioned in conjunction with drills and modified games using the batting tee. However, both the cognitive and the physical aspects of situational hitting need to be emphasized to the technically more experienced hitters in the pitched-ball hitting drills.

Any of the drills presented in this step can be done as combined drills, with fielders practicing the skills of fielding ground balls and fly balls, throwing, and catching. As the drills take on more complexity, your task of observing and cuing performances is made greater as you watch more people.

STUDENT KEYS TO SUCCESS

- Focus on ball in pitcher's hand
- Initiate swing with step and opening of hips and shoulders
- Time swing to make contact with ball ahead of front foot
- Perfect contact position
- Swing through ball
- Follow-through height of bat should match end of intended swing path

Pitched Ball Hitting Drills

1. *Bleacher Ball Drop Drill*
[Corresponds to *Softball*, Step 18, Drill 1]

Group Management and Safety Tips

- The drill can be done inside with fleece balls or whiffleballs, or outside with regulation balls.
- The setup can include just the feeder and the hitter or fielders.
- Use the home plate from a set of indoor bases, if available. Otherwise the hitter's glove can serve as home plate.
- Make sure the plate is set far enough away from the bleachers so that as the hitter swings, the bat does not hit the bleachers.
- The dropped ball simulates the slow-pitch pitch's entering the strike zone. As with the soft toss, the tosser controls the drill and must make accurate drops if the hitter is to practice effectively.

- The partner dropping the ball needs to stand in the bleachers slightly ahead of the hitter so that the ball drops down toward the hitter in a path similar to a legal pitch.

Equipment

- Bucket of 10 balls (fleece or whiffle if inside, leather or IncrediBalls® if outside), 1 per hitting station
- An empty bucket if fielder is used but does not throw back to the hitting area
- Gloves, 1 per student
- Bats, 2 or 3 of varying weights, lengths, and grip sizes per station
- Cones, hoops, ropes, or loose bases to mark target areas, if desired

Instructions and Cues to Class

- ''Tosser, drop the ball so that it simulates a slow pitch pitch's dropping into the strike zone and moving toward the back point of home plate.''
- ''Hitter, time your swing so that you make contact with the ball as it comes into the contact zone by your front foot. Remember the position you want to be in at the point of contact: feet pivoted on the ball of the back foot and the heel of the front, hips square to the line of flight of the ball, arms extended, and head down so you see the bat hit the ball.''
- ''Fielder(s), see the ball leave the bat, quickly move into position, field the ground ball or fly ball, and in one smooth, continuous motion, (a) bring it to the throwing position, then drop it in the bucket; or (b) throw the ball to the catcher. Be sure to use the overhand throw.''

Student Option

- ''Have the tosser critique your swing by focusing on your contact position and your head position.''

Student Success Goal

- 8 of 10 balls hit beyond a target distance of 100 feet or reaching the fielder

To Decrease Difficulty

- Do not use a target distance. [4]
- Lower the Success Goal. [3]

To Increase Difficulty

- Prior to dropping the ball, the tosser could specify the type of hit that must be executed—a fly ball or a ground ball. [8]
- Use specific targets that must be hit. Place them at varying distances and directions. [8]

2. Call Ball or Strike Drill

[Corresponds to *Softball*, Step 18, Drill 2]

Group Management and Safety Tips

- If desired, this drill can be done with your entire class.
- Group the class in threes, not necessarily by experience levels: a pitcher, a hitter, and a catcher.
- In the outfield, mark with cones the ends of lines parallel with and 46 feet from the outfield foul lines.
- Using the left- and right-field foul lines as the pitchers' plate (rubber), arrange the groups so that there is a minimum of 10 feet between pitchers on a line. The pitcher can use the foul line to practice the pivot foot's positioning on the rubber. The batter (with a bat) and the catcher (wearing a mask) set up on the 46-foot line directly opposite their pitcher.
- If the class is large or there are not enough catcher's masks, eliminate the bat from the drill.
- If a sufficient number of home plates are not available, have the batter use his or her glove for home plate, or place loose bases so that a corner points toward the catcher like the point of home plate.
- Have the players rotate roles after 10 pitches.

Equipment

- Regulation softball, 1 per group of three
- Extra regulation softballs
- Gloves, 1 per student
- Bats, 1 per group
- Catcher's masks, 1 per group
- Indoor-type home plates or loose bases, 1 per group

Instructions and Cues to Class

- ''Each role in the group is important. However, the purpose of the drill is to give the hitter practice watching the pitch and judging whether it is a ball or a strike.''
- ''While in the pitching role, try to throw strikes, but try to hit the corners rather than the middle of the plate. The batter will have more difficulty judging whether the pitch on the corners of the plate is a ball or strike. In addition, in a game the corner pitch is more difficult to hit, so you want to practice your placement of that pitch.''
- ''The hitter should take the stride into the pitch and initiate the swing with the hips and shoulders only—keeping the hands and arms still. *Do not swing the bat at the ball*. Watch the ball and call a ball if the pitch was outside the strike zone or a strike if it passes through the strike zone.''
- ''The catcher verifies the call of the pitch by the batter.''
- ''Remember, the slow-pitch strike zone is that area over home plate between the batter's high shoulder and the top of the knees.''

Student Options

- ''Have the catcher call the pitch and the batter verify the call.''
- ''Have the batter call the type of hit that is dictated by the pitch (only on strikes): if an inside pitch, pull the ball; if outside, hit to the opposite field; if low, ground ball; if high, go for the home run. The catcher will verify the location of the strike pitch.''
- ''Use an umpire to verify the call by the batter.''

Student Success Goals

- 6 of 10 strikes by the pitcher
- 8 of 10 hitter calls agreed to by catcher

To Decrease Difficulty

- Let the players use a larger plate (strike zone). [4]
- Let the hitter use a larger ball (this may increase difficulty for the pitcher, however). [2]

To Increase Difficulty

- Let the pitcher count only pitches that cross the corners of the plate as strikes. [4]
- Use an umpire to verify the batter's call. The batter gets no points if his or her call is not agreed to by the umpire. [6]

3. Contact Drill
[Corresponds to *Softball*, Step 18, Drill 3]

Group Management and Safety Tips

- In a class situation, this drill is best done in conjunction with other practice drills. Because the diamond is not needed for this drill, combine it on an adjacent field area with skill practice that necessitates the use of the diamond.
- Each Contact Drill station should be made up of four or five students of a similar level of experience.
- The drill is set up with a pitcher, who is 46 feet away from a hitter and a catcher, and one or two fielders to field the balls hit to an unobstructed area.
- If you set up more than one station of this drill, be sure to allow enough room between the groups so that balls hit from one group will not go into another group's area.
- Determine the scope of the fielding practice. Are throws to be included? If so, are they to be of varying distances and directions?
- See *Softball*, Step 18, Drill 13 for scoring chart.

Equipment

- Balls, 1 per student, placed in a bucket at the catcher's position and out of the way of the catcher
- Gloves, 1 per student
- Home plates, 1 per station
- Bats, 2 or 3 per station

Instructions and Cues to Class

- "Pitcher, try to throw a strike on every pitch. Remember, even though this is pitching practice for you, the major focus of the drill is on batting practice for the hitter, and the hitter should be swinging only at strikes."
- "Hitter, take a full swing at each pitch that is a strike. Try to make good contact. Focus on contacting the ball out front, opposite your front foot."

- "Watch the ball go all the way to the bat."
- "Take a smooth, fluid swing at the ball. Just make contact—do not try to hit the ball hard."
- "Hit the middle of the ball."
- "Fielders, watch the ball come off the bat. Start moving to the ball as soon as you see it leave the bat. Do not wait until the ball approaches you out in the field to start your move to the ball."
- "Try to be moving in on the ball as you catch it. This will help add force to your throw to the catcher."
- "Use a one-bounce throw if you cannot throw the ball on a line in the air to the catcher. No moon shots!"

Student Option

- "Have a partner use the hitting checklist from either Step 5 or Step 14 to reevaluate your technique.
  a. "Compare the hitting checklist done in this drill with the one you did in Step 5 or Step 14. Have you improved? Where are your major difficulties?"
  b. "Compare your technique on the checklist items with your hitting performance. Can you consistently make contact with the ball?"

Student Success Goal

- 25 points on 10 strike pitches

To Decrease Difficulty

- Do not use the scoring chart. Instead, count 1 point for every hit that goes anywhere in fair territory. [1]
- Score any ball that lands in fair territory and ends up in the outfield (see *Softball*, Step 18, Drill 4). [1]

To Increase Difficulty

- Have the batter hit line drives only (see *Softball*, Step 18, Drill 5). [3]

4. Hit the Gap Drill
[Corresponds to *Softball*, Step 18, Drill 6]

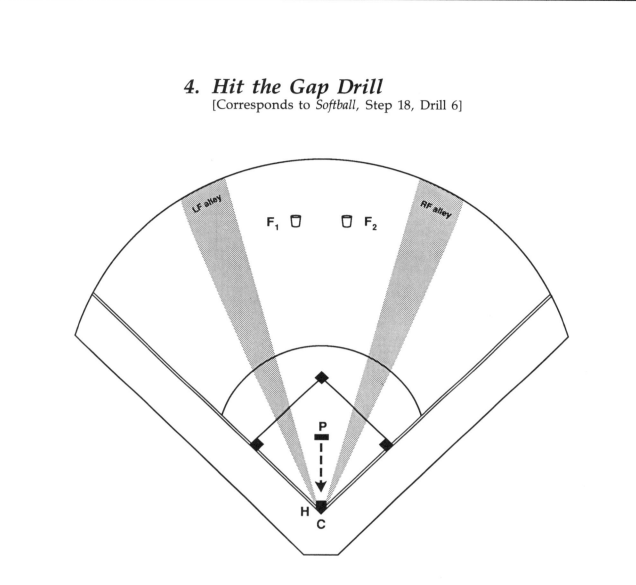

Group Management and Safety Tips
- These are same as for Drill 3.
- If you wish to include outfielders' throws, place an infielder at second base.
- See *Softball*, Step 18, Drill 6 for scoring chart.

Equipment
- This is the same as for Drill 3.
- Also, use a line marker for alley lines or cones at the outfield fence end of alleys.

Instructions and Cues to Class
- Use the instructions you did for Drill 3.
- ''Hitter, attempt to hit the ball into the target areas and all the way to the outfield fence. Not only would a ball hit into these areas result in a base hit for you, but you would also probably advance any base-runners one or more bases.''
- ''It is called 'hitting behind the runner' when you hit to the alley in right field when there is a runner on first or second base.''
- ''Fielder, retrieve the ball and place it in the empty bucket; or stand near the out-field fence, field the ball, and throw it in to a fielder covering second base.''

Student Options

- "Before the ball is pitched, determine into which alley you will attempt to place your hit."
- "Based on the location of the pitched ball, hit the ball to the appropriate alley: A right-handed batter sends an inside pitch to the left-field alley, an outside pitch to the right-field alley."

Student Success Goal

- 20 points on 10 hits

To Decrease Difficulty

- Require only 10 points on 10 hits. [3]
- Increase the size of the alley. [4]

To Increase Difficulty

- Decrease the size of the alley [4]
- Make the batter hit the ball to the appropriate alley, based on the pitch location. [8]
- Have the batter hit behind the runner (see *Softball*, Step 18, Drill 7). [1]

Step 19 **Situation-Ball Game**

As in Step 17, ''Position-Play Half-Field Games,'' this step provides practice options for the students in game play. All of the preliminary discussion in Step 17 applies to the practice involved in this step as well. It will not be repeated here, so please reread the introduction to Step 17. Additionally, the actual content for the games of the step is summarized in Step 19 of the textbook. As you read *Softball*, Step 19, pay particular attention to the sections entitled ''What to Practice,'' and the ''Reading a Situation Keys to Success Checklists.'' The items in these sections are essentially the questions you should ask the students to think about as they play the modified game (defensively and offensively).

When your students first begin situation ball, it will probably be necessary for you to set the situations that they will practice. As they become more adept at anticipating the play that the situation calls for and then reacting accordingly, you can give them a list of optional situations from which they can select those they wish to practice. Your more experienced students will undoubtedly be able to describe situations for practice. The less experienced students, however, will more than likely be dependent upon you to set the stage for their practice. You can probably use some of your more experienced players to serve as coaches for the less experienced teams. These more experienced ballplayers can then help identify game situations that need to be practiced.

The participant's book calls for a team meeting to determine which situation to practice. It would be advantageous, timewise, for you to assign the students to have this meeting completed by the beginning of the class period. If each class day you assigned different persons to serve as team captains and gave them the responsibility for the next class of surveying team members to determine the practice situations, it would certainly save class time for practice. The team captains could also make sure that the team members change positions during the game and that everyone gets a chance to participate in the game situations being practiced.

Remember, this is an opportunity for students to practice game situations. Do not allow the students simply to play. Use the time between batters to talk over the offensive and defensive situation presented. Have the students analyze the situation and identify the offensive and defensive tactics that must be involved in the following play. Try to get as many of the students as possible involved in this mental assessment of the situation. This is an opportunity for students to learn the strategy of the game of softball. If you or one or two of the students do all of the analysis and anticipation of options, then the chance for all students to become real participants in the game is lost.

1. Situation-Ball Game
[Corresponds to *Softball*, Step 19]

Groups Management and Safety Tips

- Your class must be divided into two experience-level groups.
- If there are extra players, allow them to bat whether they are in the actual game or not. Rotate them into the defensive portion of the game at each inning change.
- Encourage students to actively participate in the "thinking" part of the game. This is as important at this stage of their progress as is physical expertise in executing the skills.
- Each inning is devoted to practicing the situation set by one of the teams playing the game. The situations in odd-numbered innings are set by one team, those in even innings by the other team.
- The situation to be practiced is set at the start of each inning. Play is first made on that preset situation. The inning is played out as is appropriate for the new situations that arise in the course of play.
- Constantly reinforce for your students the necessity of analyzing every new situation. This analysis is to be done between the time the previous play was completed and the time the new batter enters the batting box. Your students will never remember all the questions on the offensive and defensive checklists, so it will be up to you to provide verbal or written cuing on those concepts. Again, large posters with the cue questions could be made. Another possibility is to have the students who are not participating read the checklists from the textbook.
- Be sure that you have two textbooks with you. One can be used at each field so that your students can look at them to remind themselves about responsibilities in various situations.

- If it is impossible to have two games going simultaneously, have the more experienced teams begin the game and play one complete inning. Then have the less experienced teams play a complete inning. The situation that was set will be practiced by all four teams before a new situation is presented. This will ensure proper reinforcement. The next day, if you play situation-ball again, have the less experienced teams begin the game.
- If you have just one game going, pair a less experienced player with a more experienced player. When the more experienced teams are on the field playing, make it the responsibility of the less experienced partner to write out the coverage, backing up, or offensive action that his or her partner should execute in the ensuing play. Then have the less experienced students analyze the actions of their partners to determine whether the action actually taken was appropriate and effective. On the other hand, when the less experienced teams are on the field, the more experienced partner could actually ask his or her partner what offensive or defensive actions are called for. This would be an opportunity for instant feedback to the less experienced player and would heighten the more experienced player's ability to read the situation correctly.
- Be sure that your students bring pencil and paper to class to write out their analyses of their counterparts' responsibilities and actual play action.
- In game play, the pitcher should be a player from the team that is at bat. The pitcher can change every inning so that everyone gets a chance to pitch and to bat.

- The catcher needs to wear a mask in this game.
- The catcher calls balls and strikes on the batter. If the full count of four balls or three strikes takes too long, shift to a two-pitch turn at bat. Each batter gets only two pitches in his or her turn at bat: Two balls equals a walk, two strikes equals an out, and one ball and one strike equals an out.

Equipment

- Gloves, 1 per student (or they can share, if they have to)
- Bats, a variety
- Sets of three bases and home plate, 1 per diamond
- Buckets of balls
- Paper and pencils for those who forgot
- Student textbooks, 2
- Large posters (windproof and rainproof) of the checklists for Reading a Defensive Situation and Reading an Offensive Situation and Reading an Offensive Situation (see *Softball*, Step 19)
- Lists of possible practice game situations

Situations That Can be Practiced

- Runner on 1st base, no one out, 1 out, 2 outs
- Runner on 2nd base, no one out, 1 out, 2 outs
- Runner on 3rd base, no one out, 1 out, 2 outs
- Runners on 1st and 2nd base, no outs, 1 out, 2 outs
- Runners on 1st and third base, no outs, 1 out, 2 outs
- Runners on 2nd and third base, no outs, 1 out, 2 outs
- Bases loaded, no outs, 1 out, 2 outs

All of the preceding situations can be practiced with the batter intending to

- hit to the outfield: right, center, left, anywhere;
- hit to the infield: 3rd base, shortstop, 2nd base, 1st base, pitcher, anywhere; or
- hit a fly ball, a ground ball, a line drive.

To Decrease Difficulty

- Have the hitter fungo hit the ball. [3]
- Let your students use a softer ball, such as an IncrediBall®. [2]
- Specify exactly where each hit is to go and whether it is to be a fly or a ground ball. [1]

To Increase Difficulty

- Do not ask for an out-loud analysis of the situation. Have the students make individual analyses mentally. After the play is completed, they discuss their actions as a group. [3, 8]

Step 20 Throwing Sidearm

The sidearm throw is a skill that should seldom be taught to beginning softball players. The sidearm throw has limited and special use in game play and is not a general utility skill. If students are taught it before they have patterned and internalized the overhand throw, they may develop bad habits from cross-skill interference. Thus, you will probably want to reserve the sidearm throw for those students who have strong and consistent overhand throws. Part of your teaching, then, can be directed toward helping your students make the adjustments for the sidearm action without interfering with the previously learned overhand pattern.

One of the reasons that the sidearm throw tends to be popular is that it is often seen in major league baseball as part of spectacular plays. The shortstop, playing ''deep in the hole,'' fires a sidearm throw to the second baseman without turning his body toward the target. The second baseman leaps into the air to avoid the sliding baserunner and whips the ball sidearm to the first baseman. These uses of the sidearm throw look spectacular, but the only reason that the major league players can execute them is that they have exceptionally strong throwing arms. Such throws put extra stress on the arm and shoulder because the body is not used to give momentum to the throw.

The special circumstances in which the sidearm throw should be used all involve throws that are short distance and require less force than the normal overhand throw would generate. Some circumstances that call for the sidearm throw include the second baseman's throw to first base after fielding a ground ball and any medium-distance feeds to a base for a force play or the first out of a double play.

As you teach the sidearm throw, it is important that you emphasize the special situations in which the throw should be used. Then be sure that you watch your students to make certain that they use the sidearm action only on relatively short throws. If their overhand throwing action begins to break down, with the throwing hand not moving high and over the throwing shoulder, you must immediately restrict their use of the sidearm action. The overhand throw is more critical to solid softball play, in both the infield and the outfield, than is the sidearm throw. A softball player can get by without a sidearm throw but cannot succeed without a solid overhand throw. Your judgment of the readiness level of your students to learn the sidearm throw should be guided by the quality of their overhand throws.

STUDENT KEYS TO SUCCESS
- Throwing body position with back flat and torso parallel to ground
- Knees bent to lower the body
- Glove side pointed toward target before throw (may require pivot)
- Arm moves from shoulder level across body in path level with ground

Throwing Sidearm Rating

CHECKPOINT	LESS EXPERIENCED	MORE EXPERIENCED
Preparation **Stance** **Body Position**	• Knees not bent enough • Erect, back straight	• Knees bent, body low • Back flat, parallel to ground
Execution **Initial Weight Shift** **Ball Position** **Body Position** **Weight Transfer** **Arm Path**	• Balanced between feet • No pivot when throwing to throwing side • Throwing arm shoulder • Not bent at waist • Steps straight ahead • Slightly high to low	• Moves to throwing-side foot • Pivot to throwing side when target is on throwing side • Throwing arm shoulder • Low, bent at waist • Steps toward target • Level with ground
Follow-Through **Weight** **Body Position** **Arm Position**	• Throwing-side foot • Erect or leaning back • Pointing to ground	• Glove-side foot • Balanced, low • Pointing to target, parallel to ground

Error Detection and Correction for Throwing Sidearm

Most sidearm errors are caused by a failure of the path of the throwing arm to be parallel to the ground. Additionally, the point of release of the ball is different in the sidearm orientation, so it may be a source of confusion for your students. The arm path's staying parallel to the ground throughout the throw is a key for your observation. If the arm remains parallel to the ground on the throw, the flight path of the ball will be slightly upward as it travels to the intended base player. On the overhand throw, the flight path of the ball on a short throw is high to low. Consequently, the sidearm throw results in a ball that is easier to catch. The arm path will result in a ball path that is the arm path's extension. The arm path cannot be level to the ground if the fielder comes to the normal, semi-erect throwing position. Thus, your cues should be focused upon the student's fielding the ball, staying low, and keeping the back parallel to the ground while preparing to throw sidearm. Then the throwing action can be parallel to the ground and across the body.

ERROR

CORRECTION

1. The trajectory of the ball is high to low.

1. Tell your student not to stand up to throw, to stay low to throw the ball, to bend at the waist, and to keep the back parallel to the ground.

2. The trajectory of the ball is too high.

2. The throwing arm must start at shoulder level, not below. Your student should not stand up while throwing. The arm should move across the body, not up to the target.

3. The ball goes to the right of the target.

3. Have your thrower step directly toward the target; snap the wrist directly at the target, not before the target (right hander); and do the Wall Drill to Glove Side, *Softball*, Step 20, Drill 1.

4. The ball goes to the left of the target.

4. The student should step directly toward the target, and snap the wrist directly at the target, not beyond the target (right hander).

ERROR	CORRECTION
5. The ball is off line on a target to the throwing side.	5. Have the thrower stay low and pivot the torso so the glove side is pointing toward the target before he or she steps to the target and throws. Assign the Wall Drill to Throwing Side, *Softball*, Step 20, Drill 2.

Throwing Sidearm Drills

1. Wall Drill to the Glove Side and the Throwing Side
[Corresponds to *Softball*, Step 20, Drills 1, 2, 3]

Group Management and Safety Tips

- The wall drills would most likely be used on rainy days when your students could not be outside practicing. In a class that is outside, the wall drills can be converted into fence drills. The wall drills are clearly explained in the textbook and would be excellent stations for more experienced players in a skill circuit done in a gymnasium.

- The only students who should practice sidearm throws are those who have well-patterned overhand throws. The more experienced players are probably the ones who could practice these drills.
- The fence drills can be done most effectively in pairs, with one partner the tosser and the other partner the thrower.

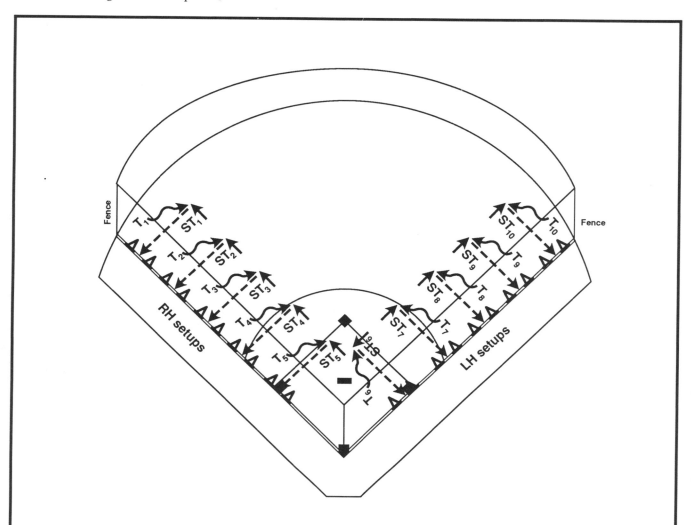

- If there is space on the outside of the outfield fence, the students practicing the sidearm throw could be stationed there. This would allow more room inside the fence for other stations in a skill circuit.
- Targets should be marked on the wall or fence. These can consist simply of two lines parallel to the ground. The lower line should be at the height of the waist of an average student in the class. The upper line should be at the height of the shoulders. These lines can be made with tape put in an interrupted line at the proper heights. Another way to mark the height is to weave a ribbon (rope, traffic ribbon) through the fence at the appropriate heights. The width of the targets should be about 5 feet and can be marked with cones or other markers placed on the ground at the base of the fence.

- The sidearm throwers are about 30 feet from the fence. Mark that throwing line with cones or other markers.
- Left-handed throwers should be at a different location, if possible, so that their throws do not cross those of the right-handers.
- Each thrower should be about 15 feet apart from others on the line.
- The sidearm thrower should first face so that the glove arm is pointing at the fence.
- The tosser is on the throwing line 10 feet away from the thrower and rolls the ball to the thrower.
- The thrower fields the ball and throws sidearm to the target.
- The tosser should roll five balls to the fielder, who fields them and throws them sidearm to the target. After the five throws are completed, the thrower should re-

trieve them at the fence. Be sure to tell them to be careful of errant throws as they collect the balls at the fence.

- The tosser and the sidearm thrower then switch positions and repeat the drill.
- The same procedure is used for sidearm throws to the throwing-arm side.
- After each partner has completed 5 sidearm throws to the glove side and the throwing-arm side, the partners can simply face one another, both on the line, and roll balls to each other. The player fields it and throws it to the fence with the appropriate sidearm action. After each has thrown two balls, they collect the balls at the fence, switch positions, and repeat the drill. This will enable them to practice the sidearm throw to the glove side and the throwing-arm side more continuously.
- If there is a player who does not have a partner, line up five softballs on the throwing line directly in front of the player. The balls should be 1 foot apart, and the player faces them. The player then simply moves up and fields the first ball and make the sidearm throw to the fence. He or she returns to the starting position and repeats the sequence. The player should first practice this moving with the glove side pointing toward the fence, then with the throwing arm pointing toward the fence.

Equipment

- Gloves, 1 per student
- Balls, 5 per student pair
- Tape or ribbon to mark target heights
- Cones or other markers to mark target widths
- Cones to mark the throwing line

Instructions and Cues to Class

- ''Field the rolling ball in a low position and stay low while you make the sidearm throw.''
- ''Keep your back flat and parallel with the ground. Don't stand up: That would make your throw go into the dirt.''

- ''After you field the ball, imagine that there is a tree limb above your head that, if you were to stand up while throwing, you will bump your head on. It's essential that you stay low while executing the sidearm throw.''
- ''Feel as though there were a table just beneath your arm and you must move your throwing arm along that table to make the throw. This will help you learn to make your arm path go horizontally across your body.''
- ''Even though this is a sidearm throw, you still need to step toward the target. Otherwise, your ball would go to the side of the target. In a game, that would mean that the player covering the base would have to move off the base to make the catch.''
- ''The throw is never as strong with a sidearm pattern as with an overhand pattern. Just remember, on a throw that is long or needs to be strong, throw overhand. On a throw that is short and needs less force, you may throw sidearm, if you want.''
- ''See how easy it is to throw sidearm to the glove side? It's not so easy when you throw to the throwing-arm side, though. Why is that? What is it about the body position that makes the sidearm throw to your throwing arm side more difficult?''
- ''It's hard to pivot the body, step toward your throwing-arm side, and not stand up when you pivot. If that's a problem, just practice the motion without the ball a few times to get the pattern.''
- ''Stay low and pivot on the throwing-arm foot. Feel yourself swinging your glove side toward the target: You are like a gate opening to the target side.''

Student Options

- ''Have your partner watch you execute the sidearm throw and give you feedback about your technique. Have him or her use the Throwing Sidearm Keys to Success Checklist in Step 20 of your textbook.''

- "Can you and your partner figure out a way to practice that forces you to stay low and keep your back parallel to the ground [see Correction 1]? Can you think of something that would help everyone in the class? If you have a good idea, show some other pairs and see what they think."
- "Maybe you know what you have to practice on and really don't need a partner to help you. How about trying to figure out a way you could practice sidearm throws in both directions by yourself? You might look at the wall drills (Drills 1, 2, 3) in Step 20 of your textbook."

Student Success Goal

- 13 of 20 fielding and on-target throwing plays
    - 7 of 10 to the glove side
    - 6 of 10 to the throwing side

To Decrease Difficulty

- Let the student use a softer ball. [2]
- Have the tosser roll the ball slower. [3]
- Make the target area larger. [4]
- Have the tosser make sure the ball rolls straight to the fielder. [3]
- On the throwing-side throw, have the tosser roll the ball more toward the fence so the fielder is already moving in the direction of the pivot. [3]

To Increase Difficulty

- Have the tosser roll the ball with more force. [3]
- Have the tosser roll the ball in the opposite direction of the throw so that the turn to make the throw is more difficult. [7]
- Have the tosser bounce the ball. [3]
- Make the target smaller. [4]
- Have the tosser vary the speed, the range, and the side to which the ball is rolled or bounced. [8]
- Have the tosser fungo hit the ball rather than toss it. [3]
- Have the tosser fungo hit with any of the preceding options (see *Softball*, Partner Drill, Step 20, Drill 4). [3]

Note: The above drill can be performed indoors in a similar manner. However, the ball will rebound off the wall after the sidearm throw. This rebound could be fielded by the tosser. As students become proficient at this drill, they can field their partner's rebounded ball and immediately throw sidearm back to the wall. The partner would then field the ball and return it sidearm as well. Thus, the partners would have a continuous drill to practice. It would be necessary for you to have them change locations on the throwing line so that they would get equal amounts of practice throwing sidearm to the glove side and to the throwing-arm side.

Similarly, the drill can be performed continuously by one person practicing in a corner of the gymnasium (or outside, if there is an "inside corner" where two buildings come together). For specifics on this type of individual practice, see *Softball*, Step 20, Drill 3.

2. Four-Player Drill
[Corresponds to *Softball*, Step 20, Drill 5]

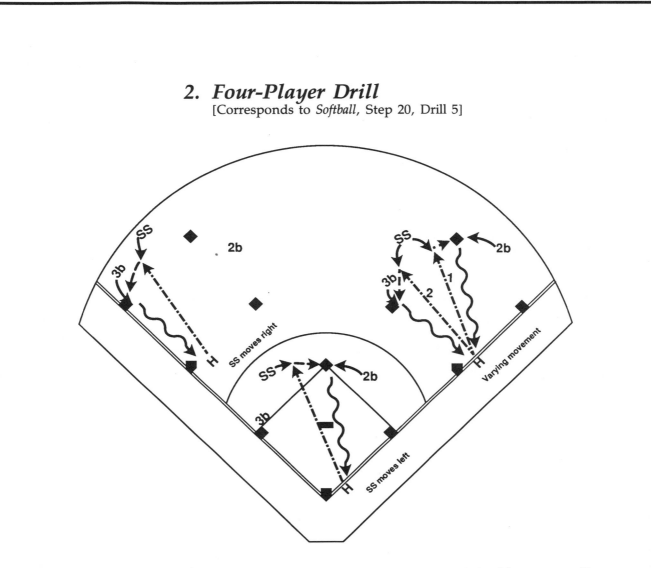

Group Management and Safety Tips

- This drill is done with two pairs of partners (total of four players). One pair is the hitter and the fielder-sidearm thrower, playing in the shortstop position. The other pair is a second baseman and a third baseman.
- This drill can be set up on the regulation diamond, but more students will be able to practice if you set it up along one foul line and an adjacent outfield fence. It can also be set up on a grass field, such as a field hockey, soccer, or football field.
- The hitter should have about four or five balls to fungo hit as ground balls to the shortstop.

- The second and third baseman will set up as if on a diamond. It is not necessary that there be bases to mark their locations; they simply need to be on either side of the shortstop.
- The shortstop fields the ground balls and makes sidearm throws to the second or third baseman. The sidearm throw should go to the base player on the side that the ground ball was hit to.
- The second and third basemen catch the sidearm throw, then roll the ball back to the fungo-hitting location.
- After 10 attempts at fielding and making the sidearm throw, the two base players switch locations, and the fungo hitter and the fielder switch positions. Then the drill is repeated.

- After the new fielder has completed 10 fields and sidearm throws, the pairs switch roles with each other, and the drill is repeated.
- For safety's sake, you need to arrange your drill setups so that all shortstops are throwing in the same direction. It is helpful to move every other set of fielders about 10 feet away from the foul line. This places them out of the line of overthrows from adjacent groups. Any errant throws will go into the area between the fungo hitter and the fielder and base players.
- The fungo hitter is the person who can see the whole field of practice, so he or she should be reminded of the need to warn people if an errant ball is headed toward a classmate.
- It would be safer to use the IncrediBall® in this drill until the fielder who is executing the sidearm throw has sufficient control to not "blast" the ball at the base player.

Equipment

- Gloves, 1 per student
- Balls, 1 per student (a soft regulation ball or an IncrediBall®)
- Bats, variety of lengths and weights

Instructions and Cues to Class

- "Fungo hitter, first hit two balls to the glove side of the shortstop. Then hit two balls to the throwing side. Finally, hit three balls randomly to either side of the shortstop. Vary the force of the hits."
- "If the player in the shortstop position can consistently field the ball and make an on-target sidearm throw to a base player, you can hit the next five balls to force the fielder to move quite a distance. Do not hit the ball out of the fielder's reach, but do try to help her or him extend the fielding range. If the fielder cannot yet consistently field the ball and make on-target throws, hit the last five balls softer."
- "Shortstop, remember to stay low on the ball as you field it and make the sidearm throw."

- "This drill helps you field the ball quickly, then make a 'catchable' throw to the appropriate base player. This means that you may be moving hard to field a ball, then have to throw the ball very softly because you have moved so close to the base."
- "Remember, the sidearm throw is not forceful. It is a short-distance throw, so you need to be sympathetic to the person who has to catch it. Don't 'blast' the ball at the baseman: He or she doesn't have enough time to react, because the ball comes so quickly."
- "Also, on most short, sidearm throws, a baserunner is coming at the receiver. If you blast the ball while the baseman is simultaneously thinking about catching the ball and the oncoming runner, he or she will have some difficulty making the catch."
- "Charge the ground ball, then reduce your momentum so you can make a soft throw to the base. You have to control your body momentum so that you can ease up on the sidearm throw to the base player who is closer to you than normal."

Student Options

- "Just before the shortstop fields the ball, the fungo hitter may call the base to which the sidearm throw should go. The fungo hitter will call out 'two' for second base or 'three' for third base."
- "Devise a way to practice in which the shortstop has to make a decision about whether to throw the ball overhand or sidearm. This is what really happens in a game. By now you are ready to design some kind of drill that allows you all to practice making the kinds of decisions that games call for. Just think about when each kind of throw is most important and what kinds of setups are needed to make a situation come about. Show your drill to another group of four, and see whether they agree that your drill works or whether they can think of a way to improve it."

Student Success Goal

- 6 of 10 fielding and sidearm throwing plays that are caught by the base player

To Decrease Difficulty

- Have the hitter roll the ball to the shortstop. [3]
- Have the shortstop slow down the action after fielding the ball. The sidearm throws to the base players could be done in slow motion. [3]
- Have the batter hit the ball directly to the shortstop, and have the base players move closer to the shortstop than they would be in a game. [4]
- Let the group use a softer ball. [2]

To Increase Difficulty

- Have the hitter vary the distance, the force, and the direction of the ground ball. [8]
- Have the hitter hit bouncing ground balls. [3]
- Have the hitter call out the base to which the sidearm throw is to be made just prior to the shortstop's fielding it. The hitter should call out "two" for second base and "three" for third base. [1]
- Add a baserunner who runs at half to one-third speed from second to third base. This baserunner can also run from first to second base when the throw is going to second base. The baserunner must wear a batting helmet and must stand up going into the base. This will force the shortstop to adjust to the runner going by as he or she fields the ball. It will also force the basemen to make targets for the throws in the proper locations and to learn to adjust to the throw and the baserunner coming in to the base at almost the same time. [6, 8]

Step 21 Double Plays

The double play, in which the defense (usually the infielders) gets two outs from continuous action, is advanced-level strategy. The actual skills needed to execute infield double plays, though, are not advanced in terms of difficulty.

Less experienced students, in their early exposure to softball, are involved primarily with learning the skills basic to the game. They have not yet developed the needed proficiency in the basic skills to execute the double play properly. This is fine because beginning-level games can be played without using the double play. The force-play strategy of making the play on the lead runner is used in beginning-level games. That strategy is a foundational concept for the more advanced double-play strategy.

The double play is presented at this time because by now your students should have gained the experience necessary to succeed. The skill and conceptual progressions basic to the double play have been developed through the previous steps in the participant's and instructor's books. The concepts and skills needed to execute the infield double plays could be presented to your more experienced students earlier. Some of the combination drills in previous steps could incorporate practice of double plays. However, a beginning unit on softball would not include double plays for the less experienced students.

Students who have mastered the basic skills and game concepts are ready for the introduction of the double play. Students who are still having difficulty throwing the ball or remembering the basic coverage and backing-up responsibilities of position play should continue to play using only the strategy of getting the lead runner out rather than move on to the double play. On the basis of these initial factors, decide which classes or which students in your classes are ready for the double play.

The bases-loaded home-to-first double play is one of the easiest to execute. The catcher and the first baseman use the same force-play skill technique previously taught. However, the second-to-first double play, with a runner on first base, is probably the double play situation that occurs most often in games. Eventual practice of all possible double play situations should be provided for your students. Beginning practice of double plays with the second-to-first double play is recommended because of the frequency of occurrence of that situation.

The special footwork and pivots used by the shortstop and second baseman are skills that have not yet been presented. Covering them all in the same class period is unrealistic. That is a lot of material to review for experienced students, never mind teach to those unfamiliar with the techniques. The drag step and the inside pivot used by the shortstop are considered easier by most softball teachers and coaches than the second baseman's pivots. The shortstop, going from his or her original fielding position to make the play at second base, is moving in the general direction of first base for the follow-up throw. On the other hand, the second baseman, coming from the first base side of second base to make the force out, must change direction to make the throw back to first base. Thus, the second baseman is making a true pivot in completing the second throw for the double play. Present the drag step and the inside pivot used by the shortstop to your students one day and the second baseman's pivots on another day.

You may decide not to group the students by experience levels for double play practice.

Rather, set up several practice stations and randomly assign students to each station. Begin the practice with the Mimetic Footwork Drill (Drill 1). Progress through the drills making sure that each student has the opportunity to practice each of the techniques used by the shortstop and to perform each of the roles required for completion of the drills assigned.

Because the use of a particular pivot technique is situation-specific (based on the source of the throw), another organizational option is to set up separate stations, each designed to practice a particular technique. Determine the number of stations needed so that half the participants are practicing the drag step and the other half are doing the inside pivot at the same time. Rotate the groups from practicing one technique to the other halfway through the class period. On a second day, cover the second baseman's pivots in the same manner.

If you wish to group your students by experience levels for each of the four double-play pivot techniques, also use the Mimetic Footwork Drill. Evaluate the double-play pivot experience levels of the students, then assign them to the appropriate practice stations to work on the pivots that show weakness. Even your more experienced students will probably not have expertise in all four of the pivots used at second base. If you find that the majority of the students lack experience in most of the pivot techniques, use one of the organizational patterns described in the previous paragraph.

Each group needs a minimum of five students to practice the beginning drill progressions. Later drills call for baserunners, which could enlarge each group to eight or more students.

STUDENT KEYS TO SUCCESS

- Proper footwork
- Smoothness in movement sequence
- Getting out of path of runner
- Strong, accurate, quickly released throw to first base

Double Play Readiness Rating	
CHECKPOINT	**READINESS CHARACTERISTIC**
Physical Skills **Throwing** **Footwork**	• Strong overhand throw • Quick release of throw • Accuracy fairly consistent • Use of opposite hand and foot in throwing is well established • Good balance • Controls weight shift
Game Concepts **Position Play**	• Demonstrates knowledge of position coverage • Demonstrates knowledge of base-coverage responsibilities • Demonstrates knowledge of basic force play concepts, executes techniques correctly

Error Detection and Correction for Double Plays

Note: This discussion of double play pivots pertains only to right-handed players. Left-handers have difficulty executing the double play techniques.

During your students' practice of double play techniques, the errors you can expect to see will be conceptually similar for all four double play skills. The specific technical footwork is different in each of the double plays, but the errors happen most often because of common problems. Thus, the errors that follow are common to all of the double play pivots. The corrections will focus on the common concepts and, if needed, on the specific double play variation of that concept.

ERROR | **CORRECTION**

ERROR	CORRECTION
1. The fielder fails to get to the base in time.	1. Have the fielder practice reacting to the ball as it is hit. When the student knows that the double play is a possibility, he or she should "cheat" by setting up to field slightly in the direction of second.
2. The fielder does not go to the ball side of the base.	2. Recommend that the student use the Mimetic Footwork Drill (Drill 1) and verbally match the source of the throw with the footing technique being used.

ERROR

CORRECTION

3. The fielder fails to move out of the baseline to throw to first base.

3. Use the Full Double Play Mimetic Drill (*Softball*, Step 21, Drill 2) for the technique being practiced; place a passive runner in the baseline 2 to 3 feet from second base and on the first base side.

a

b

c

4. The fielder does not step in the direction of the throw.

4. Have the fielder stand in a stationary position at second base and throw to first base using just the arm. Repeat, but have the fielder take a step with the throw to see the difference in the force provided by the body's moving toward first base.

ERROR 🚫   **CORRECTION**

5. When executing the second baseman's crossover pivot, the fielder does not block the forward momentum or step to first on the throw.

5. Have someone stand in the fielder's path 2 to 3 feet on the third base side of second base.

6. The fielder fails to catch the ball.

6. Check the fielder's focus as the ball approaches. Is it on the base, the runner, or the throwing target? Make the appropriate correction of focus by having the student watch the approaching ball.

Double Play Drills

1. *Mimetic Footwork Drill*
[Corresponds to *Softball*, Step 21, Drill 1]

Group Management and Safety Tips

- This drill can be done as individual, partner, or full-group practice.
- Have the students move to the base from the regular fielding position of either the shortstop or second baseman, depending upon the technique being practiced.
- Students who have little experience with the pivot footwork technique should walk through the sequence a few times before attempting it at normal speed.

Equipment

- Bases, 1 per station (anchored, if possible)

Instructions and Cues to Class

- "Without using a ball, take the regular-depth fielding positions for the shortstop and second baseman, move to second base, and execute as shortstop: drag step, inside pivot; and as second baseman: crossover step pivot, rocker pivot."
- "Repeat the technique until you feel comfortable with the footwork and do not have to look at the base as you execute it."
- "Be sure to return to your original starting position between practices."

Student Option

- "Imagine a ball hit to a specific infielder in a particular position. Execute the appropriate footwork for the double play at second base."

Student Success Goal

- 20 correctly executed pivots
  5 shortstop drag steps
  5 shortstop inside pivots
  5 second baseman crossover step pivots
  5 second baseman rocker step pivots

To Decrease Difficulty

- Let the student walk through the sequence. [3]

To Increase Difficulty

- Have the student mimetically add catching and throwing the ball to the footwork, making full double play action (see *Softball*, Step 21, Drill 2). [7]

2. *Simulated Hit Drill*
[Corresponds to *Softball*, Step 21, Drill 3]

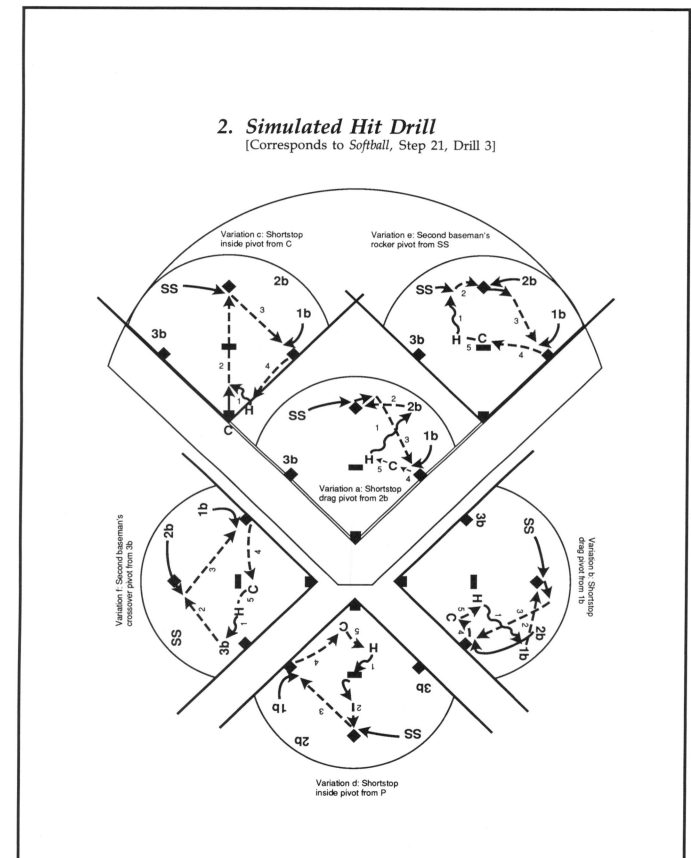

Variation c: Shortstop inside pivot from C

Variation e: Second baseman's rocker pivot from SS

Variation a: Shortstop drag pivot from 2b

Variation f: Second baseman's crossover pivot from 3b

Variation b: Shortstop drag pivot from 1b

Variation d: Shortstop inside pivot from P

Group Management and Safety Tips

- Divide your class into groups of six. Each group consists of three pairs of partners: shortstop and second baseman, a first baseman and a "hitter," and a catcher and a pitcher–third baseman.
- Set up multiple stations of full infield diamonds to accommodate your class size. Otherwise, use this drill as one station on the regular diamond, with other skill practice stations, such as pitching, fielding fly balls, or hitting in the outfield area or an adjoining field space.
- Arrange multiple stations so that overthrows at second or first base would not go into other stations
- Make a large, weatherproof chart of the feeder, pivot player, and first base coverage variations from the chart provided for this drill in the textbook. Otherwise, have a copy of the textbook available for each diamond.

Equipment

- Full diamond setups with bases and home plate, 1 per station
- Buckets of 5 balls, 1 per station

Instructions and Cues to Class

- "Today we are practicing with the [shortstop or second baseman] as the pivot player."
- "All fielders take regular-depth starting positions."
- "The'hitter' stands with a bucket of five balls 20 feet in front of the feeder. Refer to the chart for feeder, pivot player, and first base coverage variations to practice."
- "The catcher stands behind the hitter to receive the balls thrown back after the completion of each play."
- "The hitter rolls a ground ball to the feeder, who throws to the pivot player covering second base. The pivot player then throws to first base for the completion of the double play."
- "The first base cover person throws the ball to the catcher."

- "Repeat the sequence 5 times for each of the variations listed on the chart with the [shortstop or second baseman] as the pivot player."
- "After completing the variations, change positions within the pair. When one pair has completed the double play variations, rotate all roles."
- "Feeder, use an underhand toss to feed the ball to the pivot player if you are close to second base when you field the ball. Use a sidearm throw with a pivot, if necessary, for longer distance feeds."
- "Pivot player, shorten the distance of the feed throw by going to the side of second base closest to the feed player. Remember, step toward first base when making your throw."
- "First baseman, use the correct footing techniques when making your force play. Remember, when catching an off-target throw, step with the ball-side foot and tag the base with the other foot."

Student Option

- "Design a scoring system that will give you feedback on your success in all the roles of this double play drill."

Student Success Goal

- 4 of 5 successful executions of each variation (24 of 30 total)
  - 16 of 20 executions as shortstop pivot player
  - 8 of 10 as second baseman pivot player

To Decrease Difficulty

- Have the group practice only one variation per practice session. [5]
- Call out the footwork cues as the person is doing the steps. [1]
- Move the covering player closer to the base in the starting position. [4]

To Increase Difficulty

- Have the hitter vary the force and direction of the "hit" ball. [8]
- Have the hitter actually fungo hit ground balls (see *Softball*, Step 21, Drill 4). [3]

Step 22   Relays and Cutoffs

The relay and the cutoff are skills that are related in technique and execution. Because both require consistent catching and strong overhand throwing techniques, they should not be taught until your students have progressed past the less experienced level of play. It is important that your students recognize that the relay and the cutoff are defensive skills in which teamwork among three players is needed. The three players who are involved include the outfielder who fields the hit and makes the initial throw; the base player to whom the throw is ultimately intended, who takes the responsibility for lining up the relay or cutoff person; and the fielder who serves as the relay or cutoff player.

Relays and cutoffs, despite being related in technique, are different in purpose. Some persons use the terms *relay* and *cutoff* synonymously; however, they are two separate skills, and you should be sure that you clearly distinguish between them with your students.

The relay occurs when the ball goes deep into the outfield, thus requiring two or more throws to get the ball in to the intended base. The relay person is positioned in the shallow outfield to receive a throw from the deep outfielder and relay the ball by throwing it to the intended base player.

The relay player is determined by the field into which the ball goes. The shortstop is the relay player when the ball is hit to the left of center field, and the second baseman is the relay person on a ball hit to the right of center. In slow pitch, the short fielder could serve as relay person when he or she is playing in an appropriate short outfield position. This option frees the shortstop and the second baseman to cover the bases.

The players should think about the destination of the relay throw prior to the batter's hit. All outfielders and infielders should plan a relay action in the event that the ball is hit deep into the outfield. Thus, the relay action can occur as planned. A throw is made by the outfielder to the relay person, who in turn throws the ball to the intended destination.

The technique for the relay throw can certainly be taught to less experienced players prior to playing modified games. The less experienced students may not have developed the strength to throw the ball to a base even from a regular-depth outfield position, so the relay can be used effectively any time a throw is too long for one person to make. Two accurate throws are faster and more effective than one throw that is off target or "dies" as it travels to the intended base.

Much of the technique for the cutoff is the same as for the relay. Again, the purposes of the two skills are very different. The cutoff player awaits the outfielder's throw in the infield rather than in the shallow outfield. The cutoff player, when actually "cutting the ball," catches the ball and usually redirects it to a base other than the one for which the initial throw was intended. This is done because the covering base player determines that there is no chance to make a play on the lead baserunner. He or she directs the cutoff player to cut the ball and (a) throw it to another base (usually second or third base) to make a play on a runner going there or (b) hold it because there is no play on any runner at that point.

As you observe your students while they practice the relay and cutoff skills, there are a few critical actions you must focus upon. Your cues to your students should emphasize the lining-up procedure, catching the ball, and pivoting to make the overhand throw to the intended target. The most important skill here is the catch and pivot made by the cutoff or relay person.

A major difference in skill techniques between the relay and the cutoff is in the pivot. The throw by the relay person is to his or her rear; thus, a pivot to the glove side is used. The cutoff player, on the other hand, needs to make either a slight or a full pivot to the throwing side. The throw is cut 30 to 40 feet in front of home plate and is then thrown to second or third base, both of which are located in front of the cutoff player. However, the cut and throw to home on an off-target throw uses the same pivot to the glove side as does the relay.

Focus your attention on making sure that the relay or cutoff person turns the glove side toward the throwing target while making the catch and preparing for the throw. This is not easy for the relay person initially, because the body position makes tracking the ball more difficult. However, you can have the relay person begin by facing the thrower directly. Then, with each subsequent practice attempt, have him or her gradually turn the glove side toward the target.

All the correct body position and pivoting in the world will not get the out, however, if the initial, relay, or cutoff throw is off-target or high and looping. All throws in these two-part skills must be strong, accurate, overhand throws that travel a relatively straight trajectory from the thrower's hand to the glove of the receiving fielder.

The cutoff plays require a great deal of decision-making on the part of the people involved, particularly by the covering base player. Thus, it will be helpful if you have students watch others practice and silently decide, as the covering player must, whether or not to cut the ball in the situations played. Sheer repetition, with different players running bases and throwing the ball, will help the silent decision-makers learn what to look for. It is also important that you let your students

know that it is okay to make a few bad decisions early on. It is from our mistakes that we develop the ability to read the factors involved in the decision-making process. Then we will be more knowledgeable when we make such decisions in later games.

Some of the other elements of the relay and the cutoff that are critical for you to focus upon include the positioning of the relay or cutoff person. It is important that the relay or cutoff person face the outfielder and get in line with the intended base and the initial throw. This makes the throw as short as possible, thus increasing the speed at which the ball arrives at the intended base. The covering base player must be sure to call the direction the relay or cutoff person must move to get into the proper position. On the cutoff play, the covering base player must be sure to position the cutoff player just to the throwing side of the incoming ball. The covering base player must be able to see the ball as it approaches, and the cutoff person should have his or her glove side adjacent to the line of the ball. This will enable the cutoff player to catch the ball and pivot very quickly. The subsequent throw to the called base will have an increased likelihood of getting to the base before the incoming runner.

STUDENT KEYS TO SUCCESS

- Face outfielder who has the ball
- Covering base player verbally positions relay or cutoff player
- As ball approaches, extend hands to catch and begin pivot
- Catch ball, complete pivot to intended base
- Step toward target
- Throw overhand

Relay and Cutoff Rating

CHECKPOINT	LESS EXPERIENCED	MORE EXPERIENCED
Preparation Body Position Direction Faced Pivot Action for Relay Person	• Arms at sides • Outfielder with ball • None	• Arms raised and out-stretched • Outfielder with ball • As ball approaches, begins pivot by stepping toward target with glove-side foot
Execution Pivot Action for Relay Pivot Action for Cutoff Step for Relay Step for Cutoff	• Catches, then pivots • Catches, no pivot • Steps toward target • None	• As ball approaches, begins pivot, catches, and completes pivot • Catches, pivots toward intended target • Crow-hops, steps toward target • Steps in direction of throw
Follow-Through For Relay For Cutoff	• Weight forward • Facing initial thrower	• Weight forward, throwing hand points to target • Weight forward, throwing hand points to target

Error Detection and Correction for Relays and Cutoffs

ERROR

CORRECTION

1. The catch and the throw are two distinct actions.

1. Give word cues that indicate the continuous nature of the action, for example, "catch and throw" and "as you catch the ball, pivot and bring the ball to the throwing position."

2. The throw is high and looping.

2. Have the student move forward into the throw. On forward step, the body moves over the forward foot. Also, have student release the ball later, by aiming at the head or chest of the relay person.

ERROR   **CORRECTION**

3. The throw is off target.

3. Be sure the student is throwing over-hand, not sidearm. Have the student pivot and step toward the target with the glove-side foot.

4. The student pivots in the wrong direction.

4. Have the student turn the glove side slightly toward the target while waiting for the ball on the relay. Make sure that the covering player lines up the relay or cutoff person slightly off to the throwing-hand side of the incoming ball (the ball should pass on the glove side of the relay or cutoff person if it is not caught).

Relay and Cutoff Drills

The drills in this section are for practicing both the relay and the cutoff actions. However, remember that those are two separate skills; work hard to get your students to learn the differences between them. The basic skill techniques are similar except for the pivot, but when your students practice them, try to set up their orientation on the field so that they actually see that the relay goes in a straight line and the cutoff changes direction or stops. You might want to practice the two skills on different days so that your students do not associate the skill techniques as being the same and thus associate the purposes as being the same. Another option is that you can certainly teach the relay to your less experienced players earlier in the unit to help them learn to get the ball to the proper place with accurate throws, even though they might not be strong enough to throw the ball all the way to the next player. The cutoff play can be taught as a more advanced technique to the more experienced players at a point when game situations arise that make apparent its utility. Regardless of the time at which you choose to teach either or both of these skills, be certain to constantly stress the purpose of each and the differences in their techniques and uses.

1. *Mimetic Pivot Drill*
[Corresponds to *Softball*, Step 22, Drill 1]

Group Management and Safety Tips

- Your students need not be grouped according to experience level in this drill. They will, however, need to be in pairs. You might want to pair up a more experienced student with a less experienced student so that the former can help the latter with correct pivot action.
- The students can be placed anywhere in the outfield, with the outfielder partner about 30 feet from the infielder. There should be some sort of marker for home plate (a cone or home plate itself) that will orient the players as to their intended throw.

- The students may practice at their own pace because this is a mimetic drill.
- Safety concerns are limited for this practice because there are no real throws being made.
- When the students practice the relay action, locate them in what is obviously the outfield so that they will get the orientation that the relay is from the deep outfield.
- When the students practice the cutoff portion of the drill, have them relocate so that the outfielder is not as deep and the cutoff person is obviously in the infield portion of the field of play.

Equipment

- Gloves, 1 per student
- Home plate or another marker to designate home plate

Instructions and Cues to Class—Relay

- ''You are going to practice the pivot action used in the relay from the deep outfield to home plate. Concentrate on pivoting toward your glove side as you catch the ball from the deep outfielder. This enables you to prepare for the throw to home plate.''
- ''Make the catch, pivot, and throw all one continuous motion. You need to practice making the pivot as you make the catch. This is difficult but makes your throw get to home plate as fast as possible.''
- ''The outfielder needs to run toward the outfield fence to retrieve a ball, pick it up, and throw it to the relay person. This is all done with an imaginary ball, so work on visualizing the ball and your technique.''
- ''The relay person calls 'Hit the relay!' to start the practice. At that command, the outfielder runs after the ball, and the infielder moves to a shallow outfield position between home plate and the outfielder. You are both moving at the same time so that the infielder is in position waiting for the throw.''
- ''You should try to be pivoting to your glove side while 'catching' the imaginary throw from the outfielder. Then you can do the crow-hop to get your body moving in the direction of the throw. This will increase the strength of your throw.''
- ''Be sure that you imagine a runner going in to home plate. Your throw must be to the third-base side of home plate and at the catcher's knees. Direct your throwing motion to that position. 'Think' the ball to the correct location.''
- ''After 5 mimetic practices, switch roles with your partner.''

Instructions and Cues to the Class—Cutoff

- ''Next we'll practice the cutoff play. Remember, this is different from the relay. Can anyone tell us the differences between the two plays?''
- ''Right: One difference is that the cutoff person is in the infield rather than the outfield. That's because the throw from the outfield should be able to reach home (or third) if it is not cut off.''
- ''Another difference is that the relay is used when the distance the ball has to travel to its intended destination is too great for one person to throw. The cutoff, on the other hand, is used to keep the ball from getting to its intended destination. When would the cutoff person cut the ball and not allow it to continue toward home plate?''
- ''Right: The throw to home is cut off when it would not arrive in time to get the baserunner out, or when it is off target. The catcher yells 'Cut!' and indicates the base to which the ball should be thrown. It could be 'Cut third!' or 'Cut second!' or 'Cut home!' Some people would rather yell 'Cut three!' or 'Cut two!' or 'Cut four!' You and your partner decide which is better for you.''
- ''If you have to cut the ball and throw to a base other than home, be sure that you pivot and step in the direction of the throw. If you don't, your throw will be inaccurate and the cutoff will be wasted. If your throw is very inaccurate, the baserunner might advance another base.''
- ''If you are the covering base player calling 'Cut!' you must be sure you make the decision before the ball gets to the cutoff player. He or she must know whether to catch the ball or let it go through.''
- ''When you practice this drill, move so that the cutoff person is in the infield. Practice making the catch while pivoting, and throwing to the base called by your partner. In this drill, the outfield partner calls the base to which the imaginary

cutoff throw should go. (In the game, however, the call to cut would be made by the covering base player.)''

- ''Practice the pivot and throw in this drill. Imagine the ball coming in and the covering base player at the base to which you are going to throw the ball.''
- ''Practice this 5 times, with the outfielder calling different bases after the call to cut the ball. Then switch roles.''

Student Option

- ''Have a third person watch you and give you feedback on whether you seem to be pivoting as you catch the ball. That person can also tell you whether you step in the direction of the throw.''

Student Success Goal

- 4 of 5 correct performances as outfielder, relay person, and cutoff person

To Decrease Difficulty

- Practice the cutoff and relay plays on different days. [3]
- Use a third person as a covering player to call the cut action. [3]
- Have the student do the mimetic catch, pivot, and throw in slow motion. [3]

To Increase Difficulty

- Alternate the relay and cutoff plays (ME). [1, 8]
- Have the covering base player call ''Cut two'' [three, four] randomly (ME). [8]
- Have the infielder mimetically catch the ball while moving slightly toward home base, step, and throw to home plate. [7]

2. Wall Drills for Relay Pivot and Accuracy
[Corresponds to *Softball*, Step 22, Drill 2]

Group Management and Safety Tips

- This drill should be done by the less experienced players who have difficulty throwing the ball accurately to the intended base.
- This drill can be done inside as a station or it can be done in a skill circuit with a person throwing the ball at an outside wall. Use old balls and be careful of windows. Balls that are soft and scuffed up are less likely to make white marks on the wall.
- If the drill is done inside, use a Rag Ball® or an IncrediBall®.
- Your students should be positioned about 15 or 20 feet apart so that an errant throw does not hit another player when they pivot and throw.

- The students should be on a throwing line 40 feet from the target indoors, or 80 feet outdoors.
- If the drill is being done indoors, the target needs to be about 8 feet from the floor to account for the fact that the relay person is close to the wall.
- Targets outside should be put on the wall about 5 feet from the ground. The target should be a 2-foot square.
- If there is no outside wall, this drill can be done at the fence or a backstop. Then the relay person will need a bucket of balls. In such a situation, all students should retrieve the balls simultaneously.

Equipment

- Gloves, 1 per student
- Balls, 1 per student (if at a fence, 1 bucket of balls per target)
- Targets on the wall or fence
- Markers for throwing line

Instructions and Cues to Class

- ''In this drill you practice the outfielder's retrieval of the ball, the pivot, and a throw to a target representing the relay person. The pivoting action is the same for the outfielder as for the relay person. You both start with your back to the target.''
- ''Roll the ball slowly away from yourself. As the outfielder, run after it, pick it up, pivot, and throw to the target. Do this 10 times. Repeat by rolling the ball 10 times to your glove side, then 10 times to your throwing-arm side.''
- ''Be sure that, after picking up the rolling ball, you pivot to your glove side. This puts you into the correct throwing position. If you were to pivot to your throwing-arm side, you would have to take another step with your glove-side foot. You would be off balance, slower in getting your throw off to the target, and probably dizzy.''
- ''As you pivot, immediately look for the target so that you can direct your throw to it. If you weren't to look for the target until you threw, you would throw inaccurately because your head would be moving sideways while you tried to throw straight ahead, which would make the ball go off target.''
- ''It's harder to go to the throwing-arm side and then pivot toward the glove-hand side. If you have trouble with that, practice it more on your own.''

Student Options

- ''Have a partner roll the ball for you and watch to make sure that you pivot in the proper direction. Have the partner tell you at what point you look for the target.''
- ''Have a partner toss the ball in the air to you, the relay person. Have him or her watch to make sure your pivot is in the proper direction.''
- ''How can you and your partner practice fielding to the throwing-arm side and pivoting to the glove side? Can you design a practice drill that really makes you concentrate on getting into position to do an easy pivot to the glove side? If you can come up with a good drill, show it to me so it can be used to help other students.''

Student Success Goals

- 8 of 10 on-target throws off straight rolls
- 8 of 10 on-target throws off glove-side rolls
- 8 of 10 on-target throws off throwing-side rolls

To Decrease Difficulty

- Lower the number of on-target throws required for success. [3]
- The ball could be rolled more slowly. [3]
- Have the fielder run to a stopped ball. [5]
- Make the target larger. [4]
- Move the relay person closer to the target. [4]

To Increase Difficulty

- The ball could be rolled faster. [3]
- Move the relay person farther from the target. [4]
- Have a partner roll the ball and vary the direction of the roll. [3, 8]

3. *Three-Person Relay Drill*
[Corresponds to *Softball*, Step 22, Drill 3]

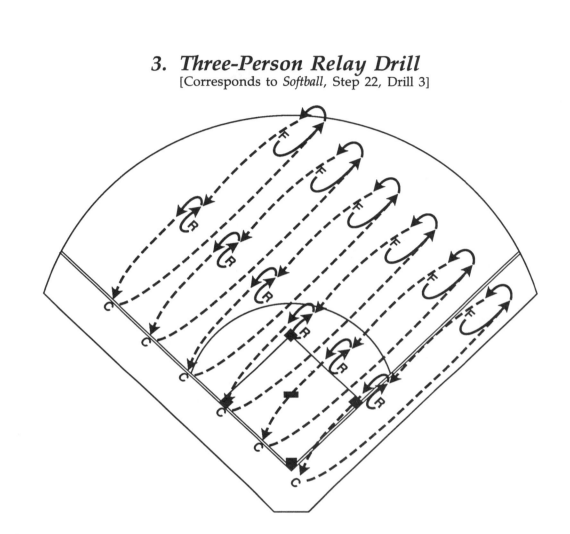

Group Management and Safety Tips

- Divide your students by experience level. Within each experience level, have the students get into threesomes.
- The students stand 100 feet apart from one another in a straight line as though they were an outfielder, a relay person, and a catcher at home plate. The relay person and the outfielder are facing the catcher.
- The three-student groups should be placed on the field so that they are all throwing in the same direction. Thus, it is probably better to do this drill across a soccer, field hockey, or football field. Then the catcher can be on the sideline and the other two can space themselves accordingly straight out from the catcher.
- The threesomes should be about 15 to 20 feet apart laterally.

Equipment

- Gloves, 1 per student
- Balls, 1 per student, or a bucket of balls at the catcher's position

Instructions and Cues to Class

- "Catcher, throw the ball past the outfielder. As the outfielder is running to retrieve the ball, you need to help the infielder get in position to relay the throw. Give verbal directions of 'Right!' or 'Left!' to position the infielder directly between you and the outfielder."
- "Relay person, you must run out to the short outfield as the outfielder is chasing the ball that has gone past him or her. Listen for the catcher's verbal cues as to the direction you need to move."

- "Outfielder, you are throwing toward home plate, so you know as you are retrieving the ball just how you should pick it up and pivot for the throw. Aim for the relay person's chest."
- "Relay person, pivot as you catch the ball so that you can crow-hop toward home plate. This will make your throw quicker and stronger."
- "Relay person, remember that there is an imaginary runner coming home, so make your throw to the third base side of home plate and at the catcher's knees."
- "All three people involved in this play must be successful to make it work. We'll keep score this way so that we can see how you do in each role: One point is scored by the outfielder when he or she fields the ball without bobbling it and makes an on-target throw to the relay person. One point is scored by the relay person when he or she makes a successful catch and accurately relays the ball to the catcher. In order for either of you to get your point, however, you must both be successful. This means points are scored only when both the outfielder and the relay person are successful."
- "The object of this drill is for all three of you to come within 2 points of one another after each completes two turns at outfielder and two turns at the relay position."
- "Do 10 sequences, then rotate. Repeat this drill 2 times."
- "Don't rush the throws. The accuracy of the throw is probably more important than rushing to get it off. When you rush the throw, you will probably direct the ball a bit off target. Then the whole object of the relay would be lost."

Student Options

- "Are there other places where a relay throw might occur? If so, can you and your partners figure out where they are? Set up and practice these other relay plays."
- "Watch other groups who seem to be successful. See whether you can determine what they do differently from you and your group. If you can see some differences, try them to see whether they make you and your partners more successful."

Student Success Goal

- 30 total points out of a possible 40 in 2 sets of 10 sequences
  15 of 20 points as outfielder
  15 of 20 points as relay person

To Decrease Difficulty

- Have the catcher throw the ball less forcefully past the outfielder. [3]
- The relay person could make a shorter throw to home plate. [4]
- Have the catcher throw the ball at consistent speed and with consistent aim so that the outfielder wouldn't need to move right or left, and the relay person would already be in proper lateral position. [3]
- Slow the sequence so that the relay person has time to think while pivoting and throwing. [3, 5]

To Increase Difficulty

- Have the catcher throw the ball forcefully past the outfielder. [3]
- Have the catcher throw the ball past the outfielder and to the right and the left so that the relay person must move farther to get into position. [3]
- Have the catcher throw the ball past the outfielder at random speeds and in random directions. [8]
- Add a baserunner to the play. The baserunner (who must wear a batting helmet) should start jogging toward home plate as the outfielder throws the ball to the relay person. [6]

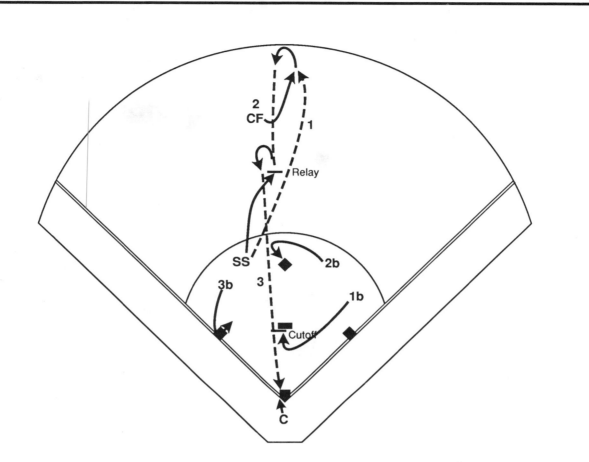

Variation: A center fielder, a relay person, a cutoff player (first baseman), a cover player (second baseman), a catcher, and a third baseman start at regulation coverage distances. The relay person throws the ball to deep outfield, and the catcher yells, ''Home!'' The relay and cutoff players line up with the outfielder and home plate and listen for further directions from the catcher. The outfielder throws the ball to the relay person, who pivots and throws home. The catcher now can call any of the following options:

- ''Cut two!'': Cutoff person cuts relay throw and throws to second base (covered by second baseman).
- ''Cut three!'': Cutoff person cuts relay throw and throws to third base.
- ''Cut four!'': Cutoff person cuts relay throw and throws home.

Step 23   Scrub and One-Pitch Games

The preface to these modified games in the participant's book contains a good explanation of the reasons for playing them. It should be given as a reading assignment prior to the students' playing these games.

By this point your students should have had opportunities to practice nearly all the skills of softball. Now they need to play modified games in which play situations occur as parts of the game. Then they will be able to react spontaneously to the situations that arise in regulation games. Spontaneous reactions, however, come about as a result of the players' analyzing the situation prior to the next player's turn at bat and determining what the actions should be if the ball is hit to them. You can reinforce this thinking process by making reference, before each batter, to the situation and asking your students to think about what their options would be if the ball were hit to them at different speeds and directions, or what offensive strategy would likely work best in this situation. Once again, as in other game play, do not take yourself out of the role of teacher by pitching or by playing. Your responsibility is to help the students learn as they play the modified games.

The various playing and strategic options possible in these games are also listed as game components for Situation Ball (see *Softball*, Step 19). Ask your students to make a list of the areas in which they are weak so that they can direct their own practice. Everyone needs to be an active participant in the cognitive aspect of game play. Cue your students, ask them questions about strategies, and have them help one another by asking questions or by reminding the team about the situation and its offensive and defensive options. One way

you can help the students get mentally involved in the game is to have them caucus prior to each batter to talk over the situation and decide what everyone's responsibilities are. This will take a great deal of time, so you don't want to do it very often. Perhaps if you call for a caucus only when there is a situation that has not occurred very often in previous play, it will be a positive learning experience.

Another way you might involve the students cognitively in the game is to pair up a more experienced player with a less experienced player. The more experienced students could be off the field of play charting the actions of their less experienced counterparts with the Offensive Player Scorecard and the Defensive Player Scorecard for Scrub (*Softball*, Step 23). In addition, the off-field partners should watch the play of their counterparts in their backing-up and baserunning play. Between innings, the off-field players can give feedback to the on-field players to help them learn more as they play the game. Perhaps you could, every other inning, have the charting students stand on the field of play, near but out of the way of the active fielders. This might be a bit awkward, but it does provide for immediate feedback to the active students. This organizational method keeps all students active in one location and provides individualized reinforcement.

The rules of the modified games are found in the participant's book. You will need to clarify any questions that arise in the course of play. In Scrub, the nature of the game forces students to play several different positions defensively. Consequently, the students will be required to use many different skills and will certainly be mentally challenged to develop a better strategic understanding of softball. This modified game can often be played as a culminating game at the end of a class period, or throughout the entire class period, if that is the need of the class. In One-pitch, however, a student could possibly stay at the same position for the entire game. You need to be observant as the students initially select their positions to make sure that the most dominant players do not usurp all "active" positions and relegate the "less involved" positions to the less dominant students. One option to prevent this is to allow the students to spend 2 innings per class period at one position, then to require them, on subsequent days, to repeat no more than one position that they have previously played.

You are the teacher of the class, and these games are not only for fun but also for student learning of game strategies. Do not play in any position in the students' game. Do not simply watch the play. Try to involve yourself by setting the stage for student analysis of every game situation. Ask the students questions so that they have to think about what the offensive and defensive strategies might be. This will help them anticipate the plays that will occur and react to them from a position of prior thought. Then the students will have a much greater chance to utilize their skills effectively in the game situation.

You can help your students succeed as total softball players. You can also help them discover their individual weaknesses and strengths. Your help in this regard should be directed toward motivating them to practice to overcome weaknesses and to recognize strengths. At this point, you are the catalyst who helps the students put together their knowledge and skills and helps them accept weaknesses as challenges for practice, not as symbols of defeat.

You can also try, at the end of each game, to help the students review the game and their roles in it. Perhaps asking them to set a goal for an individual practice in the first 10 minutes of the next class period will also help them reflect on their play and resolve to improve in areas that they know need work.

Modified Games

1. Scrub

[Corresponds to *Softball*, Step 23, Scrub]

Group Management and Safety Tips

- Your students should divide into experience-level groups. The less experienced players should play only against other less experienced students, the more experienced players should play only against other more experienced players. However, if the difference in experience levels is not great, simply divide the class into the desired number of teams.

- If it is impossible to have two fields being used simultaneously for play, have the teams play by color. One less experienced team and one more experienced team play separate innings but are one combined team (for example, the "maroon team"). The other combined team (the "gold team") also consists of one less experienced team and one more experienced team. The less experienced teams play odd-numbered innings; the more experienced even-numbered innings.

- Do not mix the two teams of a single color. The difference in skill levels heightens the chance of injury and increases your legal liability vulnerability.
- Divide the students into their experience-level groups and have them line up. Have each group number off from one end of the line, counting from 1 to 10. The number each person receives is his or her initial fielding position. The remaining persons in the experience-level group are at bat.
- Be sure to check over the fields of play to make certain that any hazards are accounted for by ground rules. Rule as out of play any obstacles that might be dangerous.
- All students must wear batting helmets while at bat and while running the bases.
- The catcher must wear a catcher's mask.

Equipment

- Gloves, 1 per player
- Sets of bases and home plate, 1 per playing field
- Balls, 3 per field (IncrediBalls® for LE, if necessary)
- Bats, varying lengths and weights
- Batting helmets, at least 4 of varying sizes per field
- Catcher's masks, 1 per field
- Pencils and checklists for the non-participating students so that they can chart a partner's play
- Participant's book, 2 copies so one can be placed at each playing field to serve as a resource

2. *One-Pitch*

[Corresponds to *Softball*, Step 23, One-Pitch]

Group Management and Safety Tips

- The students should divide into experience-level groups. The less experienced players should play only against other less experienced players; the more experienced players should play only against other more experienced players.
- If it is impossible to have two fields being used simultaneously for play, have the teams play by color as in Scrub.
- Do not mix players of different skill levels. Otherwise, the difference in skill levels would heighten the chance of injury and increase your legal liability vulnerability.
- Establish ground rules for any hazards that may affect student safety in game play.
- Review the One-pitch rules on batting. If the pitch is a ball and the batter does not swing at it, the batter gets a walk. If the pitch is a strike and the batter does not swing, he or she is out. If the pitch is hit into the field of play, it is played as in a regulation game.
- Have extra or nonparticipating students take part by umpiring, serving as base coaches, or charting the action of a counterpart on the field.
- All batters must wear batting helmets while batting and while running the bases.
- The catcher must wear a mask while catching.

Equipment

- Gloves, 1 per student
- Sets of bases and home plate, 1 per playing field
- Balls, 3 per field (IncrediBalls® for LE, if necessary)
- Bats, varying weights and lengths
- Batting helmets, at least 4 of varying sizes per field
- Catcher's masks, 1 per field
- Pencils and checklists for nonparticipants to use in charting

Step 24   Rundowns

Another skill that is not difficult but is usually restricted for more advanced play is the rundown. The rationale for placing this concept in a more advanced unit of softball is the same as that used for double plays, relays, and cutoffs: Games can be played without using these skills. When you plan your softball units for the various grade levels, you look for some things that you can introduce as new material for the later units. The motivation of your more experienced students is enhanced by their having something new to work on each year. Analyzing softball on the basis of the varying levels of game play is one way of determining a progressive order for skills and concepts.

As with most strategies or game concepts, the rundown has both a defensive and an offensive aspect. In this case, your instruction for the defense will focus on the techniques used by the fielders to put the baserunner out, and on who those fielders are to be in specific situations. The offensive aspect involves teaching the baserunner how best to get out of the rundown situation and avoid being tagged out. The best idea for the baserunner, of course, is to not get caught in that situation in the first place. You have already addressed that issue in the step on baserunning; however, even skilled runners sometimes get into rundowns and need to know how best to get out of them.

One defensive method, or system, for rundowns is presented in this step with the full acknowledgment that it is not the only one. If you are more familiar with another system that has worked well for your students, by all means use it. However, the management techniques and general format for the drills should be applicable, for the most part, regardless of the system used. The important thing is that some planned and practiced technique for your more experienced students is necessary to ensure that a runner caught off-base will be tagged out.

The fielders and the roles they play in rundowns occurring between different bases is outlined in the chart that appears in *Softball*, Step 24. Your initial observation should focus on the positions taken by the primary and, particularly, back-up fielders. The tendency for many students in the back-up role is to take up a position away from the action behind the base. It is important that you differentiate the back-up role in this play from the general backing-up role previously experienced by players. The back-up person in the rundown play is in an active play-making role and, therefore, must position himself or herself in front of the base. If the baserunner gets past the primary fielder, the back-up fielder is in the position to actually make the tag play on the runner.

Next, direct your attention to the principles outlined in the participant's book. Getting the runner out with a minimum number of throws, initiating the play by getting the runner to commit to a direction before any throw is made, keeping the runner away from the bases but closer to the base last touched, throwing the ball back and forth beside the runner rather than over the runner's head, and making the tag with a secure grip on the ball—these are the points toward which your cuing should be directed. Excess faking of the throw should be discouraged because the receiving fielder would be faked out more often than the runner.

Cuing for the baserunner should focus primarily on watching the person with the ball and deciding when to make the break for a base. The game concept of staying in the rundown until a preceding runner has the opportunity to score can be mentioned as part of your instruction. However, the opportunity for practice is limited to game situations.

Rundown Drill

1. *Full Rundown Play*
[Corresponds to *Softball*, Step 24, Drill 2]

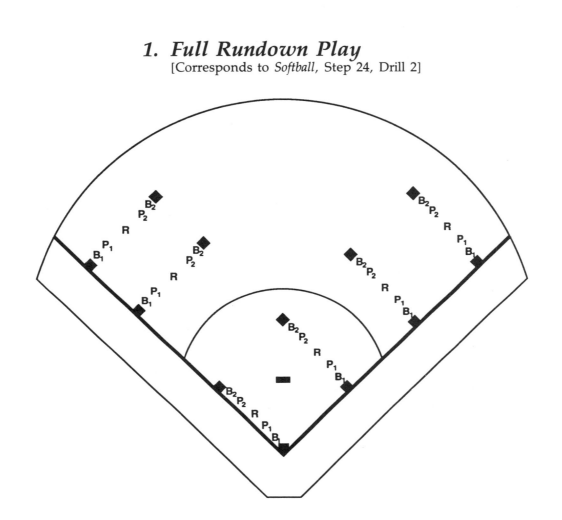

Group Management and Safety Tips

- 10 players can be accommodated for practice on the diamond by using the baseline between first base and second base as well as between home plate and third base as rundown areas.
- Additional groups can be set up in the outfield. Use the right field foul lines to position a series of bases. Establish a second line of bases in the field of play, parallel to and 60 feet from the right field foul line.
- Assign groups of five students per station.
- Have a chart of the fielders' involvement in rundown plays available at each station.

Equipment

- Bases, 2 per station
- Balls, 1 per station (extras available from instructor)
- Gloves, 1 per student (or minimum of four per station)
- Batting helmets of varying sizes at each station

Instructions and Cues to Primary Fielders

- "The primary fielder with the ball initiates the drill by moving toward the baserunner, thus forcing the runner to begin movement toward a base. Hold up the ball in your throwing hand where the receiving fielder can see it."
- "When the runner starts moving toward the other primary fielder (the 'receiving' fielder), throw the ball so that it passes by the runner's shoulder and arrives shoulder-high to the receiving fielder."
- "Throw the ball while the runner is still a few feet from the fielder."
- "Be ready for a return throw if the runner comes back toward you."
- "Primary receiving fielder, give a good open-glove target at your shoulder on the same side as the throwing hand of the throwing fielder."
- "Watch the ball and close the distance to the runner. Stop your movement as the runner approaches within a few feet of you; anticipate the throw from your partner. Catch the ball and tag the runner, if possible. If no tag is made, chase the runner toward your partner and continue the rundown play."
- "Try to make the baserunner return to the base he or she left."

Instructions and Cues to Baserunners

- "Baserunners must wear a batting helmet while participating in this drill. The throws are intended to pass *beside* your body, but the helmet will protect your head from off-target throws."
- "Baserunner, watch the fielder with the ball. Continuing to watch the ball, retreat away from that player when he or she moves in your direction while holding the ball."
- "If the player throws the ball to the other fielder prior to making any movement in your direction, immediately run toward the fielder who just made the throw and try to reach the base. Two long throws

will have to be made to put you out. You should be able to pass the primary fielder before a return throw is made."
- "Watch the back-up fielder's eyes and glove movement to determine whether the throw is approaching and to make your decision whether to continue to the base or stop and continue in the rundown."

Instructions and Cues to Back-Up Fielders

- "Play in front of the base and be ready to move into the primary fielding role if the baserunner passes the primary fielder at your base."
- "If, in the role of primary fielder, you are passed by the runner, rotate your position around behind the original back-up fielder. You now assume the back-up role. Remember to take up your position in front of the base, not behind it, because tagging the runner after he or she reaches the base is of no use."

Student Option

- "Each student is to think of one situation in which a rundown could occur. Choose the primary and back-up fielders and place them in position at the bases. Direct the practice of the group for your situation."

Student Success Goals

- The goal of the defense is to tag the runner out in 30 seconds, having used no more than two throws.
- The runner's goal is to reach base safely or to stay in the rundown for 30 seconds without being tagged out.

To Decrease Difficulty

- Have the group practice the Rotation Drill without a baserunner (see *Softball*, Step 24, Drill 1). [6]
- Have the group practice the Rotation Drill with a baserunner moving in slower motion. [3]

To Increase Difficulty

- Have the group practice the Full Rundown Play Number 2 using a sixth person as the player who has the ball and initiates the play (see *Softball*, Step 24, Drill 3). This initiator might represent the cutoff person who has cut the ball on a throw to home plate and catches the batter-baserunner rounding first base and attempting to advance to second base. [6, 8]

Step 25   Coed Slow Pitch Game

Throughout this instructor's book, we have stressed that you should not let your students simply play. Our view has been that you are in an instructional setting with something meaningful to teach. The skills, game concepts, strategies, and rules needed to play the regulation game constitute the major content areas for your softball unit, not the game itself. Full game play has its place, especially as part of your more advanced units, but it is not the primary content of your softball unit, regardless of the students' experience level. The student's prerequisites for playing the official game are skill proficiency, decision-making ability in the strategies of game play, and the ability to participate in accordance with the rules of play.

The full game selected for the final step in the participant's text is the coed slow pitch game. The coed game is especially appropriate because many classes today are coeducational. Softball is one of the few team sports (volleyball is another) that have official games designed specifically for coed play. The official coed rules have undoubtedly been developed on the assumption that members of one sex are stronger and more skillful than members of the other sex. Therefore, teams are made up of equal numbers of players of each gender. These assumptions may not always be valid in your class situation. However, some social awareness for your students could be provided by males and females participating together in a sport setting and working toward common goals. You may need to look beyond "maleness" and "femaleness" to equate your teams, but in so doing try to maintain the coed makeup of the teams.

The major rules for coed play are outlined in *Softball*, Step 25, and are not repeated here. The focus is on what you, the instructor, can do with the game. For one thing, use this coed game as a true culminating experience. Now is finally the time to let your students simply play. Determine the interest your upper-level classes have in competition. Set up a tournament for the last week(s) of the unit. Provide an alternate activity for students not wishing to be highly competitive. Instead of a tournament with leagues and ultimate winners, set up games day by day and let the students direct the focus of the games. Their focus might be on playing with friends, playing for fun, or even working further on certain aspects of the game (an unlikely but possible choice).

Regardless of the focus of the games, your primary role as teacher is to establish a safe environment and make sure the games are conducted with both the safety and the enjoyment of the participants in mind.

- Monitor the team selection and make adjustments to ensure equal skill levels on the teams.
- Provide sufficient numbers on ''permanent'' teams to take care of possible student absenteeism.
- Set up the alternate field (you will probably need the regular diamond plus an adjacent field for most classes) with hazards eliminated.
- Establish ground rules for each field of play, with safety as a primary focus.
- Encourage participation
- Encourage student involvement in the organization and conduct of the games. Provide for student coaches, officials, and so forth, if desired by the more competitive teams.
- Encourage student decision making in all levels of game play.
- Encourage play with a purpose, be it winning the tournament or having fun with friends every day in class.

Evaluation Ideas

Evaluation is one of the most difficult tasks a physical educator faces in teaching. How does one use evaluations in ways that are supportive of rather than threatening to students' efforts to improve their skills and, at the same time, that gather data that indicate the students' achievement of the objectives of the unit? That is the $64,000 question. In an educational setting, there is no way to assess student acquisition of skills and knowledge (learning) without utilizing some form of evaluation.

First and foremost, evaluation should be linked to the objectives you have set for the softball unit. It would not be fair to students to test them on skills and knowledge that have not been covered. Additionally, it is unlikely that students will do their best on tests administered in setups unrelated to those they have used when practicing the skills. Consequently, skill testing and knowledge testing should be based upon the actual content of your softball unit and conducted in ways that reflect the type of practice that the students have experienced.

It is important that you share with your students the goals and objectives you have established for the softball unit. It may help them to know the things on which they will be evaluated. A discussion of the course objectives and the items of evaluation could help the students see that these are related. Similarly, telling the students that the evaluation will be based upon their current experience levels and the progress they have made, rather than upon their being compared to everyone else in the class, may help allay their fears about evaluation.

The objectives you set for the softball unit will depend upon the age and experience levels of the students in your classes. Consequently, as you plan the unit, you need to be explicit in your expectations for student skill and knowledge acquisition. Then you can select or design evaluation tools that are specifically tailored to your classes.

You are the person who is most directly affected by the evaluation data you collect. Such data can help you assign students' grades and assess the degree of skill and knowledge acquired by your students. This will help you plan both during the unit and after it is completed. The progress your students show in the softball activities should enable you to adjust your daily lesson planning to reflect their learning. Similarly, the same evaluation data can be used to modify your Scope and Teaching Sequence (see Appendices B.1 and B.2) for future softball units.

TESTING PROCEDURES

The sport of softball requires that students exhibit both psychomotor skills and cognitive understanding of rules and tactics as they practice and play. Thus, it is important to assess both during the unit. There are numerous ways of determining skill proficiency and testing cognitive knowledge. The method you select is likely to reflect your approach to teaching and the value you place on evaluation. Both qualitative and quantitative evaluations can be done throughout the unit by using the many skill checklists and student success goals found in the participant's textbook. If you use this formative evaluation approach, you might also allow students to repeat the "tests" and record the best scores they achieve. It might also be possible to allow students to select skills tests to perform for evaluation from a larger list of drills that can be used as skills tests. Thus, they will be able to practice specific tests and do their best for evaluation purposes. In addition, the use of assessment throughout the unit will help your students determine the areas in which they have strengths and the areas in which they need more practice or study.

Perhaps you will want some indication of the technical proficiency of your students as they execute the skills. There are many skill checklists in the steps of the participant's book. Many of the suggested Student Options in this instructor's book involve students working together to help one another analyze and improve their skill technique. There is little reason for students not to be used to provide evaluation data on the technical proficiency of their peers. Should you have them do this, or should you use the Student Success Goals as skills tests, you will want to encourage your students to bring their textbooks to class. This will help them know what to look for and how the skill should be done. You will have to establish a rating scale of some sort for the checklists so that the student assessors or the other raters will be able to quantify their observations. Additionally, if you allow the students to repeat a "drill–skill test" or rating checklist after they have had additional practice time (even time practicing other skills, because so many of the same skills are used in different combinations in softball), you can get data that describes the students' progress or lack thereof.

The rules and tactics of softball are applied when the skills are combined and used in game-like situations. It would be useful to assess your students' cognitive understanding of a rule or a strategy when it is relevant to the material being covered or practiced. This means that you would probably give a series of knowledge quizzes throughout the unit, at the point in the unit when the tactics or rules in question are inherent in the practice and play being done. You can also, in such quizzes, include questions on skill technique to ascertain whether the students understand the desired skill execution. Such quizzes and a final or culminating test can be developed by selecting appropriate questions from the bank of test questions that follows. As you read the questions in the test bank, you will realize that some are designed for less-experienced students and some are more appropriate for more experienced students. The questions in the test bank are certainly not exhaustive; therefore, you will more than likely want to develop questions of your own that reflect the intent of your unit.

It is not necessary to test on every skill taught, particularly because many skills are used not in isolation but in combination with other skills. Often you can evaluate students' skill proficiency while they are involved in modified game play. There are several ways to do this:

1. You can have students observe partners and record Success Goals or assess technique.

2. You can watch as students play; assess the skill or cognitive aspect you are interested in. In order to ensure that you focus your evaluation observation, it is best that you key on two or three common offensive and defensive skills or tactics to be demonstrated by students in the course of playing the modified game. Then, you are eliminating some subjectivity as you do the assessment. A three-point rating scale (proficient, or ✔ +; acceptable, or ✔; needs work, or ✔ −) is usually as specific as one can get in such game play observation sessions.

3. You can videotape the modified game so that you can make your rating assessments later outside of class.

4. You can also use the videotape replay in class to test your students' knowledge by having them identify particular skill errors or describe the appropriate offensive and defensive tactics called for in a particular situation. You would probably want to select a clear model from the tape, then provide some sort of question that the students could respond to as they watch the replay. An example would be a shot of a player throwing the ball sidearm from the outfield. The students would look at the tape and identify the demonstrated technique error by choosing from a multiple-choice list such as this:

a. The outfielder is stepping toward the target with the incorrect foot.

b. The outfielder is not following through after releasing the ball.

c. The outfielder is releasing the ball too early.

d. The outfielder is not throwing the ball overhand.

ADMINISTERING TESTS

There are ways for you to administer the quizzes and tests throughout the unit rather than simply at the beginning and the end. If there are opportunities for your students to do individual practice, you can give them the option to take a "drill–skill test" or to repeat one or more that they have already done. There are times when all of your students may not be able to practice in the modified games going on because of a lack of field space for enough game setups. If there are adjacent practice areas, the students not playing the modified games could take the skill tests, or, if they wish to improve their scores, they could repeat any test they have previously completed.

This format can also be utilized for administrating cognitive quizzes and written tests. Rather than having all students in the class take written quizzes and tests at the same time, have half of the class take the quiz or test while the other half of the class is involved in skill practice or modified game play. Then, midway through the class session, the students playing the game or practicing could switch roles with the test takers. You could have the less experienced students take the written test while the more experienced practice or play, and vice versa. This format will enable you to have all students involved in meaningful activity throughout the class period.

The strongest indicator of student learning is progress in skill proficiency and cognitive understanding. However, progress is often difficult to measure for one of two reasons: Students either tend to be skill-test "smart," or they get nervous and do poorly on the pretest. If students know that you are looking for improvement, they will often intentionally do poorly on the initial test so that they can show increased levels of proficiency on later repeats of the test.

There are ways to deal with the fears of those who do poorly on the pretest. First, if the skill test is one the students can practice and repeat, they tend to worry less about "blowing" the first attempt. Second, if the skill test has criteria appropriate to the skill experience level of the students, they can see that improvement is possible. For example, you can reduce the Success Goals of some drills for the less experienced students or increase the Success Goals for the more experienced students in order to help them believe that they can reach the goal established.

Third, in order to discourage intentional pretest "flunkies," you can weight the progress of students according to their experience level. For example, the less experienced student can be expected to improve to a greater degree (not to a higher skill level) than can the more experienced student. Weighting the amount of improvement accordingly and assigning points to be calculated into the grade according to the weighting can account for differences in the degree of improvement possible. For example, at first a less experienced player successfully fielded 1 out of 10 fungo-hit ground balls; after practicing, the same person successfully fielded 9 out of 10 fungo-hit ground balls. A more experienced student, on the other hand, successfully fielded 7 out of 10 ground balls on his or her initial attempt; after practicing, that same student successfully fielded 10 out of 10 ground balls. The less experienced student improved a total of 8, whereas the more experienced student improved by only 3. The improvement scores are then weighted so that for less experienced students, an improvement score of 0-4 equals 1 point, an improvement score of 5-7 equals 2 points, and an improvement score of 8 or more equals 3 points. For more experienced students, an improvement score of 1 equals 1 point, of 2 equals 2 points, and of 3 equals 3 points. This would mean that the students in the previous example would both acquire 3 points for their improvement on the drill–skill test. Now they are both able to get "good" grades although they ended at different skill levels and one had more room for improvement. This technique works well if you are interested in using progress as an element in evaluation.

Regardless of the types and formats for evaluation that you choose to utilize, it is essential that they be based on the goals and objectives that you have established for the softball course and for your students' involvement in it. Additionally, if you use a number of different things to evaluate your students, no single skill test, technique evaluation, or written test will have an inordinate impact on a student's overall assessment. This should help reduce the students' fear that one bad day will "kill" them in terms of a grade.

Test Bank

The following sections feature questions about softball rules, strategies, and techniques of skill execution. Note that a particular rule, strategy, or technique idea may be found in more than one section. You can select questions from this test bank to develop a quiz or a test. You can also get ideas for making up questions of your own to supplement those you select from the test bank.

WRITTEN EVALUATION QUESTIONS

Multiple Choice Directions: Please write in the correct letters in the space at the left side of the question number.

_____ 1. Your keys to success for catching a ball include
   a. meeting the ball out in front of your body.
   b. using your glove hand only.
   c. pointing your fingers up if the ball is above your waist.
   d. bringing the ball to the throwing position using a four-finger grip.

_____ 2. Your keys to success for executing the overhand throw include
   a. stepping in the direction of the throw with the throwing-side foot.
   b. stepping in the direction of the throw with the glove-side foot.
   c. using a four-finger grip.
   d. using a two-finger grip.

_____ 3. Fielding a ground ball is made easier by
   a. having your throwing-side foot ahead as you field the ball.
   b. keeping your legs straight and your hips high.
   c. watching the ball go into your glove.
   d. waiting until the last minute to move into position to field the ball.

_____ 4. Your position for the contact point in hitting should include
   a. hips square to the intended line of flight of the ball.
   b. arms extended.
   c. eyes focused on the area in the field where you want the ball to go.
   d. front leg straight, back leg bent at the knee.

_____ 5. In slow pitch, the inside pivot is used by the shortstop at second base on a double play ball hit to the
   a. first baseman.
   b. second baseman.
   c. pitcher.
   d. third baseman.

_____ 6. The drag-step pivot is used by the shortstop at second base on a double play ball hit to the

   a. first baseman.
   b. second baseman.
   c. pitcher.
   d. third baseman.

_____ 7. The rocker-step pivot is used by the second baseman at second base on a double play ball hit to the

   a. first baseman.
   b. shortstop.
   c. pitcher.
   d. third baseman.

_____ 8. The crossover-step pivot is used by the second baseman at second base on a double play ball hit to the

   a. first baseman.
   b. shortstep.
   c. pitcher.
   d. third baseman.

_____ 9. With a runner on first base and less than two outs, in a game for less experienced players, when a ground ball is hit to the shortstop, the covering player for the force-out on the lead runner going into second base is the

   a. first baseman.
   b. second baseman.
   c. pitcher.
   d. third baseman.

_____ 10. With a runner on first base and less than two outs, in a game for less experienced players, the shortstop covers second base for the force-out on the lead runner when a ground ball is hit to the

   a. first baseman.
   b. second baseman.
   c. pitcher.
   d. third baseman.

_____ 11. A hit ball would be declared a fair ball when

   a. a ground ball hits third base and goes into foul territory.
   b. a pop-up lands on home plate and goes back to the backstop.
   c. a bunt, in fast pitch, lands in foul territory but comes to rest in fair territory in the infield.
   d. a ground ball down the first base line hits a rock in fair territory and is then touched by the first baseman on foul ground.
   e. a fly ball in fair territory in the outfield goes off the glove of the left fielder (standing in fair territory) and is picked up by that fielder.

_____ 12. With runners on first and second in a slow pitch game, the batter hits a ball to the fence. The center fielder fields the ball and prepares to make the play to home plate. In this situation,

    a.   the shortstop is the relay person.

    b.   the second baseman is the relay person.

    c.   the first baseman is the cutoff person.

    d.   the third baseman is the cutoff person.

    e.   the first baseman backs up home.

    f.   the pitcher backs up home.

    g.   the second baseman covers second for a cutoff throw.

    h.   the shortstop covers second for a cutoff throw.

_____ 13. When executing the overhand throw, do _not_

    a.   rotate your throwing arm back.

    b.   step in the direction of the throw.

    c.   lead with the ball as your arm comes forward.

    d.   extend your forearm.

_____ 14. The softball vocabulary does not include

    a.   home run.

    b.   double play.

    c.   hole in one.

    d.   tag play.

_____ 15. It is recommended that less experienced softball students first learn how to throw

    a.   overhand.

    b.   underhand.

    c.   sidearm.

    d.   a lob toss.

_____ 16. In fielding a fly ball, the outfielder should

    a.   get behind the ball and be moving toward the infield when catching it.

    b.   field the ball over the glove-side shoulder.

    c.   be looking at the intended target of the throw while moving toward the fly.

    d.   field the ball with the glove hand only.

_____ 17. On a ball hit between the left fielder and the center fielder that travels to the fence, the relay person is the

    a.   third baseman.

    b.   shortstop.

    c.   second baseman.

    d.   first baseman.

_____ 18. On a ball hit to right field with a subsequent play at home plate, the cutoff person is the
    a. shortstop.
    b. third baseman.
    c. second baseman.
    d. first baseman.

_____ 19. With runners on first and second base and no outs, a ground ball is hit sharply to the pitcher. The play should go
    a. to third, then first.
    b. to second, then first.
    c. to first, then second.
    d. to third, then second.

_____ 20. In slow pitch, when there are no runners on base, the player backing up the first baseman when a ground ball is hit to the shortstop is the
    a. pitcher.
    b. second baseman.
    c. right fielder.
    d. catcher.

_____ 21. The pitching distance required in slow pitch softball is
    a. 40 feet.
    b. 46 feet.
    c. 52 feet.
    d. 60 feet.

_____ 22. The proper method of rounding a base is to
    a. run straight to the base, then make a sharp turn toward the next base.
    b. approach the base on the outside of the base path and touch the inside corner of the bag with the left foot.
    c. approach the base on the outside of the base path and touch the inside corner of the bag with the right foot.
    d. approach the base on the inside of the base path and touch the inside corner with the right foot.

_____ 23. A regulation softball game consists of
    a. six innings.
    b. seven innings.
    c. nine innings.
    d. ten innings.

_____ 24. The bases that may be overrun without the runner's liability of being tagged out are
    a. first and second.
    b. first and third.
    c. second and third.
    d. first and home.

_____ 25. When defining the "infield fly rule," which of the following statements are correct:

    a. There must be less than two outs.

    b. There must be two outs.

    c. There are runners on first and third.

    d. There are runners on first and second.

    e. The bases are loaded.

    f. The batter hits a fair or foul fly ball that is playable by an infielder.

    g. The batter hits a fair fly ball playable by an infielder.

    h. The batter is out only if the fielder catches the ball.

    i. The baserunners may advance at the risk of being put out.

    j. The baserunners may not advance.

_____ 26. In a slow pitch game, there is a runner on first base with no outs, and a left-handed player is up to bat. The batter hits a sharp ground ball to the first baseman, who is playing deep behind the baseline between first and second. In the ensuing play,

    a. the first baseman fields the ball, steps on first, and throws to second for a force play on the runner going to second.

    b. the second baseman covers second.

    c. the first baseman throws to second base for a force play.

    d. the shortstop covers second base on the inside (infield side) of the base.

    e. the shortstop covers second base on the outside (outfield side) of the base.

    f. the first baseman covers first base for the return throw for a double play.

    g. the shortstop backs up the throw to second base.

    h. the left fielder backs up the throw to second.

    i. the right fielder backs up the throw to second.

_____ 27. The fielder's glove fingers should point down when the player catches a ball

    a. at the waist.

    b. below the waist.

    c. above the waist.

_____ 28. On a ground ball hit to the third baseman, the covering player at second base for a force play is the

    a. first baseman.

    b. second baseman.

    c. third baseman.

    d. shortstop.

_____ 29. The covering player at second base for a force play on a ground ball hit to the pitcher is the

    a. first baseman.

    b. second baseman.

    c. third baseman.

    d. shortstop.

_____ 30. The infield fly rule is intended to prevent an infielder from intentionally dropping a pop fly and then making a
  a. play on the batter at first base.
  b. force play on the batter at first base.
  c. double play.
  d. tag play on the lead runner.

True/False Directions: Please write ''True'' or ''False'' in the space at the left side of the question number.

_____ 1. While running out a ground ball hit to the shortstop, the batter should run directly over first base, turn to the right, then return to the base to avoid being liable to be tagged out.

_____ 2. With a runner on first base, a ground ball is hit to the third baseman. The shortstop covers second base for the force play there.

_____ 3. A baserunner is called out when, running in fair territory, he or she is hit by a batted ball that has been missed by the first baseman.

_____ 4. In fast pitch, the strike zone is that space over home plate between the shoulders and the top of the knees of a batter assuming a normal batting stance.

_____ 5. The throw to third base for a tag play should be thrown so that it arrives shoulder-high to the covering player.

_____ 6. The two basic pitching styles in fast pitch softball are the windmill and the slipshot.

_____ 7. In a slow pitch game, 10 players constitute a team, and the right fielder is the player in Position 10.

_____ 8. The positioning of the infielders for the start of a slow pitch game is more similar to baseball than to fast pitch softball.

_____ 9. When tagging up and advancing on a caught fly ball, the runner leaves the base when the fielder contacts the ball.

_____ 10. A pop-up lands in fair territory between home and third base, rolls into foul territory, then is touched by the catcher. It is a fair ball.

_____ 11. A runner is on second base with no outs. The batter hits a long foul fly ball to right field. The runner on second tags up and advances to third base after the catch, arriving at the base before the right fielder's throw. The runner is safe at third.

_____ 12. A fly ball is hit down the line into left field. The ball lands in fair territory but rolls into foul territory, where it is picked up by the left fielder. It is a foul ball.

_____ 13. A batter-baserunner, while running in fair territory to first base, is hit by a ball thrown to make the play at first. The batter-baserunner is out.

_____ 14. In slow pitch, the baserunner may advance on a passed ball.

_____ 15. In a slow pitch, there is a batter with a count of two strikes. The batter swings and fouls off the next pitch. The batter is out.

_____ 16. A regulation softball game consists of nine innings.

_____ 17. A baserunner in slow pitch may not lead off the base until the ball reaches home plate or is hit by the batter.

_____ 18. A baserunner in fast pitch may not lead off the base until the ball leaves the pitcher's hand.

_____ 19. The pitcher and catcher are sometimes called the *battery*.

_____ 20. In slow pitch, the strike zone is that space over home plate between the shoulders and the top of the knees of a batter assuming a normal batting stance.

_____ 21. A pitcher may change to another position, then return to pitch in the same game.

_____ 22. On a ground ball hit to the shortstop, the first baseman's stretch is timed with the fielding of the ball by the shortstop.

_____ 23. Bunting is not permitted in the game of slow pitch.

_____ 24. Executing the double play at second base is usually easier for the shortstop than for the second baseman.

_____ 25. A slow pitch team fields 10 players, whereas a fast pitch team fields only 9.

_____ 26. There is no limit on the height of the pitch in slow pitch as long as it has an arc of at least 3 feet.

_____ 27. If a hitter having trouble hitting consistently pops up, the trouble may be due to overstriding.

_____ 28. Slow pitch strategy commonly employs four outfielders, who can be located in a variety of positions on the field.

_____ 29. In slow pitch softball, the batter is declared out if he or she chops downward when hitting the pitched ball.

_____ 30. The batter is entitled to first base if hit by a pitch in fast pitch softball, but not in slow pitch.

_____ 31. A batted ball that hits third base and bounces into foul territory is a fair ball.

_____ 32. When a batter-baserunner attempting to stretch a hit is tagged out going into third base, he or she is credited with a triple.

_____ 33. The catcher makes an overthrow to first base that remains in fair territory and travels down the right field line. The baserunner may advance only to second base.

_____ 34. With a baserunner on second base, a ground ball is hit to the shortstop. In an attempt to field the ball in the baseline, the shortstop runs into the baserunner. The decision of the umpire is that the baserunner is out for interference.

_____ 35. The defensive leader of a softball team is normally the catcher.

_____ 36. A baserunner running from first to second base is hit by a batted ball after the second baseman makes a misplay in fielding the ball. The decision of the umpire is that the runner is out.

_____ 37. The sidearm throw should be used when a long-distance throw is needed.

_____ 38. The basic defensive strategy used by less experienced players in game situations is to get one out at a time by making the force-out on the lead runner.

_____ 39. The relay is a defensive play used when the distance is too great for the outfielder to throw the ball all the way to home.

_____ 40. You should try to pull the ball on an outside pitch.

_____ 41. The second baseman uses the sidearm throw when fielding a ground ball and making a throw to first base.

_____ 42. The cutoff is a defensive play used when there is no play on the lead runner (usually going into third or home) but there is the possibility of a play on another runner.

_____ 43. A baserunner running in fair territory, hit by a batted ball prior to its passing a fielder other than the pitcher, is out.

_____ 44. The delayed steal is a tag play used by the defense to put out a runner caught between bases.

_____ 45. The modified game that gives participants experience playing every different position is called Scrub.

_____ 46. The crow-hop is used by the pitcher when delivering the ball to the batter.

Diagram Directions: Complete the diagrams provided with each of the following questions. Carefully read and follow the directions for labeling each diagram.

1. Diagram the regular-depth, straight-away starting positions for the defensive players at the time of the first pitch of a slow pitch softball game. Use the position numbers to mark the *exact* positions of the fielders. Accompany each position number with the corresponding symbol (e.g., P for pitcher).

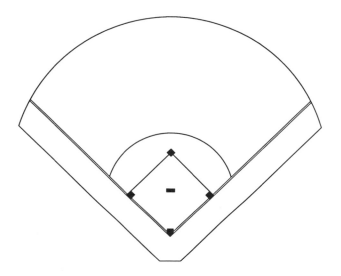

2. Diagram the positions for all players (including baserunners) in a bases-loaded, no-out situation in the second inning of play. Place the symbols (e.g., P for pitcher, B for baserunner) in the *exact* positions the players would take for the first pitch to the next batter.

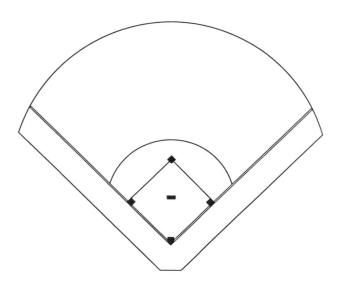

3. There is a runner on first base with no outs in the first inning of a slow pitch game for more experienced players. The batter hits a ground ball to the second baseman, who is in the regular-depth position. Indicate all fielders' starting positions before the ball was hit with the appropriate symbols for each position. Diagram the double play attempt by the fielders. Show the path of the hit ball by a line of alternating dots and dashes, with an arrow showing the direction (– · – · – · – · ➤); the path of the thrown ball by a dashed line with an arrow showing the direction (– – ➤); and the paths of the fielders moving to cover their bases by solid lines, with arrows showing the directions (——➤). Mark the *exact* positions taken by the covering fielders at the bases by large solid dots (●).

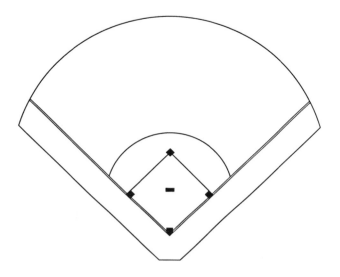

4. A strong, right-handed pull hitter is at bat with a runner on first base. The defense over-shifts. Use the correct position numbers to diagram the *exact* positions of the fielders for the first pitch to the batter.

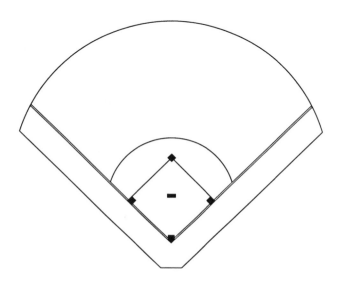

ANSWER KEY FOR WRITTEN EVALUATION QUESTIONS

Multiple Choice

1. a, c
2. b, d
3. c
4. a, b, d
5. c
6. a, b
7. b
8. d
9. b
10. a, b, c
11. a, c, e
12. a, c, f, g
13. c
14. c
15. a
16. a
17. b
18. d
19. a
20. d
21. b
22. b
23. b
24. d
25. a, d, e, g, i
26. c, e, f, h
27. b
28. b
29. d
30. c

True/False

1. False
2. False
3. False
4. False
5. False
6. False
7. False
8. True
9. True
10. False
11. True
12. False
13. True
14. False
15. True
16. False
17. True
18. True
19. True
20. False
21. True
22. False
23. True
24. True
25. True
26. False
27. True
28. True
29. True
30. True
31. True
32. False
33. False
34. True
35. True
36. False
37. False
38. True
39. True
40. False
41. True
42. True
43. True
44. False
45. True
46. False

Diagrams

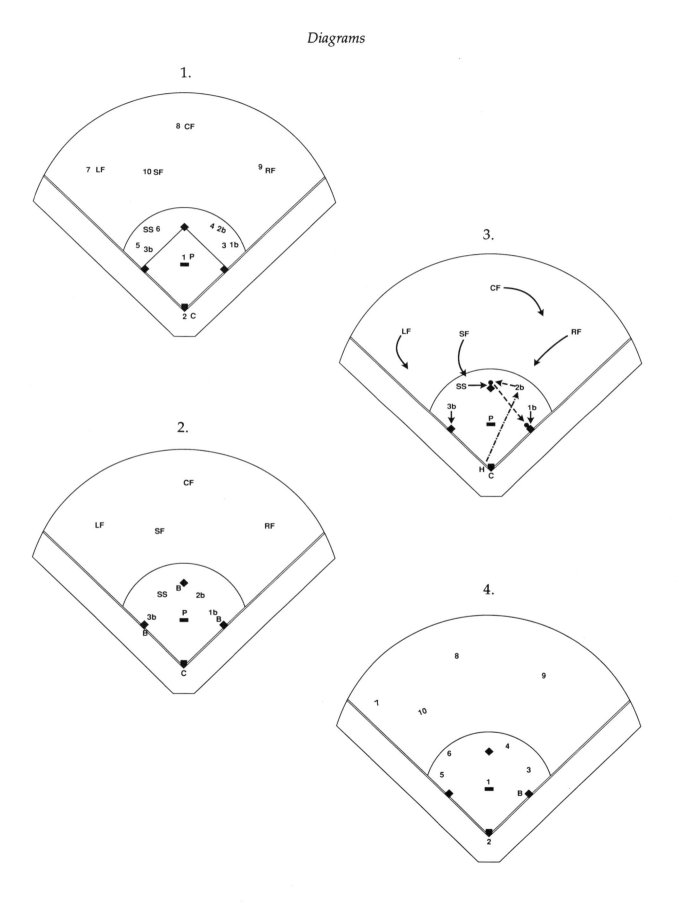

Appendices

A   Knowledge Structure of Softball (Overview)
B.1 Sample Scope and Teaching Sequence
B.2 Scope and Teaching Sequence (Blank)
C.1 Sample Individual Program
C.2 Individual Program (Blank)
D.1 Sample Lesson Plan
D.2 Lesson Plan (Blank)

Appendix A
How to Use the Knowledge Structure Overview

A knowledge structure is an instructional tool—by completing one you make a very personal statement about what you know about a subject and how that knowledge guides your decisions in teaching and coaching. The knowledge structure for softball outlined here has been designed for a teaching environment, with teaching progressions that emphasize technique and performance objectives in realistic settings. In a coaching environment, you would need to emphasize more physiological and conditioning factors, with training progressions that prepare athletes for competition.

The Knowledge Structure of Softball shows the first page or an *overview* of a completed knowledge structure. The knowledge structure is divided into broad categories of information that are used for all of the participant and instructor guides in the Steps to Success Activity Series. Those categories are

- physiological training and conditioning,
- background knowledge,
- psychomotor skills and tactics, and
- psycho-social concepts.

Physiological training and conditioning has several subcategories, including warm-up and cool-down. Research in exercise physiology and the medical sciences has demonstrated the importance of warming up and cooling down after physical activity. The participant's books and instructor's guides present principles and exercises for effective warm-up and cool-down, which, because of time restrictions, are usually the only training activities done in the teaching environment. In a more intense coaching environment, additional categories should be added—training principles, injury prevention, training progressions, and nutrition principles.

The background-knowledge category presents subcategories of information that represent essential background knowledge that all instructors should command when meeting their classes. Softball background knowledge includes playing the game, basic rules and safety, softball today, and equipment.

Under psychomotor skills and tactics, all the individual skills in an activity are named. For softball, the offensive skills are hitting and baserunning. The defensive skills are catching, throwing overhand, fielding ground balls, fielding fly balls, pitching, and throwing sidearm. These skills are also presented in a recommended order of presentation. In a complete knowledge structure, each skill is broken down into subskills, delineating selected technical, biomechanical, motor learning, and other teaching and coaching points that describe mature performance. These points can be found in the Keys to Success or in the Keys to Success Checklists within the participant's book.

Once individual skills are identified and analyzed, then selected basic tactics (team techniques) of the activity are also identified and analyzed. For softball, the offensive tactics are place hitting, overrunning a base, rounding a base, hitting behind the runner, tagging up on a fly ball, and running in a rundown. The defensive tactics are covering and backing up, getting the lead runner, force plays, tag plays, relays, cutoffs, rundowns, and three types of situation position play. Notice that they are arranged to reflect the decision making strategies and capabilities of learners as they become more proficient.

The psycho-social category identifies selected concepts from the sport psychology and sociology literature that have been shown to contribute to learners' understanding of and success in the activity. These concepts are built into the key concepts and the activities for teaching. For softball, the concepts are anticipation before the pitch: read and prepare; and anticipation during the play: read and react.

In order to be a successful teacher or coach, you must convert what you have learned as a student or done as a player or performer to a form of knowing that is both conscious and appropriate for presentation to others. A knowledge structure helps you with this transition and speeds your *steps to success*. You should view a knowledge structure as the most basic level of teaching knowledge you possess for a sport or activity. For more information on how to develop your own knowledge structure, see the textbook that accompanies this series, *Instructional Design for Teaching Physical Activities*.

Knowledge Structure of Softball (Overview)

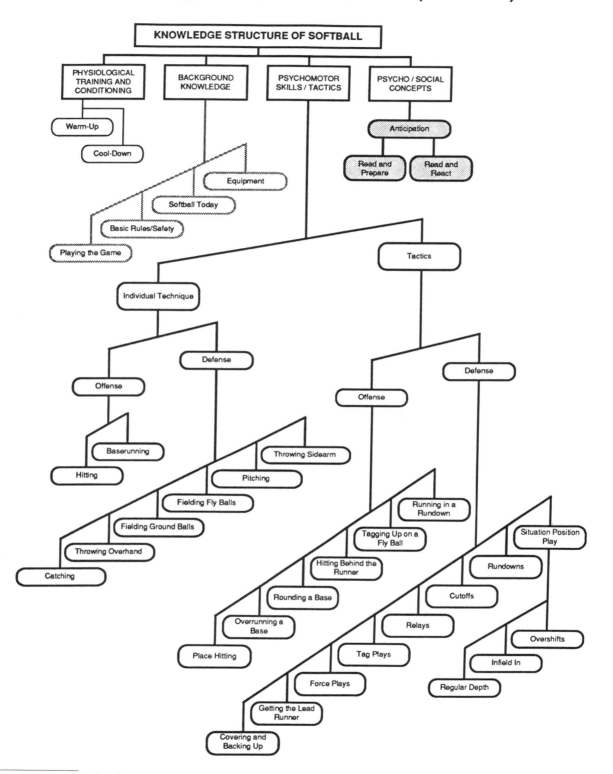

Note. From "The Role of Expert Knowledge Structures in an Instructional Design Model for Physical Education" by J.N. Vickers, 1983, *Journal of Teaching in Physical Education*, **2**(3), pp. 25, 27. Copyright 1983 by Joan N. Vickers. Adapted by permission. This Knowledge Structure of Softball was designed specifically for the Steps to Success Activity Series by Joan N. Vickers, Judy P. Wright, Diane L. Potter, and Gretchen A. Brockmeyer.

Appendix B.1

Sample Scope and Teaching Sequence

NAME OF ACTIVITY Softball
LEVEL OF LEARNER Less Experienced

Legend:
- **N** New
- **R** Review
- **C** Continue
- **P** Student-Directed Practice in Stations (with number of stations)
- **NP** New material practiced in stations (with number of stations)

Note: "Combining Two Basics" serves as the Warm-Up Every Class Session (continues across all sessions, indicated by arrows).

Step	Activity / Session Number	1	2	3	4	5	6	7	8	9	10	11	12	13	14	15	16	17	18	19	20	21	22	23	24	25	26	27	28	29	30
1	Catching	N	N	R	C	C	C	C			C	C	C	C			C	C	C	C	C	C	C	C	C	C	C	C	C	C	C
2	Throwing Overhand	N	N	R	C	C	C	C			C	C	C	C			C	C	C	C	C	C	C	C	C	C	C	C	C	C	C
1–3	Combining Two Basics			N	R	C	C	C	→	Warm-Up Every Class Session																				↑	
4	Fielding a Ground Ball			N	R	C	C	C		C	C	C					C	C	C	C	C		C	C	P_2	C	C	C	C	C	C
5	Hitting and Using the Batting Tee			R	P_1	N	P_1	R		C	C	C																			
6	Fungo Hitting a Ground Ball					N	P_2	R		C												C									
1–7	Four-Skill Combination							N	P_1	C																					
8	Pitching								NP_1			P_3				P_1	C	C	C	C	C	C	C	C		C	C	C	C	C	C
9	Baserunning								NP_2		C	C				C	C	C	C	C	C	C	C	C	C	C	C	C	C	C	C
10	Position Play									N	C	C			N	C	C	C	C	C	C	C	C	C	C	C	C	C	C	C	C
11	Force Play and Tag Play									NP_2	R	C				C	C	C	C	C	C	C	C	C	C	C	C	C	C	C	C
12	Grounders-Only T-Ball									N	P_2	C																			
13	Fielding a Fly Ball											NP_1	R	C	C	C	C	C	C	C	C		C	C	P_2	C	C	C	C	C	C
14	Hitting a Soft Toss												N	C	C	C															
15	Fungo Hitting a Fly Ball													N	C	C						C									
14–16	Fielding Hit Fly Balls														P_2	N															
17	Position-Play Half-Field Games															N	C														
18	Hitting a Pitched Ball																N	C	C	C	C		C	C	C	C	C	C	C	C	C
19	Situation-Ball Game																	N	C	N	R	R	C	C	P_2	C	C	C	C	C	C
20	Throwing Sidearm										N					R	N	N	C												
21	Double Plays																		N SS	N 2b	C	C	C	P_1	P_2	C	C	C	C	C	C
22	Relays and Cutoffs															N					C	C	C/N	C	P_2	C	C	C	C	C	C
23	Scrub and One-Pitch Games																			N	N		C	C			C	C	C		
24	Rundowns																								NP_1	N					
25	Coed Slow Pitch Game																									N	C	C	C	C	C

Notes:

Appendix B.2
How to Use the Scope and Teaching Sequence Form

A completed scope and teaching sequence is, in effect, a master lesson plan. It lists all the individual skills to be included in your course, recorded (vertically) in the progressive sequence in which you have decided to present them and showing (horizontally) the manner and the sessions in which you will teach them.

The Sample Scope and Teaching Sequence (Appendix B.1) illustrates how the chart is to be used. When read vertically, this chart indicates that in Session 9, for example, the class will continue (C) working on the skills presented in Steps 1, 2, 3, 4, 5, and 6 by practicing (P_1) them as a part of the combination skill of fielding and hitting (fungo or tee-hit) ground balls. The subscript beside the ''P'' indicates that this practice is one station of a lesson and the students at that station are responsible for directing their practice. In that same Session 9, force plays and tag plays are introduced as a second station (NP_2). When read horizontally, the chart also indicates, for example, that the skills in Step 11 are worked on for 17 sessions, 1 session being an introduction and 16 sessions being a review and continuations.

A course scope and teaching sequence chart (use the blank form in Appendix B.2) will help you to plan your daily teaching strategies better (see Appendices D.1 and D.2). It will take some experience to predict accurately how much material you can cover in each session. However, by completing a plan like this, you can compare your progress to your plan and revise the plan to fit the next class better.

The chart will also help you tailor the amount of material to the length of time you have to teach it. Notice that this particular sample indicates that all the skills listed are covered in 30 sessions. Your less experienced students may not be able to progress that rapidly. Your more experienced students may be able to progress faster. You may not have 30 sessions to devote to your softball unit; thus, you might want to teach some skills one year and other skills in softball units in later years. Be sure that your course's scope and teaching sequence allots ample time for reviewing and practicing each skill and/or concept.

Appendix B.2

Scope and Teaching Sequence

NAME OF ACTIVITY _____

LEVEL OF LEARNER _____

New **N**   Review **R**   Continue **C**   Student Directed Practice **P**

Session Number 1 2 3 4 5 6 7 8 9 10 11 12 13 14 15 16 17 18 19 20 21 22 23 24 25 26 27 28 29 30

Steps: 1 2 3 4 5 6 7 8 9 10 11 12 13 14 15 16 17 18 19 20 21 22 23 24 25

Notes:

Note. From *Badminton: A Structures of Knowledge Approach* (pp. 60-61) by J.N. Vickers and D. Brecht, 1987, Calgary, AB: University Printing Services. Copyright 1987 by Joan N. Vickers. Adapted by permission.

Appendix C.1

Sample Individual Program

INDIVIDUAL COURSE IN ___ Softball ___   GRADE/COURSE SECTION ___

STUDENT'S NAME ___   STUDENT ID # ___

I. DEMONSTRATED BY PHYSICAL SKILLS

Physical Skills	TECHNIQUE AND PERFORMANCE OBJECTIVES	WT* × %		POINT PROGRESS**			= FINAL SCORE***
			1	2	3	4	
Overhand Throw	*Technique:* Number out of 10 trials student demonstrates 75% or more of the items on the checklist.	2.5	LE 3 / ME 5	4 / 6	5 / 7	6+ / 8+	
	Performance: Number out of 10 trials thrown from a distance of 60 feet into a 3 feet by 3 feet target 3 feet above the ground.	2.5	LE 3 / ME 5	4 / 6	5 / 7	6+ / 8+	
Fielding Ground Balls	*Technique:* Number out of 10 trials student demonstrates 75% or more of the items on the Fielding Ground Balls Checklist.	7.5	LE 3 / ME 5	4 / 6	5 / 7	6+ / 8+	
	Performance: Number out of 10 trials cleanly fielded and accurately thrown from the shortstop position to a fielder at first base.	7.5	LE 3 / ME 5	4 / 6	5 / 7	6+ / 8+	
Fielding Fly Balls	*Technique:* Number out of 10 trials student demonstrates 75% or more of the items on the Fielding Fly Balls Checklist.	5	LE 3 / ME 5	4 / 6	5 / 7	6+ / 8+	
	Performance: Number out of 5 trials fielded without error and thrown accurately in the air a distance of 80 feet from the center field position to a fielder at a second base; number out of 5 trials fielded without error and accurately thrown, using a one-bounce throw, a distance of 165 feet from the center field position to a fielder at home plate.	5	LE 1	1 / 2	2 / 3	3+ / 4+	
		5	LE 1 / ME	2	3	3+ / 4+	

Skill	Criteria	Weight	Level				
Hitting	Technique: Number out of 10 soft-toss hitting trials student demonstrates 75% or more items on the checklist.	7.5	LE	3	4	5	6+
			ME	5	6	7	8+
	Performance: Percentage of balls hit fair during modified or regulation game play.	7.5	LE	30	40	50	60+
			ME	50	60	70	80+
Pitching	Technique: Number out of 10 trials student demonstrates 75% or more items on the checklist.	5	LE	3	4	5	6+
			ME	5	6	7	8+
	Performance: Number of strikes out of 10 pitches from a distance of 46 feet.	5	LE	3	4	5	6+
			ME	5	6	7	8+
Baserunning	Technique: Number out of 5 trials student demonstrates 75% or more items on the Overrunning First Base Checklist; number out of 5 trials demonstrating 75% or more items on the Rounding a Base Checklist.	1	LE		1	2	3+
			ME	1	2	3	4+
		1.5	LE		1	2	3+
			ME	1	2	3	4+
	Performance: Percentage of times overrunning the base is appropriately used in modified or regulation games; percentage of times rounding a base is appropriately used in modified or regulation games.	1	LE	30	40	50	60+
			ME	50	60	70	80+
		1.5	LE	30	40	50	60+
			ME	50	60	70	80+

SUBTOTAL PHYSICAL SKILLS = 65%

(Cont.)

Sample Individual Program (cont.)

II. CONCEPTS
DEMONSTRATED
COGNITIVELY

Concept	Performance	WT				
Position Play	Performance: Percentage of correct answers on quiz regarding position play and areas of responsibility.	2.5 LE ME	40 60	50 70	60 80	70+ 90+
Covering and Backing Up	Performance: Percentage of correct answers on quiz regarding defensive covering and backing-up responsibilities.	2.5 LE ME	40 60	50 70	60 80	70+ 90+
Force Plays and Tag Plays	Performance: Percentage of correct answers on quiz regarding force play and tag play.	2.5 LE ME	40 60	50 70	60 80	70+ 90+
Double Plays	Performance: Percentage of correct answers on quiz regarding double plays.	2.5 LE ME	40 60	50 70	60 80	70+ 90+
Relays and Cutoffs	Performance: Percentage of correct answers on quiz regarding relay and cutoff play.	2.5 LE ME	40 60	50 70	60 80	70+ 90+
Rundowns	Performance: Percentage of correct answers on quiz regarding rundown plays.	2.5 LE ME	40 60	50 70	60 80	70+ 90+
Culminating Knowledge Test	Performance: Percentage of correct answers on final examination.	20	--------			

SUBTOTAL COGNITIVE = 35%

TOTAL = 100%

*WT = Weighting of an objective's degree of difficulty.

**PROGRESS = Ongoing success, which may be expressed in terms of (a) accumulated points (1, 2, 3, 4); (b) grades (D, C, B, A); (c) symbols (merit, bronze, silver, gold); (d) unsatisfactory/satisfactory; and others as desired.

***FINAL SCORE equals WT times PROGRESS.

Appendix C.2
How to Use the Individual Program Form

To complete an individual program for each student, you must first make five decisions about evaluation:

1. How many skills or concepts can you or should you evaluate, considering the number of students and the time available? The larger your classes and the shorter your class length, the fewer objectives you will be able to use.

2. What specific quantitative or qualitative criteria will you use to evaluate specific skills? See the Sample Individual Program (Appendix C.1) for ideas.

3. What relative weight is to be assigned to each specific skill, considering its importance in the course and the amount of practice time available?

4. What type of grading system do you wish to use? Will you use letters (A, B, C, D), satisfactory/unsatisfactory, a number or point system (1, 2, 3, etc.), or percentages (10%, 20%, 30%, etc.)? Or, you may prefer a system of achievement levels indicated by colors (red, white, blue), softballs (Dudley, Diamond, Worth), or medallions (gold, silver, bronze).

5. Who will do the evaluating? You may want to delegate certain quantitative evaluations to the students' peers, up to a predetermined skill level (e.g., a ''B'' grade), with all qualitative evaluations and all top-grade determinations being made by you.

Once you have made these decisions, draw up an evaluation sheet (using the blank form in Appendix C.2) that will fit the majority of your class members. Then decide whether you will establish a minimum level as a passing/failing point. Calculate the minimum passing score and the maximum attainable score, and divide the difference into as many grade categories as you wish. If you use an achievement-level system, assign a numerical value to each level for your calculations.

The blank Individual Program form is intended not to be used verbatim (although you may do so if you wish), but rather to suggest ideas that you can use, adapt, and integrate with your own ideas to tailor your program to you and your students.

Make copies of your program evaluation system to hand out to each student at your first class meeting. Be prepared to make modifications for those who need special consideration. Such modifications could include changing the weight assigned to particular skills, substituting one skill for another, or varying the criteria used for evaluating those students. Thus, individual differences can be recognized within your class.

You, the instructor, have the freedom to make the decisions about evaluating your students. Be creative. The best teachers always are.

Appendix C.2

Individual Program

INDIVIDUAL COURSE IN _____

STUDENT'S NAME _____

GRADE/COURSE SECTION _____

STUDENT ID # _____

SKILLS/CONCEPTS	TECHNIQUE AND PERFORMANCE OBJECTIVES	WT* ×	POINT PROGRESS** 1	2	3	4	=	FINAL SCORE***

Note. From "The Role of Expert Knowledge Structures in an Instructional Design Model for Physical Education" by J.N. Vickers, 1983, *Journal of Teaching in Physical Education,* **2**(3), p. 17. Copyright 1983 by Joan N. Vickers. Adapted by permission.

*WT = Weighting of an objective's degree of difficulty.

**PROGRESS = Ongoing success, which may be expressed in terms of (a) accumulated points (1, 2, 3, 4); (b) grades (D, C, B, A); (c) symbols (merit, bronze, silver, gold); (d) unsatisfactory/satisfactory; and others as desired.

***FINAL SCORE equals WT times PROGRESS.

Appendix D.1
Sample Lesson Plan

Lesson plan _____9_____ of _____30_____ Activity: ____Softball____

Class _____

Equipment: Batting tees; bats; balls—regulation or IncrediBalls®; gloves; loose bases

Objectives: By the completion of class, students will have practiced the following:

1. Fielding ground balls hit directly at them, hit to their glove and nonglove sides, and hit short to them; then, making overhand throws to a catcher 70 feet away.
2. Hitting ground balls off a batting tee or from a self-toss (a fungo hit) in varying directions to a fielder.
3. Catching balls thrown from shortstop distance.
4. Moving to cover the base and do the footwork of a force play at 1st, 2nd, and 3rd base.
5. Moving to cover the base and do the footwork of a tag play at 1st, 2nd, and 3rd base.

Skill or concept	Learning activity	Teaching points	Time (min)
1. Outline objectives of class, and warm-up	• Jog to increase heart rate, and stretching routine	• Static stretch	5
2. Management	• Divide students into 2 groups (12-15 people per station): Read the directions and set up groups of 3 (according to Diagram D.1) at each station.	• Hitters need to be careful that no one is in their swing path.	3
3. Station practice			
Station 1	Review:	Review major cues:	20
Hitting ground balls either fungo hitting or off the tee, then fielding ground balls and throwing overhand	• Direct Grounders Drill (Step 7, Drill 1) • Moving to the Ball Drill (*Softball* Step 7, Drill 2) • Groups of 3 (H = hitter, C = catcher, F = fielder)	• Hitter, direct grounders accurately so fielder practices appropriately. • Catcher, give fielder a good target. • Fielder, get in front of ball, watch it go into glove, make smooth transition to overhand throw.	

- Each hit 5 ground balls

    directly at fielder,

    to glove side,

    to nonglove side, and

    short (fielder charges ball).
- Rotate C to H to F to C

- When moving laterally, get to ball quickly, be stationary when fielding ball, step in direction of throw.
- Hitter be careful not to hit into another fielder's area.

Station 2

Force plays and tag plays

New material:
- Mimetic Footwork Drill (Step 11, Drill 1)
- Groups of 3 (T = tosser; F1, F2 = fielders)

Tosser:
- Stands near pitching rubber, faces home, ball on ground
- "Fields" ball and tosses it to base to cover fielder for force play
- 4 repetitions (2 from SS and 2 from 2b) for each fielder

Fielder:
- Assumes regular-depth fielding position
- Begins moving to base as tosser picks up ball
- Rotates from F1 to F2 to T to F1

Repeat entire sequence quence for tag play.

Force play: 20
- Throw ball so arrives   6 (at
  chest-high to fielder.   each
- Fielder, move to corner of base closest to tosser.
- Stretch to catch ball.
- Catch ball with 2 hands.

Tag play:
- Throw ball toward fielder's knee.
- Fielder move to straddle, or stand adjacent to, base.
- Face direction of incoming runner.
- At 1b, runner is returning to base.

	Rotate to next base and repeat (1b to 3b to 2b to 1b).	
	Students rotate stations (1 to 2, and 2 to 1).	2
	Practice at second station.	20
4. Closing	All students group together at equipment distribution location.	For next class bring textbook, and dress for playing a game.	2
5. Dismissal		

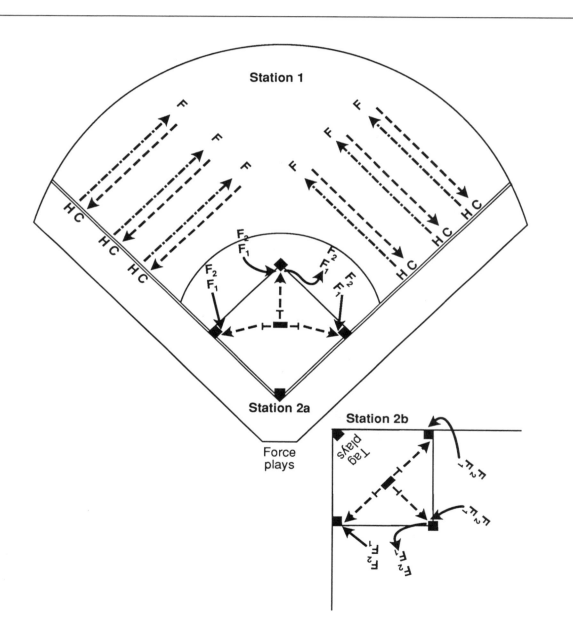

Diagram D.1 Station setup for lesson nine.

Appendix D.2
How to Use the Lesson Plan Form

All teachers have learned in their training that lesson plans are vital to good teaching. This is a commonly accepted axiom, but there are many variations in the form that lesson plans can take.

An effective lesson plan sets forth the objectives to be attained or attempted during the session. If there is no objective, then there is no reason for teaching and no basis for judging whether the teaching is effective.

Once you have named your objectives, list specific activities that will lead to attaining each. Every activity must be described in detail: What will take place and in what order, and how will the class be organized for optimum learning situations. Record key words or phrases as focal points and brief reminders of the applicable safety precautions.

Finally, set a time schedule that allocates a segment of the lesson for each activity to guide you in keeping to your plan. It is wise also to include in your lesson plan a list of all the equipment you will need; this list will serve as a reminder for you to check for the availability and location of the equipment before class.

An organized, professional approach to teaching requires preparing daily lesson plans. Each lesson plan provides you with an effective overview of your intended instruction and a means to evaluate it when class is over. Having lesson plans on file allows someone else to teach in your absence and offers a degree of protection in liability suits.

You may modify the blank lesson plan shown here to fit your own needs. You might also add, on the back, student options for practice and ways to decrease or increase the level of difficulty of the tasks you have established.

Lesson Plan

| LESSON PLAN _____ OF _____   OBJECTIVES: |
| ACTIVITY _____ |
| CLASS _____ |

SKILL OR CONCEPT	LEARNING ACTIVITIES	TEACHING POINTS	TIME

Note. From *Badminton: A Structures of Knowledge Approach* (p. 95) by J.N. Vickers and D. Brecht, 1987, Calgary, AB: University Printing Services. Copyright 1987 by Joan N. Vickers. Reprinted by permission.

References

Goc-Karp, G. , & Zakrajsek, D.B. (1987). Planning for learning: Theory into practice. *Journal of Teaching in Physical Education*, **6**(4), 377-392.

Housner, L.D., & Griffey, D.C. (1985). Teacher cognition: Differences in planning and interactive decision making between experienced and inexperienced teachers. *Research Quarterly for Exercise and Sport*, **56**(1), 45-53.

Imwold, C.H., & Hoffman, S.J. (1983). Visual recognition of a gymnastic skill by experienced and inexperienced instructors. *Research Quarterly for Exercise and Sport*, **54**(2), 149-155.

Rink, J. (1985). *Teaching physical education for learning*. St. Louis, MO: Times Mirror/ Mosby.

Suggested Readings

Allan, E. (1969). *Baseball play and strategy*. New York: Ronald Press.

Allen, A. (1959). *Handbook of baseball drills*. Englewood Cliffs, NJ: Prentice-Hall.

American Alliance for Health, Physical Education, Recreation and Dance. (1988). *NAGWS softball guide*. Reston, VA: Author.

Anderson, R. (1985). *Stretching*. Bolinas, CA: Shelter Publications.

Dobson, M., & Sisley, B. (1971). *Softball for girls*. New York: Ronald Press.

Drysdale, S., & Harris, K. (1982). *Complete handbook of winning softball*. Rockleigh, NJ: Longwood.

Houseworth, S., & Rivkin, F. (1985). *Coaching softball effectively*. Champaign, IL: Leisure Press.

Jones, B.J., & Murray, M.J. (1978). *Softball concepts for coaches and teachers*. Dubuque, IA: William C. Brown.

Joyce, J., Anquillare, J., & Klein, D. (1975). *Winning softball*. Chicago: Henry Regnery.

Kneer, M., & McCord, C. (1987). *Softball: Slow and fast pitch*. Dubuque, IA: William C. Brown.

Linde, K., & Hoehn, R. (1985). *Girls' softball: A complete guide for players and coaches*. West Nyack, NY: Parker.

Meyer, R. (1984). *The complete book of softball*. Champaign, IL: Leisure Press.

Noren, A.T. (1966). *Softball with officiating rules*. New York: Ronald Press.

Polk, R., & Lopiano, D. (1983). *Baseball-softball playbook*. Mississippi State: Mississippi State University.

Wenk, R. (1984). *Coaching youth softball*. Champaign, IL: Leisure Press.

Whiddon, N.S., & Hall, L.T. (1980). *Teaching softball*. Minneapolis, MN: Burgess.

Williams, T., & Underwood, J. (1986). *The science of hitting*. New York: Simon & Schuster.

About the Authors

Diane L. Potter, EdD, is professor of physical education at Springfield College in Springfield, Massachusetts. A teacher with over 27 years of experience in physical education professional preparation with responsibility for softball skills and coaching classes, Dr. Potter also coached the Springfield College softball team for 21 years. In addition, she was a player for 15 years in Amateur Softball Association (ASA) Class A Fast Pitch. Dr. Potter has been an international clinician in softball, conducting clinics in Italy and The Netherlands and taking teams to The Netherlands in 1971, 1975, and 1982. In 1982 she was awarded the Silver Medaillen by the Koninklijke Nederlandse Baseball en Softball Bond (the Royal Dutch Baseball and Softball Association); she is the only woman so honored.

Dr. Potter is an outstanding leader in women's sport; she has served as a member of the AIAW Ethics and Eligibility Committee and was inducted into the National Association of Collegiate Directors of Athletics Hall of Fame in 1986. She is an outstanding teacher and coach and has served as a role model for many fine women teacher-coaches who have been her students and her players. Her recreational activities include horseback riding, fishing, camping, and listening to classical music.

Gretchen A. Brockmeyer, EdD, is an associate professor of physical education at Springfield College, in Springfield, Massachusetts. She has been a teacher educator for over 20 years, with primary responsibility for secondary physical education methods and supervision of field-based teaching experience. A coach of many different sports, she served as assistant coach for the Springfield College softball team for 7 years. Dr. Brockmeyer is an exceptional teacher educator and role model. She is committed to helping her students become physical educators who possess the skills and the professional commitment necessary to provide meaningful learning opportunities for those they teach. Her students have consistently confirmed her faith in their abilities by becoming successful teachers who are caring human beings. Dr. Brockmeyer's leisure time is devoted to golfing, reading, music, and nurturing Seth and Alyssa.